FUNDAMENTALS OF
ENGLISH GRAMMAR
Second Edition

WORKBOOK Volume A

Betty Schrampfer Azar
Donald A. Azar

Longman

To Immee, Amelia Azar

Publisher: *Tina B. Carver*
Managing editor, production: *Sylvia Moore*
Editorial/production supervisor: *Janet Johnston*
Editorial assistants: *Shelley Hartle, Athena Foley*
Prepress buyer: *Ray Keating*
Manufacturing buyer: *Lori Bulwin*
Scheduler: *Leslie Coward*
Illustrator: *Don Martinetti*
Cover supervisor: *Marianne Frasco*
Cover designer: *Joel Mitnick Design*
Interior designer: *Ros Herion Freese*

©1999 by Prentice-Hall, Inc.
A Pearson Education Company
Pearson Education
10 Bank Street, White Plains, NY 10606

Printed in the United States of America

10

ISBN 0-13-347071-7

Contents

Chapter 3 FUTURE TIME

Chapter 4 NOUNS AND PRONOUNS

PRACTICE	PAGE

Chapter 5 MODAL AUXILIARIES

Chapter 8   COUNT/NONCOUNT NOUNS AND ARTICLES

Preface

This *Workbook* consists of exercises to accompany *Fundamentals of English Grammar (2nd edition)*, a developmental skills text for mid-level ESL/EFL students. The exercises are designated SELFSTUDY (answers given) or GUIDED STUDY (answers not given). The SELFSTUDY practices are intended for students to use independently. The answers are in a separate, detachable *Answer Key* booklet at the back of this book. The GUIDED STUDY practices may be selected by the teacher for additional classwork, homework, or individualized instruction. Answers to the GUIDED STUDY practices, as well as suggestions for using the *Workbook*, can be found in the *Teacher's Guide*.

Many of the initial practices in each unit are tightly controlled and deliberate, intended to clarify form and meaning. Control is then loosened as the manipulative and clarifying practices lead to others that promote free, creative use of the target structures. The *Workbook* also contains suggestions for writing and various group activities such as games and discussions.

ACKNOWLEDGMENTS

I am grateful to the many people who enable me to pursue the work I love. I am especially indebted to my husband, mainstay, and co-author, Don, who kept me afloat through the recent illness and loss of my much loved mother and provided the support system in which our work together could continue and prosper.

I am also greatly indebted to Shelley Hartle, our editorial assistant, without whom it would have been impossible to keep to production schedule. Though still new to the team, she adapted quickly and handled everything with aplomb, from proofing galleys and compiling indexes to tending the ducks when we had to be away.

Many thanks go to Janet Johnston, our production editor, who kept everything running smoothly on her end and was wonderfully supportive and understanding. Thanks similarly go to Sylvia Moore, managing editor. Special thanks also go to Tina Carver, publisher, who has been consistently supportive not only as a friend but as a top-notch publishing professional whose sound judgment I highly respect.

My appreciation goes, too, to Ray Adame, Barbara Barysh, Nancy Baxer, Eric Bredenberg, Karen Chiang, Athena Foley, Norman Harris, Terry Jennings, Gordon Johnson, Ray Keating, Andy Martin, Don Martinetti, Gil Muller, Ed Perez, Jack Ross, Jerry Smith, and Ed Stanford. In addition, my gratitude goes to Joy Edwards, Barbara Matthies, and R.T. Steltz. Chelsea Parker has been splendid. Finally, I am lovingly grateful to my father for his continuing support and involvement in my endeavors. Many of his ideas and suggestions are reflected in the text.

BETTY SCHRAMPFER AZAR

Once again, I begin by expressing my gratitude to Betty for her continued patience and guidance, and for the same incredible expertise that she brings to all phases of this project. Much of this was accomplished during a difficult time. Her ability and persistence got the book out. I continue to marvel and to learn.

I want to thank my father-in-law, Bill Schrampfer, for numerous handwritten ideas for topics and sentences. His agile mind provided much fodder. Inspiration apeared from many sources, R.T. Steltz, Tom Hemba, and my uncle Elias George among them, as well as Fred Lockyear, Gary Althen and other colleagues whose brains I often pick without knowing why until I start putting sentences down.

And special thanks still go to Chelsea Parker. She continues to endure our commitment to these projects and always provides joy and support.

DONALD A. AZAR

CHAPTER **1**
Present Time

◇ **PRACTICE 1—SELFSTUDY:** Interview questions and answers.

Directions: Complete the sentences with appropriate words.

A: Hi. My name _____ *is* _____ Kunio.

B: Hi. My _____ *name* _____ is Maria. I _____ glad to meet you.

KUNIO: I _____ glad to _____ you, too. Where _____?

MARIA: I _____ from Mexico. Where _____?

KUNIO: I _____ Japan.

MARIA: Where _____ living now?

KUNIO: On Fifth Avenue in _____ apartment. And you?

MARIA: I _____ living in a dorm.

KUNIO: _____ your field of study?

MARIA: Business. After I study English, I _____ going to attend the School of Business Administration. How _____ you? _____ your major?

KUNIO: Chemistry.

MARIA: _____ you like to do in your free time? _____ you have any hobbies?

KUNIO: I _____ to swim. How _____ you?

MARIA: I read a lot and I _____ stamps from all over the world.

KUNIO: Really? _____ you like some stamps from Japan?

MARIA: Sure! That would be great! Thanks.

KUNIO: I have _____ write your full name on the board when I introduce _____ to the class. _____ do you spell your name?

MARIA: My first _____ is Maria. M-A-R-I-A. My last _____ is Lopez. L-O-P-E-Z.

KUNIO: My _____ name is Kunio. K-U-N-I-O. My _____ name is
Akiwa. A-K-I-W-A.

MARIA: Kunio Akiwa. _____ that right?

KUNIO: Yes, it _____. It's been nice talking with you.

MARIA: I enjoyed it, too.

◇ **PRACTICE 2—GUIDED STUDY:** Introducing yourself.

Directions: Write answers to the questions. Use your own paper.

1. What is your name?
2. Where are you from?
3. Where are you living?
4. Why are you here (in this city)?
   a. Are you a student? If so, what is your major field of study?
   b. Do you work? If so, what is your job?
   c. Do you have another reason for being here?
5. What do you like to do in your free time?
6. What is your favorite season of the year? Why?
7. What are your three favorite books?
8. Describe your first day at this school.

◇ **PRACTICE 3—GUIDED STUDY:** Present verbs. (Charts 1–1 → 1–3)

Directions: All of the following sentences contain mistakes. Find the mistakes and rewrite each
sentence correctly.

Example: I no like cold weather. → ***I don't like cold weather.***

1. I no living at home right now.
2. I be living in this city.
3. Student at this school.
4. I am study English.
5. I am not knowing my teacher's name.
6. (*supply name*) teach our English class.
7. She/He★ expect us to be in class on time.
8. We always are coming to class on time.
9. Tom does he going to school?
10. Tom no go to school.
11. My sister don't have a job.
12. Does Sara has a job?

_____
★Choose the appropriate pronoun for your teacher, *he* or *she*.

13. Does you have a job?

14. Is Canada does it be north of the United States?

15. I never to go to my office on Saturday.

16. Ahmed, Toshi, Ji, Ingrid, and Pedro eats lunch together every day.

◇ PRACTICE 4—SELFSTUDY: Present verbs. (Charts 1–1 → 1–3)

Directions: Use the given verb to complete the sentence that follows. Use the SIMPLE PRESENT or the PRESENT PROGRESSIVE.

1. *sit*   I _____ *am sitting* _____ at my desk right now.

2. *read*   I _____ the second sentence in this exercise.

3. *look*   I _____ at sentence 3 now.

4. *write*   Now I _____ the right completion for this sentence.

5. *do*   I _____ a grammar exercise.

6. *sit*   I usually _____ *sit* _____ at my desk when I do my homework. And right

now I _____ *am sitting* _____ at my desk to do this exercise.

7. *read*   I often _____ the newspaper, but right now I

_____ a sentence in my grammar workbook.

8. *look*   I _____ at the newspaper every day. But right now I

_____ at my grammar workbook.

9. *write*   When I do exercises in this workbook, I _____ the answers in my

book and then I check them in the *Answer Key*.★ Right now I _____

an answer in the book.

10. *do*   I _____ grammar exercises every day. Right now I

_____ Practice 4 in this workbook.

◇ PRACTICE 5—SELFSTUDY: Forms of the simple present. (Chart 1–1)

Directions: Review the basic forms of the SIMPLE PRESENT TENSE by completing the sentences with the correct form of the verb "SPEAK."

PART I: STATEMENT FORMS

1. I (*speak*) _____ *speak* _____ English.

2. They (*speak*) _____ English.

3. He (*speak*) _____ English.

4. You (*speak*) _____ English.

5. She (*speak*) _____ English.

★The *Answer Key* to the selfstudy practices is in the back of this book.

PART II: NEGATIVE FORMS

1. I (speak, not) ___*do not (don't) speak*___ your language.

2. They (speak, not) _____ English.

3. He (speak, not) _____ English.

4. You (speak, not) _____ English.

5. She (speak, not) _____ English.

PART III: QUESTION FORMS

1. (you, speak) ___*Do you speak*___ English?

2. (they, speak) _____ English?

3. (he, speak) _____ English?

4. (we, speak) _____ English?

5. (she, speak) _____ English?

◇ **PRACTICE 6—SELFSTUDY:** Simple present. (Charts 1–1 → 1–3)

Directions: Write -S/-ES in the blanks where necessary and make any other needed changes in the verb. If the verb does not need -S/-ES, put a slash (/) in the blank.

1. Alan like__*s*__ to play soccer.

2. My son watch__*es*__ too much TV.

3. Rita do__*es*__n't like __/__ coffee.

4. Monkeys climb____ trees.

5. Do____ you like____ to climb trees?

6. Do____ Paul like____ to cook?

7. Alex like____ to dance

8. Mike wash____ his own clothes.

9. Rita go____ to school at seven.

10. Bees make____ honey.

11. A bee visit____ many flowers in one day.

12. Tina get____ her work done on time.

13. Tina and Pat get____ their work done.

14. Do____ Bill get____ his work done?

15. Eric do____n't get____ it done on time.

16. David carry____ a briefcase to work.

17. Janet play____ tennis every day.

18. A frog catch____ flies with its tongue.

19. Frogs are small green animals that live____ near water.

20. A turtle is another animal that live____ near water.

◇ **PRACTICE 7—GUIDED STUDY:** Final forms with *-s/-es.* (Charts 1–1 → 1–3)

Directions: Complete the sentences in COLUMN A with the words from COLUMN B.
- Capitalize the first word of the sentence.
- Add final **-S/-ES** to the verb if necessary.
- Add a period or question mark at the end of the sentence.

Example: 1. ***A star shines in the sky at night.***

COLUMN A	**COLUMN B**
1. a star	A. cause air pollution
2. a hotel	B. stretch when you pull on it
3. newspaper ink	C. support a huge variety of marine life
4. bees	✔ D. shine in the sky at night
5. do automobiles	E. cause great destruction when it reaches land
6. does physical exercise	F. use its long trunk like a hand to pick things up
7. a rubber band	G. improve your circulation and general health
8. a river	H. stain my hands when I read the paper
9. oceans	I. produce one-fourth of the world's coffee
10. Brazil	J. gather nectar from flowers
11. does an elephant	K. flow downhill
12. a hurricane	L. supply its guests with clean towels

◇ **PRACTICE 8—SELFSTUDY:** Forms of the present progressive. (Charts 1–1 and 1–2)

Directions: Review the basic forms of the PRESENT PROGRESSIVE by completing the sentences with the correct form of the verb ''SPEAK.''

PART I: **STATEMENT FORMS**

1. I (*speak*) _____ ***am speaking*** _____ English right now.

2. They (*speak*) _____ English right now.

3. She (*speak*) _____ English right now.

4. You (*speak*) _____ English right now.

PART II: **NEGATIVE FORMS**

1. I (*speak, not*) _____ ***am not speaking*** _____ English right now.

2. They (*speak, not*) _____ English right now.

3. He (*speak, not*) _____ English right now.

4. You (*speak, not*) _____ English right now.

PART III: **QUESTION FORMS**

1. (*you, speak*) _____ ***Are you speaking*** _____ English right now?

2. (*they, speak*) _____ English right now?

3. (*she, speak*) _____ English right now?

4. (*we, speak*) _____ English right now?

◇ **PRACTICE 9—SELFSTUDY: Simple present and present progressive. (Charts 1–1 → 1–3)**

Directions: Complete the sentences with **DO, DOES, IS,** or **ARE.** If no completion is needed, put a slash (/) in the blank.

1. Jack ____**does**____ not work at his father's store.

2. ____**Do**____ you have a job?

3. Kate ____/____ works at a restaurant.

4. Tom ____**is**____ working this afternoon.

5. _____ you working today?

6. Emily and Sara _____ working at the ice cream store this summer.

7. _____ Eric planning to get a job this summer?

8. _____ you plan to get a job, too?

9. Denise _____ wears jeans to work every day.

10. She _____ a carpenter.

11. Today she _____ working at the Hills' house.

12. She and her partner Scott _____ building a new porch for Mr. and Mrs. Hill.

13. Denise and Scott usually _____ work together on small construction jobs.

14. A turtle _____ lays eggs.

15. _____ snakes lay eggs?

16. _____ a lizard lay eggs?

17. _____ a lizard a reptile?

18. _____ turtles and snakes reptiles?

19. Turtles, snakes, and lizards _____ all reptiles.

20. Almost all reptiles _____ lay eggs.

21. Reptiles _____ cold-blooded.

22. Their body temperature _____ the same as the temperature of their surroundings.

◇ **PRACTICE 10—GUIDED STUDY: Simple present and present progressive. (Charts 1–1 → 1–3)**

Directions: Complete the sentences with **DO, DOES, IS,** or **ARE.** If no completion is needed, put a slash (/) in the blank.

1. A mosquito _____ flying around Sam's head.

2. Mosquitoes _____ pests.

3. They _____ bother people and animals.

4. _____ a male mosquito bite?

5. No, male mosquitoes _____ not bite.

6. Only female mosquitoes _____ bite animals and people.

7. A female mosquito _____ lays 1,000 to 3,000 eggs in her lifetime.

8. How long _____ mosquitoes live?

9. A female mosquito _____ lives for 30 days.

10. A male mosquito _____ not live as long as a female.

11. How long _____ a male mosquito live?

12. It _____ dies after 10 to 20 days.

13. Hillary _____ wearing mosquito repellent.

14. The mosquito repellent _____ smells bad, but it _____ works.

15. The mosquito repellent _____ effective.

16. Mosquitoes _____ stay away from people who _____ wearing mosquito repellent.

17. _____ you ever wear mosquito repellent?

18. _____ mosquito repellent work?

◇ **PRACTICE 11—SELFSTUDY: Frequency adverbs. (Charts 1–1 and 1–2)**

Directions: Complete each sentence with an appropriate FREQUENCY ADVERB* from the list.

    always   usually   often   sometimes   seldom   rarely   never

1. I see one or two movies every week.   → I _____**often**_____ go to the movies.

2. I let my roommate borrow my car one time last year.

   → I _____**rarely**_____ let my roommate borrow my car.

3. Maria eats cereal for breakfast seven days a week.

   → Maria _____ eats cereal for breakfast.

4. Four out of five visitors to the museum stay for three hours or longer.

   → Museum visitors _____ stay for at least three hours.

5. We occasionally have quizzes in Dr. Jacobs's history class.

   → Dr. Jacobs _____ gives quizzes in history class.

_____

*See Chart 7–8 for more information about frequency adverbs.

6. If the teacher is on time, the class begins at 8:00 A.M. Once in a while, the teacher is a few mintues late.   → The class _____ begins at 8:00 A.M.

7. The train from Chicago has been late ninety percent of the time.

   → The train from Chicago is _____ on time.

8. In the desert, it rains only two days between May and September every year.

   → It _____ rains there in the summer.

9. James asks me to go the the sailboat races every year, but I don't accept his invitation because I think sailboat racing is boring.

   → I _____ go to sailboat races with James.

10. Every time I go to a movie, I buy popcorn.

    → I _____ buy popcorn when I go to a movie.

11. Andy and Jake are friends. They go out to dinner at least three times a week.

    → Andy and Jake _____ go out to dinner with each other.

12. Andy and Jake do business with each other every once in a while. Most of the time they don't discuss business when they go out to dinner with each other.

    → They _____ discuss business during dinner.

◇ PRACTICE 12—GUIDED STUDY: Simple present: frequency adverbs. (Charts 1–1 and 1–2)

Directions: Make sentences about yourself. Use FREQUENCY ADVERBS with the given ideas.

Example: wear sandals in the summer
   → *I usually wear sandals in the summer.*
Example: read poetry in my spare time
   → *I rarely read poetry in my spare time.*

FREQUENCY ADVERBS:

   always   usually   often   sometimes   seldom   rarely   never

1. wear a suit to class

2. go to sleep at ten-thirty

3. read mystery stories before I go to sleep

4. hand in my school assignments on time

5. listen to the radio in the morning

6. speak to strangers at a bus stop

7. believe the things I read in newspapers

8. call a friend if I feel lonely or homesick

9. wear a hat when the weather is chilly

10. have chocolate ice cream for dessert

Directions: Use the PRESENT PROGRESSIVE to identify the actions in the pictures.

He is swimming.
He's doing the crawl.

1. _____

2. _____

3. _____

4. _____

5. _____

6. _____

7. _____

8. _____

◇ PRACTICE 14—GUIDED STUDY: Present progressive. (Charts 1-1 and 1-2)

Directions: Use the PRESENT PROGRESSIVE to identify the actions in the pictures.

1. _____

2. _____

3. _____

4. _____

5. _____

6. _____

7. _____

8. _____

◇ **PRACTICE 15—SELFSTUDY: Simple present and present progressive. (Charts 1–1 → 1–4)**

Directions: Complete the sentences with the SIMPLE PRESENT or PRESENT PROGRESSIVE form of the verbs in the list. Each verb is used only one time.

belong	need	see	✓take
bite	play	shine	understand
drive	prefer	sing	watch
look	rain	✓snow	write

1. Look outside! It _____***is snowing***_____. Everything is beautiful and all white.

2. My father _____***takes***_____ the 8:15 train into the city every weekday morning.

3. On Tuesdays and Thursdays, I walk to work for the exercise. Every Monday, Wednesday, and

   Friday, I _____ my car to work.

4. A: Charlie, can't you hear the telephone? Answer it!

   B: You get it! I _____ my favorite TV show. I don't want to miss

   anything.

5. A: What kind of tea do you like?

   B: Well, I'm drinking black tea, but I _____ green tea.

6. I'm gaining weight around my waist. These pants are too tight. I _____

   a larger pair of pants.

7. A: Dinner's ready. Please call the children.

   B: Where are they?

   A: They _____ a game outside in the street.

8. It's night. There's no moon. Emily is outside. She _____ at the sky. She

   _____ more stars than she can count.

9. Michael has a good voice. Sometimes he _____ with a musical group in

   town. It's a good way to earn a little extra money.

10. A: Ouch!

    B: What's the matter?

    A: Every time I eat too fast, I _____ my tongue.

11. Alicia always _____ in her diary after dinner.

12. Thank you for your help in algebra. Now I _____ that lesson.

13. This magazine isn't mine. It _____ to Colette.

14. I can see a rainbow because the sun _____ and it _____

    at the same time.

◇ PRACTICE 16—SELFSTUDY: Present verbs: questions and short answers. (Chart 1–5)

Directions: Complete the questions with **DO, DOES, IS,** or **ARE.** Then complete both the affirmative and negative short answers.

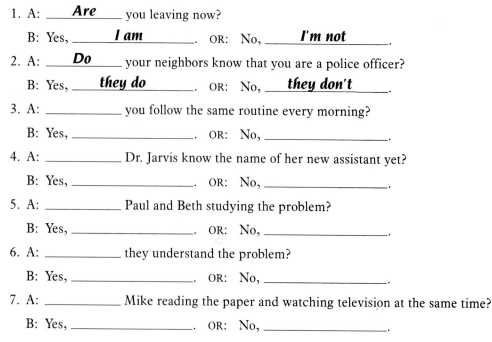

1. A: _____*Are*_____ you leaving now?

   B: Yes, _____*I am*_____. OR: No, _____*I'm not*_____.

2. A: _____*Do*_____ your neighbors know that you are a police officer?

   B: Yes, _____*they do*_____. OR: No, _____*they don't*_____.

3. A: _____ you follow the same routine every morning?

   B: Yes, _____. OR: No, _____.

4. A: _____ Dr. Jarvis know the name of her new assistant yet?

   B: Yes, _____. OR: No, _____.

5. A: _____ Paul and Beth studying the problem?

   B: Yes, _____. OR: No, _____.

6. A: _____ they understand the problem?

   B: Yes, _____. OR: No, _____.

7. A: _____ Mike reading the paper and watching television at the same time?

   B: Yes, _____. OR: No, _____.

8. A: _____ you listening to me?

   B: Yes, _____. OR: No, _____.

9. A: _____ that building safe?

   B: Yes, _____. OR: No, _____.

10. A: _____ the weather affect* your mood?

    B: Yes, _____. OR: No, _____.

◇ **PRACTICE 17—GUIDED STUDY: Present progressive.   (Charts 1–1 and 1–2)**

Directions: In small groups, pretend to perform actions. One member of the group pretends to do
something, and the rest of the group tries to guess what the action is and describe it using the
PRESENT PROGRESSIVE.

Example: painting a wall

STUDENT A: (pretends to be painting a wall)
OTHERS: You're conducting an orchestra. (No.)
             Are you washing a window? (No.)
             You're painting a wall. (Yes!)

SUGGESTIONS FOR ACTION:

    painting a wall   *playing the piano*
    drinking a cup of tea/coffee   *swimming*
    petting a dog   *driving a car*
    dialing a telephone   *watching a tennis match*
    climbing a tree   *pitching a baseball*

---

*The word *affect* is a verb: *The weather **affects** my mood.*
The word *effect* is a noun: *Warm, sunny weather has **a good effect** on my mood.*

◇ **PRACTICE 18—GUIDED STUDY:** Present progressive. (Charts 1-1 and 1-2)

Direction: Practice the PRESENT PROGRESSIVE in pairs or groups.

FIRST: In a small group of your classmates, pretend to perform any usual, common human activity and describe aloud what you are doing.

Example: I'm standing in front of an unpainted wall. I'm opening a can of paint. Now I'm picking up a paintbrush. I'm dipping the brush in a can of paint. I'm lifting the brush. Now I'm painting the wall.

SECOND: Perform the action again while your classmates describe what you are doing.

Example: You're standing in front of an unpainted wall. You're opening a can of paint. Now you're picking up a paintbrush. You're dipping the brush in a can of paint. You're lifting the brush. Now you're painting the wall.

◇ **PRACTICE 19—SELFSTUDY:** Present verbs. (Charts 1-1 → 1-5)

Directions: Use either the SIMPLE PRESENT or the PRESENT PROGRESSIVE of the verbs in parentheses.

1. It (be) _____**is**_____ a cool autumn day. The wind (blow) _____**is blowing**_____, and the leaves (fall) _____**are falling**_____ to the ground.

2. My roommate (eat) _____ breakfast at exactly seven o'clock every morning. I usually (eat, not) _____ breakfast at all. What time (eat, you) _____ in the morning?

3. A: (shop, you) _____ at this store every week?

   B: No. I _____. I (shop, usually) _____ at the store near my apartment.

   A: Why (shop, you) _____ here now?

   B: I (try) _____ to find something special for my father's birthday.

4. A: Flowers! Flowers for sale! Yes sir! Can I help you?

   B: I'll take those—the yellow ones.

   A: Here you are, mister. Are they for a special occasion?

   B: I (buy) _____ them for my wife. I (buy) _____ her flowers on the first day of every month.

5. A: I like to read. How about you? (*read, you*) _____ a lot?

   B: Yes, I _____. I (*read*) _____ at least one novel each week,

   and I (*subscribe*) _____ to several magazines. And I always (*look*)

   _____ at the newspaper during breakfast.

6. A: Knock, knock! Anybody home? Hey, Bill! Hi! It's me. Where are you?

   B: I (*be*) _____ in the bedroom!

   A: What are you doing?★

   B: I (*try*) _____ to sleep!

   A: Oh. Sorry. I won't bother you. Tom, shhh. Bill (*rest*) _____.

7. Before you begin to study, you should ask yourself two questions. First, "Why (*study, I*)

   _____ this subject right now?" Second, "What (*want, I*)

   _____ to learn about this topic?" Students (*need*) _____

   to understand the purpose of their study.

8. In cold climates, many trees (*lose*) _____ their leaves in winter. They (*rest*)

   _____ for several months. Then they (*grow*) _____ new leaves

   and flowers in the spring. Some trees (*keep*) _____ their leaves during the

   winter and (*stay*) _____ green all year long. In some regions of the earth, trees

   (*grow, not*) _____ at all. For example, some desert areas (*have, not*)

   _____ any trees. (*grow, trees*) _____ on all of the

   continents in the world?★★

◇ PRACTICE 20—GUIDED STUDY: Present verbs. (Charts 1–1 → 1–4)

   Directions: Use either the SIMPLE PRESENT or the PRESENT PROGRESSIVE of the verbs in parentheses.

   1. Ann is a painter. She (*go*) _____ to the opening of every new art show in the

      city. She (*like*) _____ to see the latest work of other artists. Right now she

      (*prepare*) _____ for her own show of her new paintings next month.

   2. A: What book (*read, you*) _____?

      B: It's about Spain. I (*think*) _____ you would enjoy it.

      A: I (*see*) _____ sailing ships on the cover.

      B: Yes. It (*be*) _____ about Spanish explorations in the 17th century.

   3. A: I (*leave*) _____ now. (*want, you*) _____ to go

      with me into town?

      B: No, thanks. I can't. I (*wait*) _____ for my sister to call from the

      airport so that I can pick her up.

   _____

   ★In rapid, informal spoken English, *What are you doing* can sound like "**What**cha do-un?"
   ★★No trees grow in Antarctica.

4. I work for an agricultural equipment company called Ballco. Right now, Ballco (*try*)

_____ to establish business contacts throughout South America. At the

present time, our sales manager (*travel*) _____ in Brazil and (*talk*)

_____ to potential customers. He (*know*) _____ both

Spanish and Portuguese.

5. A: Does the earth turn around and around?

   B: Yes, Jimmy. The earth (*spin*) _____ around and around on its axis as it

   circles the sun. The earth (*spin*) _____ rapidly at this very moment.

   A: I (*feel, not*) _____ anything. (*try, you*) _____

   to fool me?

   B: Of course not! (*think, you, really*) _____ that the earth isn't

   moving?

   A: I guess so. Yes. I can't see it move. Yes. It isn't moving.

   B: (*believe, you*) _____ only those things that you can see? Look at

   the trees out the window. All of them (*grow*) _____ at this very

   moment, but you can't see the growth. They (*get*) _____ bigger and

   bigger with every second that passes. You can't see the trees grow, and you can't feel the

   earth spin, but both events (*take*) _____ place at this moment while

   you and I (*speak*) _____.

   A: Really? How do you know?

6. A: Look at Della! Where (*go, she*) _____ and why (*walk, she*)

   _____ so fast?

   B: She (*rush*) _____ to a meeting with the company vice-president.

   Every morning at this time, she (*submit*) _____ a report on the

   previous day's activities and (*present*) _____ the daily

   recommendations.

   A: But I (*hear, usually*) _____ the daily recommendations from the

   president himself at the ten o'clock staff meetings.

   B: Every day, the vice-president (*rewrite*) _____ Della's comments and (*take*)

   _____ them to the president. At every ten o'clock meeting, the president

   simply (*read*) _____ the same recommendations that Della stayed up

   working on the night before, and he (*act*) _____ like he's been up for hours

   comtemplating those ideas.

   A: Well, I'll be darned! That (*seem, not*) _____ fair!

   B: It (*be, not*) _____. But that's the way it works.

◇ **PRACTICE 21—GUIDED STUDY: Present verbs. (Charts 1–1 → 1–4)**

Directions: Change the verb tenses. Use the same verb, but change other words in the sentence to make the neaning of the new verb tense clear.

PART I: Change the italicized verb from the SIMPLE PRESENT to the PRESENT PROGRESSIVE. Change other words to make the meaning of the new verb tense clear.

Example: Jane *walks* to work almost every day.
→ *Right now it's 7:45 in the morning, and Jane **is walking** to work.*

1. I *study* English every day.
2. The sun *shines* from morning until night every day.
3. The earth *rotates* on its axis.
4. Dr. Li *talks* to high school students all over the country about the dangers of drugs.
5. When Ted is tired, he *sleeps* wherever he is.

PART II: Change the *italicized* verb from the PRESENT PROGRESSIVE to the SIMPLE PRESENT. Change other words to make the meaning of the new verb tense clear.

Example: Right now, Luigi's team *is winning* the soccer game by a score of one to nothing.
→ *Luigi's team always **wins** a lot of soccer games during the year.*

6. Sue and her husband aren't home. They *are traveling* in South America.
7. Listen. Sam *is playing* the piano.
8. We don't have class today because our physics professor *is running* in a marathon this afternoon.
9. My friend Adam *is wearing* jeans today.
10. I'*m doing* a grammar exercise.

◇ **PRACTICE 22—GUIDED STUDY: Present verbs. (Charts 1–1 → 1–4)**

Directions: Complete the sentences in your own words, using the SIMPLE PRESENT or the PRESENT PROGRESSIVE form of a verb, whichever is appropriate.

Example: . . . every day before . . . .
→ *My brother George eats a large breakfast every day before he leaves for work.*

1. . . . usually . . . before . . . .
2. . . . always . . . when . . . .
3. . . . every Wednesday afternoon.
4. . . . at this very moment.
5. . . . every other day or so.
6. Why . . . right now?
7. How often . . . ?
8. . . . sometimes . . . after . . . .
9. . . . rarely . . . when . . . .
10. At the present time, ...

◇ PRACTICE 23—SELFSTUDY: Prepositions. (Chapter 1)

Directions: Complete the sentences with appropriate PREPOSITIONS.*

1. My eight-year-old son Mark is afraid _____*of*_____ thunder and lightning.

2. My mother really likes my friend Ahmed because he is always so polite _____ her.

3. Fifty miles is equal _____ eighty kilometers.

4. A: How do I get to your house?

   B: Are you familiar _____ the big red barn on Coles Road? My house is just past that
   and on the left.

   A: Oh, sure. I know where it is.

5. It's so hot! I'm thirsty _____ a big glass of ice water.

6. My boss was nice _____ me after I made that mistake, but I could tell she wasn't pleased.

7. Are you angry _____ me?

8. A: Harry, try some of this pasta. It's delicious.

   B: No, thanks. My plate is already full _____ food.

9. Four council members were absent _____ the meeting last night.

10. A: Why are you so friendly with Mr. Parsons? He's always so mean to everybody.

    B: He's always been very kind _____ me, so I have no reason to treat him otherwise.

11. My sister is so mad _____ me. She won't even speak to me.

12. Is everybody ready _____ dinner? Let's eat before the food gets cold.

---

*See Appendix 1 for a list of preposition combinations.

CHAPTER **2**
Past Time

◇ **PRACTICE 1—SELFSTUDY: Simple past. (Charts 2–1 → 2–3)**

Directions: Change the sentences to PAST TIME. Use a SIMPLE PAST verb. Choose *yesterday* or *last*.

PRESENT	PAST
every day	*yesterday*
every morning	*yesterday morning*
every afternoon	*yesterday afternoon*
every night	*last night*
every week	*last week*
every Monday, Tuesday, etc.	*last Monday, Tuesday, etc.*
every month	*last month*
every year	*last year*

1. I **walk** to my office **every morning**.

   → I _____*walked*_____ to my office (*yesterday,*) ~~*last*~~ morning.

2. I **talk** to my parents on the phone **every week**.

   → I _____*talked*_____ to my parents on the phone *yesterday,* (*last*) week.

3. The post office **opens** at eight o'clock **every morning**.

   → The post office _____ at eight o'clock *yesterday, **last** *morning.

4. Mrs. Hall **goes** to the fruit market **every Monday**.

   → Mrs. Hall _____ to the fruit market *yesterday,* ***last*** Monday.

5. The company executives **meet** at nine o'clock **every Friday morning**.

   → The executives _____ at nine o'clock *yesterday,* ***last*** Friday morning.

6. I **make** my own lunch and **take** it to work with me **every morning**.

   → ***Yesterday,*** ***Last*** morning, I _____ my own lunch and _____ it to work with me.

7. Mr. Clark **pays** his rent on time **every month**.

   → Mr. Clark _____ his rent on time *yesterday,* ***last*** month.

8. The baby *falls* asleep at three o'clock *every* afternoon.

   → ***Yesterday,*** ***Last*** afternoon, the baby _____ asleep at three o'clock.

9. The last bus to downtown **leaves** at ten o'clock **every night**.

   → The last bus to downtown _____ at ten o'clock *yesterday,* ***last*** night.

◇ PRACTICE 2—SELFSTUDY: Simple past: regular and irregular verbs. (Charts 2–1 → 2–4)

Directions: Write the SIMPLE PAST form of the given verbs.

1. start	_started_	13. sing	_____
2. go	_went_	14. explore	_____
3. see	_____	15. ask	_____
4. stand	_____	16. bring	_____
5. arrive	_____	17. break	_____
6. win	_____	18. eat	_____
7. have	_____	19. watch	_____
8. make	_____	20. build	_____
9. finish	_____	21. take	_____
10. feel	_____	22. pay	_____
11. fall	_____	23. leave	_____
12. hear	_____	24. wear	_____

◇ PRACTICE 3—SELFSTUDY: Simple past forms. (Charts 2–1 → 2–4)

Directions: Use the given words to make questions and give answers.

1. you/answer

A: _____**Did you answer**_____ the question?

B: Yes, _____**I did**____. _____**I answered**_____ the question. OR:

No, ____**I didn't**____. _____**I didn't answer**_____ the question.

2. he/see

A: _____ the fireworks?

B: Yes, _____. _____ the fireworks. OR:

No, _____. _____ the fireworks.

3. they/watch

A: _____ the game?

B: Yes, _____. _____ the game. OR:

No, _____. _____ the game.

4. you/understand

A: _____ the lecture?

B: Yes, _____. _____ the lecture. OR:

No, _____. _____ the lecture.

5. you/be

A: _____ at home last night?

B: Yes, _____. _____ at home last night. OR:

No, _____. _____ at home last night.

◇ **PRACTICE 4—SELFSTUDY: Simple past: regular and irregular verbs. (Charts 2–1 → 2–4)**

Directions: Complete the sentences by using the SIMPLE PAST of the verbs below. Use each verb only one time.

call	hold	sell	swim
fight	jump	✔shake	teach
freeze	ride	stay	think

1. Paul _____**shook**_____ the bottle of soda so hard that it sprayed all over his clothes.

2. Carol didn't want to go on vacation with us, so she _____ home alone all week.

3. Since I hurt my knee, I can't go jogging. Yesterday, I _____ in the pool for an hour instead.

4. I was terrified just standing over the pool on the high diving board. Finally, I took a deep breath, held my nose, and _____ into the water.

5. The climber, who was fearful of falling, _____ the rope tightly with both hands.

6. Johnny pushed Alan, and the two boys _____ for a few minutes. Neither boy was hurt.

7. Before Louise started her own company, she _____ chemistry at the university.

8. It was extremely cold last night, and the water we put out for the cat _____ solid.

9. Before I made my decision, I _____ about it for a long, long time.

10. John _____ your house three times to ask you to go to the movie with us, but there was no answer, so we went ahead without you.

11. My car wouldn't start this morning, so I _____ my bicycle to work.

12. I needed money to pay my tuition at the university, so I _____ my motorcycle to my cousin.

◇ **PRACTICE 5—GUIDED STUDY: Simple past: regular and irregular verbs. (Charts 2–1 → 2–4)**

Directions: Complete the sentences by using the SIMPLE PAST of the verbs below. Use each verb only one time.

ask	dig	play	spend
build	forgive	quit	steal
choose	lose	✔ring	talk

1. The phone _____**rang**_____ eight times before anybody answered it.

2. Oh my gosh! Call the police! Someone _____ my car!

3. The architectural firm that I work for designed this building. My brother's construction company _____ it. It took them two years to complete it.

4. The children _____ baseball until dark and didn't want to stop for dinner.

5. After I gave a large bone to each of my three dogs, they went to separate corners of the backyard and _____ holes to bury their bones.

6. A: Why isn't Bill here for the meeting? He's supposed to give the weekly report.

   B: I _____ to him last night on the phone, and he said he'd be here.

7. After looking at all the chairs in the furniture store, I finally _____ the red one. It was a difficult decision.

8. A: How are you getting along in your relationship with Carla?

   B: Not bad. Last night I _____ her again to marry me, and she said "maybe."

9. The players are depressed because they _____ the game last weekend. Next time they'll play better.

10. A: How can you take a three-month vacation? What about your job?

    B: I won't be going back to that job ever again. I _____ yesterday.

11. I can't afford a new car because I _____ all my money on new furniture for my apartment.

12. A: Is Elizabeth still angry with you?

    B: No, she _____ me for what I did, and she's speaking to me again.

◇ **PRACTICE 6—SELFSTUDY: Simple past: irregular verbs. (Charts 2–1 → 2–4)**

Directions: Complete the sentences with the SIMPLE PAST of any of the verbs in Chart 2–4.

1. I _____ *swept* _____ the kitchen floor with a broom.

2. A bird _____ into our apartment through an open window.

3. I _____ the bird in my hands and put it back outside.

4. My father _____ me how to make furniture.

5. It got so cold last night that the water in the pond _____.

6. When I heard about Sue's problem, I _____ sorry for her.

7. Alex _____ a map for us to show us how to get to the museum.

8. A few minutes ago, I _____ on the radio about a bad plane accident.

9. Joe had an accident. He _____ off the roof and _____ his leg.

10. Sam _____ the race. He ran the fastest.

11. Ted _____ his car to Alaska last summer.

12. The soldiers _____ the battle through the night and into the morning.

13. I used to have a camera, but I _____ it because I needed the money.

14. Jane didn't want anyone to find her diary, so she _____ it in a shoe box in her closet.

15. There was a cool breeze last night. I opened the window, but Colette got cold and _____ it.

16. Rita _____ faster than anyone else in the 100-meter dash.

17. None of the other runners was ever in front of Rita during the race. She _____ all of the other runners in the race from start to finish.

18. Greg is a penny pincher. I was very surprised when he _____ for my dinner.

19. Frank was really thirsty. He _____ four glasses of water.

20. Karen had to decide between a blue raincoat and a tan one. She finally _____ the blue one.

21. Ann _____ a beautiful dress to the wedding reception.

22. My pen ran out of ink, so Sam _____ me an extra one he had.

◇ **PRACTICE 7—GUIDED STUDY:** *Simple past: irregular verbs. (Charts 2–1 → 2–4)*

Directions: Complete the sentences with the SIMPLE PAST of any of the verbs in Chart 2–4.

1. We _____ at the new restaurant last night. The food wasn't very good.

2. Jason _____ an excellent job of glueing the broken vase together.

3. The sun _____ at 6:21 this morning.

4. My wife gave me a painting for my birthday. I _____ it on a wall in my office.

5. Laurie has circles under her eyes because she _____ only two hours last night. She was studying for her final exams.

6. John is a good carpenter. He _____ the house in which he and his family live.

7. Matt lost his watch. He looked everywhere for it. Finally, he _____ it in the washing machine as he was removing the wet clothes to put them into the dryer. He had washed his watch, but it was still ticking.

8. Joy was barefoot. She stepped on a piece of broken glass and _____ her foot.

9. Danny and I are old friends. We _____ each other in 1975.

10. My friend told me that he had a singing dog. When the dog _____ to sing, I _____ my hands over my ears and _____ the room.

11. My friend _____ a note and passed it to me in class.

12. I didn't want anyone else to see the note, so I _____ it into tiny pieces and _____ it in the wastebasket.

13. My mother _____ all the letters I wrote to her while I was in England. She didn't throw any away.

14. The student with the highest grade point average _____ a speech at the graduation ceremony. She _____ about her hopes for the future of the world.

15. No, I didn't buy these tomatoes. I _____ them in a pot on the balcony outside my apartment.

16. Paul was in a hurry to get to class this morning. He _____ to comb his hair.

17. Last week I _____ an interesting book about the volcanoes in Iceland.

18. When Erica and I were introduced to each other, we _____ hands.

19. Mike is in jail because he _____ a car.

20. The fish I caught was too small. I carefully returned it to the water. It quickly _____ away.

21. I _____ the doorbell for a long time, but no one came to the door.

22. Amanda _____ a lie. I didn't believe her because I _____ the truth.

23. Steve _____ the campfire with only one match. Then he _____ on the fire to make it burn.

◇ **PRACTICE 8—GUIDED STUDY:** Regular verbs: pronunciation of -ed endings. (Chart 2–3)

Directions: Practice pronouncing final **-ED** by saying the words in the list aloud.

PRONUNCIATION NOTES: Final **-ed** has three different pronunciations: /**t**/, /**d**/, and /**əd**/.

- Final **-ed** is pronounced /**t**/ after most voiceless sounds. Voiceless sounds are made by pushing air through your mouth; no sound comes from your throat. Examples of voiceless sounds: /**p**/, /**k**/, /**f**/, /**s**/, /**sh**/, /**ch**/. Pronunciation: *stopped* = *stop* + /**t**/ ("stopt"); *talked* = *talk* + /**t**/ ("talkt").
- Final **-ed** is pronounced /**d**/ after most voiced sounds. Voiced sounds come from your throat. If you touch your neck when you make a voiced sound, you can feel your voice box vibrate. Your voice box produces voiced sounds. Examples of voiced sounds: /**b**/, /**v**/, /**n**/, and all vowel sounds. Pronunciation: *robbed* = *rob* + /**d**/ ("robd"); *lived* = *live* + /**d**/ ("livd").
- Final **-ed** is pronounced /**əd**/ after words that end in "t" or "d." /**əd**/ adds a whole syllable to a word. Pronunciation: *wanted* = *want* + /**əd**/ ("want-ud"); *needed* = *need* + /**əd**/ ("need-ud").

1. stopped = *stop* + /**t**/
2. robbed = *rob* + /**d**/
3. wanted = *want* + /**əd**/
4. talked = *talk* + /**t**/
5. lived = *live* + /**d**/
6. needed = *need* + /**əd**/
7. passed = *pass* + /**t**/★
8. pushed = *push* + /**t**/
9. watched = *watch* + /**t**/
10. thanked = *thank* + /**t**/

11. finished = *finish* + /**t**/
12. dreamed = *dream* + /**d**/
13. killed = *kill* + /**d**/
14. turned = *turn* + /**d**/
15. played = *play* + /**d**/
16. continued = *continue* + /**d**/
17. repeated = *repeat* + /**əd**/
18. waited = *wait* + /**əd**/
19. added = *add* + /**əd**/
20. decided = *decide* + /**əd**/

◇ **PRACTICE 9—GUIDED STUDY:** Regular verbs: pronunciation of *-ed* endings. (Chart 2–3)

Directions: Practice pronouncing final **-ED** by reading the sentences aloud.

1. I **watched** TV. Jean **listened** to the radio. Nick **waited** for the mail.
   watch/t/   listen/d/   wait/əd/

2. I **tasted** the soup. It **seemed** too salty.
   taste/əd/   seem/d/

3. James **planned** for his future. He **saved** money and **started** his own business.
   plan/d/   save/d/   start/əd/

4. I **asked** a question. Joe **answered** it. Then he **repeated** the answer for Ted.
   ask/t/   answer/d/   repeat/əd/

5. I **stared** at the sculpture for a long time. Finally, I **touched** it.
   stare/d/   touch/t/

6. Mary **prepared** a long report for her boss. She **completed** it late last night.
   prepare/d/   complete/əd/

7. After Dick **parked** the car, I **jumped** out and **opened** the door for my mother.
   park/t/   jump/d/   open/d/

8. After I **finished** reading Rod's poem, I **called** him and we **talked** for an hour.
   finish/t/   call/d/   talk/t/

9. Earlier today, I **cleaned** my apartment.
   clean/d/

10. I **washed** the windows, **waxed** the wood floor, and **vacuumed** the carpet.
    wash/t/   wax/t/   vacuum/d/

11. I **expected** to hear from Dr. Li about a scholarship.
    expect/əd/

12. I **crossed** my fingers and **hoped** for good news.
    cross/t/   hope/d/

13. I **poured** water into the glass and **filled** it to the top. I **offered** it to Sara.

14. Tim **dropped** the book. I **picked** it up and **dusted** it off with my hand.

15. She **handed** us the tests at the beginning of class and **collected** them at the end.

16. I **guessed** at most of the answers. I **realized** I should have **studied** harder.

★The words "passed" and "past" have the same pronunciation.

◇ PRACTICE 10—SELFSTUDY: Spelling of *-ing* and *-ed* forms. (Chart 2–5)

Directions: Complete the chart. Refer to Chart 2–5 if necessary.

END OF VERB	DOUBLE THE CONSONANT?	SIMPLE FORM	-ING	-ED
-e	**NO**	excite	***exciting***	***excited***
Two Consonants		exist		
Two Vowels + One Consonant		shout		
One Vowel + One Consonant		ONE-SYLLABLE VERBS pat		
		TWO-SYLLABLE VERBS (STRESS ON **FIRST** SYLLABLE) visit		
		TWO-SYLLABLE VERBS (STRESS ON **SECOND** SYLLABLE) admit		
-y		pray pry		
-ie		tie		

◇ PRACTICE 11—SELFSTUDY: Spelling of *-ing*. (Chart 2–5)

Directions: Write one ''t'' or two ''t's'' in the blanks to spell the **-ing** verb correctly. Then write the simple form of the verb in each sentence.

SIMPLE FORM

1. I'm wai__*t*__ing for a phone call.   1. _____*wait*_____

2. I'm pa__*tt*__ing my dog's head.   2. _____*pat*_____

3. I'm bi____ing my nails because I'm nervous.   3. _____

4. I'm si____ing in a comfortable chair.   4. _____

5. I'm wri____ing in my book.   5. _____

6. I'm figh____ing the urge to have some chocolate ice cream.   6. _____

7. I'm wai____ing to see if I'm really hungry.   7. _____

8. I'm ge____ing up from my chair now.   8. _____

9. I'm star____ing to walk to the refrigerator.   9. _____

10. I'm permi____ing myself to have some ice cream.   10. _____

11. I'm lif____ing the spoon to my mouth.   11. _____

12. I'm ea____ing the ice cream now.   12. _____

13. I'm tas____ing it. It tastes good.   13. _____

14. I'm also cu____ing a piece of cake.   14. _____

15. I'm mee____ing my sister at the airport tomorrow.   15. _____

16. She's visi____ing me for a few days. I'll save some cake   16. _____

and ice cream for her.

◇ **PRACTICE 12—SELFSTUDY:**   Simple present vs. simple past. (Charts 2-1 → 2-4)

Directions: Use the SIMPLE PRESENT or the SIMPLE PAST form of the verb in parentheses, whichever is appropriate.

1. A: (hear, you) _____**Did you hear**_____ the thunder last night?

   B: No, I _____**didn't**_____. I (hear, not) _____**didn't hear**_____ anything all night. I

   (be) _____**was**_____ asleep.

2. A: Listen! (hear, you) _____**Do you hear**_____ a siren in the distance?

   B: No, I _____**don't**_____. I (hear, not) _____**don't hear**_____ anything at all.

3. A: (build, you) _____ that bookshelf?

   B: No, I _____. My uncle (build) _____ it for me.

4. A: (be, a fish) _____ slippery to hold?

   B: Yes, _____. It can slip right out of your hand.

   A: How about frogs? (be, they) _____ slippery?

   B: Yes, _____.

   A: What about snakes?

   B: I (know, not) _____. I've never touched a snake.

5. A: I (want) _____ to go to the mall this afternoon and (look) _____

   for a new bathing suit. (want, you) _____ to go with me?

   B: I can't. I (have) _____ an appointment with my English teacher. Besides, I

   (buy) _____ a new bathing suit last year. I (need, not) _____

   a new one this year.

6. I (offer) _____ to help my older neighbor carry her groceries into her house

   every time I see her return from the store. She (be) _____ always very

   grateful. Yesterday, she (offer) _____ to pay me for helping her, but of course I

   (accept, not) _____ the offer.

7. Last Monday night, I (*take*) _____ my sister and her husband to my favorite restaurant for dinner and (*find*) _____ the doors locked. I (*know, not*) _____ it then, but my favorite restaurant (*be, not*) _____ open on Mondays. We (*want, not*) _____ to eat anywhere else, so we (*go*) _____ back to my house. I (*make*) _____ a salad and (*heat*) _____ some soup. Everyone (*seem*) _____ satisfied even though I (*be, not*) _____ a wonderful cook.

8. My daughter is twenty-one years old. She (*like*) _____ to travel. My wife and I (*worry*) _____ about her a little when she (*be*) _____ away from home, but we also (*trust*) _____ her judgment.

   Last year, after she (*graduate*) _____ from college, she (*go*) _____ to Europe with two of her friends. They (*travel, not*) _____ by train or by car. Instead, they (*rent*) _____ motor scooters and slowly (*ride*) _____ through each country they visited.

   While she (*be*) _____ away, my wife and I (*worry*) _____ about her safety. We (*be*) _____ very happy when we (*see*) _____ her smiling face at the airport and (*know*) _____ that she was finally safe at home.

◇ **PRACTICE 13—SELFSTUDY: Past progressive. (Charts 2–6 and 2–7)**

Directions: Complete the sentences by using the PAST PROGRESSIVE of the verbs below. Use each verb only one time.

answer	count	look	✔stand
begin	drive	melt	walk
climb	eat	sing	

1. Fortunately, I didn't get wet because I _____**was standing**_____ under a large tree when it began to rain.

2. I saw Ted at the student cafeteria at lunch time. He _____ a sandwich.

3. Mr. Cook asked an interesting question. The professor _____ Mr. Cook's question when Mr. Gray rudely interrupted.

4. Robert didn't answer the phone when Sara called. He _____ his favorite song in the shower and didn't hear the phone ring.

5. A: I saw a whale!

   B: Really? Neat! When?

   A: This morning. I _____ on the beach when I heard a sudden ''whoosh!'' It was the spout of a huge gray whale.

6. Three people _____ the east side of the mountain when the avalanche occurred. All three died.

7. A: Were you on time for the play last night?

   B: I drove as fast as I could. The play _____* just as we walked in the door of the theater.

8. Robert came in while I _____ the money from the day's receipts. I completely lost track and had to start all over again.

9. It was difficult to ski because the temperature was rising and the snow _____.

10. A: What do you think was the cause of your accident?

    B: I know what caused it. Paul _____ at the scenery while he _____ the car. He simply didn't see the other car pull out from the right.

◇ PRACTICE 14—GUIDED STUDY: Present progressive and past progressive. (Charts 1–2, 2–6, and 2–7)

Directions: Complete the dialogues by making up answers to the questions. Use the PRESENT PROGRESSIVE or the PAST PROGRESSIVE of the verb in parentheses.

1. A: Why were you at the airport so late last night?

   B: I _was waiting for my brother's plane._ _____ (wait)

2. A: Hi, Eric. I didn't expect to run into you at the airport. Why are you here today?

   B: I _'m waiting for my brother's plane._ _____ (wait)

3. A: Ted saw you around nine yesterday morning. Were you on your way to work when he saw you?

   B: No, I _____ (walk)

4. A: Hi, Greg. How are you this morning? Are you on your way to work?

   B: No, I _____ (walk)

5. A: Why are you laughing? What's so funny?

   B: We _____ (watch)

6. A: Why were you and your friends laughing so loudly a little while ago?

   B: We _____ (watch)

7. A: Where are Ann and Rob? I haven't seen them for a couple of weeks. Are they in town?

   B: No, they _____ (travel)

8. A: Where were Ann and Rob when you got back from your trip? Were they in town?

   B: No, they _____ (travel)

---

*Spelling note: There are **three n's** in the word *beginning*.

9. A: What was I saying when the phone interrupted me? I lost my train of thought.

   B: You _____ (describe)

10. A: What's Marilyn talking about?

    B: She _____ (describe)

◇ **PRACTICE 15—SELFSTUDY: Past time using time clauses. (Charts 2–1 → 2–8)**

Directions: Combine the two sentences in any order, using the time expression in parentheses.

1. The doorbell rang. I was climbing the stairs. (*while*)
   → *While I was climbing the stairs, the doorbell rang.* OR:
   → *The doorbell rang while I was climbing the stairs.*
2. I gave Alan his pay. He finished his chores. (*after*)
3. The firefighters checked the ashes one last time. They went home. (*before*)
4. Mr. Novak stopped by our table at the restaurant. I introduced him to my wife. (*when*)
5. The kitten was sitting on the roof. An eagle flew over the house. (*while*)
6. My father was listening to a baseball game on the radio. He was watching a basketball game on television. (*while*)

◇ **PRACTICE 16—SELFSTUDY: Simple past vs. past progressive. (Charts 2–1 → 2–8)**

Directions: Complete the sentences with the SIMPLE PAST or the PAST PROGRESSIVE form of the verb in parentheses.

1. It (*begin*) _____**began**_____ to rain while Amanda and I (*walk*) _____**were**_____ _____**walking**_____ to school.

2. While I (*wash*) _____ dishes, I (*drop*) _____ a plate and (*break*) _____ it.

3. I (*hit*) _____ my thumb while I (*use*) _____ the hammer. Ouch!

4. While I (*walk*) _____ under an apple tree, an apple (*fall*) _____ and (*hit*) _____ me on the head.

5. Last month, both my brother and my next-door neighbor were in Thailand, and neither one of them (*know*) _____ that the other was there. While they (*attend*) _____ my daughter's wedding reception last weekend, my neighbor (*mention*) _____ her trip, and my brother was very surprised. It seems that they (*be*) _____ in Bangkok for three days at exactly the same time and (*stay*) _____ in hotels that were only a few blocks away from each other.

6. While I (*look*) _____ at the computer screen, I (*start*) _____ to feel a little dizzy, so I (*take*) _____ a break. While I (*take*) _____ a short break outdoors and (*enjoy*) _____ the warmth of the sun on my face, an elderly gentleman (*come*) _____ up to me

and (*ask*) _____ for directions to the public library. After I (*tell*)

_____ him how to get there, he (*thank*) _____ me and

(*go*) _____ on his way. Soon a big cloud (*come*) _____ and

(*cover*) _____ the sun, so I (*go*) _____ back inside to work.

◇ **PRACTICE 17—GUIDED STUDY: Simple past vs. past progressive. (Charts 2-1 → 2-8)**

Directions: Complete the sentences with the SIMPLE PAST or the PAST PROGRESSIVE of the verbs in parentheses.

Late yesterday afternoon while I (*1. prepare*) _____ dinner, the doorbell

(*2. ring*) _____ . I (*3. put*) _____ everything down and (*4. rush*)

_____ to answer it. I (*5. open*) _____ the door and (*6. smile*)

_____ at the stranger standing in my doorway. He (*7. hold*) _____

a small vacuum cleaner. While he (*8. tell*) _____ me about this wonderful

vacuum cleaner that he wanted to sell to me, the phone (*9. ring*) _____ . I

(*10. excuse*) _____ myself and (*11. reach*) _____ for the phone. While

I (*12. try*) _____ to talk on the phone and listen to the vacuum cleaner

salesman at the same time, my young son (*13. run*) _____ up to me to tell me about

the cat. The cat (*14. try*) _____ to catch a big fish in my husband's prized

aquarium. The fish (*15. swim*) _____ on the bottom to avoid the cat's paw.

I (*16. say*) _____ goodbye to the vacuum salesman and (*17. shut*)

_____ the door. I (*18. say*) _____ goodbye to the person on the

phone and (*19. hang*) _____ up. I (*20. yell*) _____ at the cat and

(21. shoo)* _____ her away from the fish. Then I (22. sat) _____

down in an easy chair and (23. catch) _____ my breath. While I (24. sit)

_____ there, the doorbell (25. ring) _____ again. Then the

phone (26. ring) _____. Then my son said, "Mom! Mom! The dog is in the

refrigerator!" I (27. move, not) _____. "What's next?" I said to myself.

◇ **PRACTICE 18—GUIDED STUDY: Present and past verbs. (Chapters 1 and 2)**

Directions: Complete the sentences with the SIMPLE PRESENT, PRESENT PROGRESSIVE, SIMPLE PAST, or PAST PROGRESSIVE.

PART I:

SITUATION: Right now Toshi (1. sit) _____ ***is sitting*** _____ at his desk. He (2. write)

_____ in his grammar workbook. His roommate, Oscar, (3. sit)

_____ at his desk, but he (4. study, not) _____. He

(5. stare) _____ out the window. Toshi (6. want) _____ to

know what Oscar (7. look) _____ at. Here is their dialogue:

TOSHI: Oscar, what (8. you, look) _____ at?

OSCAR: I (9. watch) _____ the bicyclists. They are very skillful. I

(10. know, not) _____ how to ride a bike, so I (11. admire)

_____ anyone who can. Come over to the window. Look at that guy

in the blue shirt. He (12. steer) _____ his bike with one hand while

he (13. drink) _____ a Coke with his other. And all the while, he

(14. weave) _____ in and out of the heavy street traffic and the

pedestrian traffic. He (15. seem) _____ fearless.

TOSHI: Riding a bike (16. be, not) _____ as hard as it (17. look) _____.

I'll teach you to ride a bicycle if you'd like.

OSCAR: Really? Great.

TOSHI: How come you don't know how to ride a bike?**

OSCAR: I never (18. have) _____ a bike when I (19. be) _____ a

kid. My family (20. be) _____ too poor. One time I (21. try)

_____ to learn on the bike of one of my friends, but the other kids all

(22. laugh) _____ at me. I never (23. try) _____ again

because I (24. be) _____ too embarrassed. But I'd love to learn now!

When can we start?

_____

*"Shoo! Shoo!" means "Go away! Leave!" When the woman *shooed* the cat, that means she said "Shoo! Shoo!" and made the cat leave.

**"How come?" means "Why?" For example, "How come you don't know how to ride a bike?" means "Why don't you know how to ride a bike?"

PART II:

Yesterday Toshi (*25. sit*) _____ **was sitting** _____ at his desk and (*26. write*) _____

in his grammar workbook. His roommate, Oscar, (*27. sit*) _____ at his desk,

but he (*28. study, not*) _____. He (*29. stare*) _____ out

the window. He (*30. watch*) _____ bicyclists on the street below.

Toshi (*31. walk*) _____ over to the window. Oscar (*32. point*) _____

out one bicyclist in particular. This bicyclist (*33. steer*) _____ with one

hand while he (*34. drink*) _____ a Coke with the other. And all the while,

he (*35. weave*) _____ in and out of the heavy traffic. To Oscar, the bicyclist

(*36. seem*) _____ fearless.

Oscar never (*37. learn*) _____ how to ride a bike when he (*38. be*)

_____ a kid, so Toshi (*39. offer*) _____ to teach him how.

Oscar (*40. accept*) _____ gladly.

◇ **PRACTICE 19—SELFSTUDY:** Past habit with *used to.* (Chart 2–9)

Directions: Using the given information, complete the sentences. Use **USED TO**.

1. When James was young, he hated school. Now he likes school.

→ James _____ **used to hate school** _____.

2. When I was young, I thought that people over forty were very old.

→ I _____ that people over forty were very old.

3. Ann was a secretary for many years, but now she owns her own business.

→ Ann _____, but now she owns her own business.

4. Rebecca had a rat as a pet when she was ten. The rat died, and she hasn't had another rat as a
pet since that time.

→ Rebecca _____ as a pet.

5. Before Adam got married, he went bowling five times a week.

→ Adam _____ five times a week.

6. A long time ago, we raised chickens in our yard.

→ We _____ in our yard.

7. When we raised our own chickens, we had fresh eggs every morning.

→ We _____ every morning when we raised our own
chickens.

8. When Ben was a child, he often crawled under his bed and put his hands over his ears when
he heard thunder.

→ Ben _____ and _____
_____ when he heard thunder.

◇ **PRACTICE 20—GUIDED STUDY:** Past habit with *used to*. (Chart 2–9)

Directions: Combine the given ideas into a sentence with "USED TO . . . , BUT NOW . . . ."

1. Years ago, I smoked two packs of cigarettes a day. Now, I don't smoke at all.
   → *I used to smoke two packs a day, but now I don't smoke at all.*

2. Amanda always stayed up late when she was a student. When she got a job after she graduated, she had to go to bed early.
   → *Amanda used to stay up late, but now she goes to bed early.*

3. My neighbor Bill drove his car to work every day last year. Now, he rides the bus.

4. At the beginning of the semester, Eric worked hard. Now, he is too busy with his social life.

5. Millions of years ago, dinosaurs ruled the world. Millions of years ago, they also became extinct.

6. The Allens had a large house when their children lived at home, but they moved to a small three-room apartment after the children grew up and left home.

7. Susan ate a balanced diet when she was a child. Now she's a teenager and eats a lot of junk food.

8. When I was a child, I didn't stay up late. Now, I'm up late every night because I have to study a lot.

9. Hiroki never wore cowboy boots when he lived in Japan. When he moved to Texas, he started wearing cowboy boots every day.

10. When I was a kid, I didn't have a job in the summer. I went swimming every day during the summer. Now I have to go to work, so I can go swimming only on weekends.

◇ **PRACTICE 21—GUIDED STUDY:** Past habit with *used to*. (Chart 2–9)

Directions: Write about or discuss in small groups the following topics. Use USED TO. Try to think of at least two or three differences for each topic.

1. Compare past and present means of transportation.
   (e.g., *People used to take long trips across the Atlantic by ship, but now they fly from one continent to another in a few hours.*)

2. Compare past and present clothing.
   (e.g., *Shoes used to have buttons, but now they don't.*)

3. Compare your grandparents' lives when they were teenagers to the lives of teenagers today.
   (e.g., *My grandparents didn't use to watch rented movies on TV with their friends, but today teenagers often watch movies together for entertainment.*)

4. Compare past and present beliefs.
   (e.g., *Some people used to believe the moon was made of cheese, but now we know that the moon is not made of cheese.*)

◇ **PRACTICE 22—GUIDED STUDY:** Verb tense review. (Chapters 1 and 2)

Directions: Complete the sentences with the verbs in parentheses. Use the SIMPLE PAST, SIMPLE PRESENT, or PAST PROGRESSIVE.

(1) Once upon a time, a king and his three daughters (*live*) _____ **lived** _____ in a castle in a faraway land. One day while the king (*think*) ___ **was thinking** ___ about his daughters, he (*have*) _____ **had** _____ an idea. He (*form*) _____ **formed** _____ a plan for finding husbands for them.

(2) When it (come) _____ **came** _____ time for the three daughters to marry, the king (announce) _____ **announced** _____ his plan. He said, "I'm going to take three jewels to the center of the village. The young men (meet) _____ **meet** ★ _____ at the fountain there every day. The three young men who find the jewels will become my daughters' husbands."

(3) The next day, the king (choose) _____ three jewels—an emerald, a ruby, and a diamond—and (take) _____ them into the village. He (hold) _____ them in his hand and (walk) _____ among the young men. First he (drop) _____ the emerald, then the ruby, and then the diamond. A handsome man (pick) _____ up the emerald. Then a wealthy prince (spot) _____ the ruby and (bend) _____ down to pick it up. The king (be) _____ very pleased.

(4) But then a frog (hop) _____ toward the diamond and (pick) _____ it up. The frog (bring) _____ the diamond to the king and said, "I (be) _____ the Frog Prince. I claim your third daughter as my wife."

(5) When the king (tell) _____ Tina, his third daughter, about the Frog Prince, she (refuse) _____ to marry him. When the people of the land (hear) _____ the news about the frog and the princess, they (laugh) _____ and (laugh) _____. "Have you heard the news?" the people (say) _____ to each other. "Princess Tina is going to marry a frog!"

(6) Tina (feel) _____ terrible. "I (be) _____ the unluckiest person in the world," she (sob) _____. She (believe) _____ no

---

★The simple present is used here because the story is giving the king's exact words in a quotation. Notice that quotation marks (" . . . ") are used. See Chart 15–1 for more information about quotations.

one (*love*) _____ her and her father (*understand, not*) _____

her. She (*hide*) _____ from her friends and (*keep*) _____ her pain

in her heart. Every day she (*grow*) _____ sadder and sadder. Her two sisters

(*have*) _____ grand weddings. Their wedding bells (*ring*) _____

with joy across the land.

(7) Eventually, Tina (*leave*) _____ the castle. She (*run*) _____

away from her family and (*go*) _____ to live by herself in a small cottage in the

woods. She (*eat*) _____ simple food, (*drink*) _____ water from the

lake, (*cut*) _____ her own firewood, (*wash*) _____ her own clothes,

(*sweep*) _____ the floor, (*make*) _____ her own bed, and (*take*)

_____ care of all her own needs. But she (*be*) _____ very lonely

and unhappy.

(8) One day Tina (*go*) _____ swimming. The water (*be*) _____

deep and cold. Tina (*swim*) _____ for a long time and (*become*) _____

very tired. While she (*swim*) _____ back toward the shore, she (*lose*)

_____ the desire to live. She (*quit*) _____ trying to swim to safety.

She (*drown*) _____ when the frog suddenly (*appear*) _____

and, with all his strength, (*push*) _____ Tina to land. He (*save*) _____

her life.

(9) "Why (*save, you*) _____ my life, Frog?"

"Because you (*be*) _____ very young and you (*have*) _____ a

lot to live for."

"No, I (*do, not*) _____," said the princess. "I (*be*) _____ the

most miserable person in the whole universe."

(10) "Let's talk about it," (*say*) _____ the frog, and they (*begin*) _____

to talk. Tina and the Frog Prince (*sit*) _____ together for hours and hours. Frog

(*listen*) _____ and (*understand*) _____. He (*tell*)

_____ her about himself and his own unhappiness and loneliness. They (*share*)

_____ their minds and hearts. Day after day, they (*spend*) _____

hours with each other. They (*talk*) _____, (*laugh*) _____, (*play*)

_____, and (*work*) _____ together.

(11) One day while they (*sit*) _____ near the lake, Tina (*bend*)

_____ down and, with great affection, (*kiss*) _____ the frog on his

forehead. Suddenly the frog (*turn*) _____ into a man. He (*take*) _____

Tina in his arms and said, "You (*save*) _____ me with your kiss. Outside, I (*look*)

_____ like a frog. But you (*see*) _____ inside and (*find*)

_____ the real me. Now I (*be*) _____ free. An evil wizard turned

me into a frog until I found the love of a woman with a truly good heart." When Tina (*see*)

_____ through outside appearances, she (*find*) _____ true love.

(12) Tina and the prince (*return*)

_____ to the castle and (*get*)

_____ married. Her two sisters, she

discovered, (*be*) _____ very

unhappy. The handsome husband (*ignore*)

_____ his wife and (*talk, not*)

_____ to her. The wealthy

husband (*make*) _____ fun of his wife

and (*give*) _____ her orders all the

time. But Tina and her frog prince (*live*)

_____ happily ever after.

◇ **PRACTICE 23—GUIDED STUDY: Past time.   (Chapter 2)**

Directions: In a small group, make up a story that happens in past time.

FIRST: One member of the group should begin the story, then the next student continues the story, and then the next ones until the story is finished.
SECOND: One member of the group should repeat the whole story orally while the others listen.
THIRD: The group should discuss any changes they want to make in the story.
FOURTH: Then each member of the group should write this story; in other words, each member of the group should write **the same story**.

Story suggestions:

1. A creative story about fictional people and events.
    Possible beginning: *One day a person named Joe decided he had a boring life, so he decided to do something new and different every day for the rest of his life. The next morning was a Monday. Joe got up and left his apartment . . . .*

2. An inventive tale about people and talking animals.
    Possible beginning: *Once upon a time, a bear named Jane and a crow named Frank became friends. They got tired of their lives in the wilderness, so they decided to go to a city . . . .*

3. A humorous story about a fictional student in your class who constantly has bad luck.
    Possible beginning: *There is a student named . . . in our class who always seems to have bad luck. One day he wanted to sharpen his pencil, but he forgot what he was doing. The pencil got shorter and shorter. Then finally (. . .)'s finger was in the pencil sharpener. He sharpened his finger to a point before he realized what he was doing. Now he has one finger that is pointed at the end . . . .*

4. A murder mystery with various suspects.
    Possible beginning: *On a dark and stormy night, Mr. Fox lit a candle and took his money box from its hiding place. He unlocked it and slowly counted each gold coin. He didn't hear footsteps coming up the stairs. The door creaked open . . . .*

◇ **PRACTICE 24—GUIDED STUDY: Past time.   (Chapter 2)**

Directions: With your classmates, write a story that happens in the past. Each student should write one paragraph of three to five sentences at a time. One student begins the story. Then he or she passes the paper on to another student, who will then write a paragraph and pass the paper on—until everyone in the class has had a chance to write a paragraph. Use the story suggestions in Practice 23 above or make up your own story beginning.

◇ **PRACTICE 25—SELFSTUDY: Prepositions of time.   (Chart 2–10)**

Directions: Complete the sentences with appropriate PREPOSITIONS.

1. Jack goes shopping ___***on***___ Saturdays.

2. Elaine and I had a light lunch _____ noon, and then we played tennis _____ the afternoon.

3. A: Hi, John. It's good to see you again. When I saw you _____ December, you were working at the department store. Are you still working there?

    B: No. I quit _____ January 1st. _____ present, I'm working at Joe's Music Shop.

    _____ the future, I hope to have my own music store.

4. _____ 1988, we moved to this city. We arrived _____ night and couldn't find our new house. We got a hotel room and found the house _____ the morning.

5. I like to visit friends _____ the evening. I don't like to stay home by myself _____ night.

6. Excuse me. Are you busy _____ the moment?

7. A: When did you and your family go to New York?

   B: _____ 1990.

   A: _____ the spring or fall?

   B: We arrived _____ June 15 and left _____ the 21st.

8. What are the most important events that occurred _____ the nineteenth century?

◇ **PRACTICE 26—SELFSTUDY: Prepositions. (Chapters 1 and 2)**

Directions: Complete the sentences with appropriate PREPOSITIONS.

1. Richard got mad ___*at*___ me when I asked him to get up early ___*in*___ the morning.

2. I'm ready _____ a change and a better job. I'll choose more carefully _____ the future.

3. A: Are you prepared to answer all questions for the court?

   B: Yes, I am.

   A: Where were you _____ February 3, 1991, _____ exactly 8:12 P.M.?

   B: I was having dinner with friends.

   A: Don't you usually work _____ the evening?

   B: I was absent _____ work. I was angry _____ a co-worker and didn't go to work that day. I left my friends _____ midnight.

   A: No more questions for this witness, Your Honor.

4. A: Are you familiar _____ the new musical play downtown?

   B: I'm told it's very good. We're going to see it _____ the summer.

5. A: What do you do _____ Sunday afternoons?

   B: I go to the amusement park with my family almost every Sunday.

   A: Oh. Isn't the park full _____ people _____ Sundays? I hate crowds.

   B: It's not so bad _____ the early afternoon. It gets worse later in the day.

6. My son was afraid _____ dogs _____ the past, but now he's asking me to get him one.

CHAPTER 3
Future Time

◇ **PRACTICE 1—SELFSTUDY:** Present, past, and future. (Chapters 1, 2, and 3)

Directions: Complete the sentences with the given verbs. Use:
a. the SIMPLE PRESENT
b. the SIMPLE PAST, and
c. **BE GOING TO/WILL.**

1. *arrive*
   a. Joe _____*arrives*_____ on time **every day.**
   b. Joe _____*arrived*_____ on time **yesterday.**
   c. Joe _____*is going to arrive*_____ on time **tomorrow.** OR:
      Joe _____*will arrive*_____ on time **tomorrow.**

2. *arrive?*
   a. _____ Joe _____ on time **every day?**
   b. _____*Did*_____ Joe _____*arrive*_____ on time **yesterday?**
   c. _____ Joe _____ on time **tomorrow?** OR:
      _____ Joe _____ on time **tomorrow?**

3. *arrive, not*
   a. Mike _____ on time **every day.**
   b. Mike _____ on time **yesterday.**
   c. Mike _____*isn't going to be*_____ on time **tomorrow.** OR:
      Mike _____ on time **tomorrow.**

4. *eat*
   a. Ann _____ breakfast **every day.**
   b. Ann _____ breakfast **yesterday.**
   c. Ann _____ breakfast **tomorrow.** OR:
      Ann _____ breakfast **tomorrow.**

5. *eat?*
   a. _____ you _____ breakfast **every day?**
   b. _____ you _____ breakfast **yesterday?**
   c. _____ you _____ breakfast **tomorrow?** OR:
      _____ you _____ breakfast **tomorrow?**

6. *eat, not*
   a. I _____ breakfast **every day.**
   b. I _____ breakfast **yesterday.**
   c. I _____ breakfast **tomorrow.** OR:
      I _____ breakfast **tomorrow.**

◇ **PRACTICE 2—SELFSTUDY:** Present, past, and future. (Chapters 1, 2, and 3)

Directions: Complete the sentences with forms of the verb in italics. Use the SIMPLE PRESENT, SIMPLE PAST, and **BE GOING TO.**

1. A: I *got* up at five this morning.

   B: Oh? ____**Do**____ you _____**get**_____ up at five every morning?

   A: Yes, I ___**do**___. I _____**get**_____ up at five every morning.

   B: ____**Did**____ you _____**get**_____ up at five yesterday morning?

   A: Yes, I ___**did**___. I _____**got**_____ up at five yesterday morning.

   B: ____**Are**____ you _____**going to get**_____ up at five tomorrow morning?

   A: Yes, I ___**am**___. I _____**'m going to get**_____ up at five tomorrow morning.

2. A: I *studied* last night.

   B: Oh? _____ you _____ every night?

   A: Yes, I _____. I _____ every night.

   B: _____ you _____ last Saturday night?

   A: Yes, I _____. I _____ last Saturday night.

   B: _____ you _____ tomorrow night?

   A: Yes, I _____. I _____ tomorrow night.

◇ **PRACTICE 3—GUIDED STUDY:** Present, past, and future. (Chapters 1, 2, and 3)

Directions: Write a dialogue by completing the sentences with your own words.

A: I . . . yesterday.
B: Oh? . . . you . . . every day?
A: Yes, I . . . . I . . . every day.
B: . . . you . . . two days ago?
A: Yes, I . . . . I . . . two days ago.
B: . . . you . . . tomorrow?
A: Yes, I . . . . I . . . tomorrow.

◇ **PRACTICE 4—SELFSTUDY:** *Be going to.* (Chart 3–1)

Directions: Complete the sentences with **BE GOING TO** and the words in parentheses.

1. A: What (*you, do*) _____**are you going to do**_____ this afternoon?

   B: I (*finish*) _____**am going to finish**_____ my report.

2. A: Where (*Ryan, be*) _____ later tonight?

   B: He (*be*) _____ at Kim's house.

3. A: (*you, have*) _____ a hamburger for lunch?

   B: I (*eat, not*) _____ lunch. I don't have enough time.

4. A: (*you, finish*) _____ this exercise soon?

   B: I (*finish*) _____ it in less than a minute.

5. A: When (*you, call*) _____ your sister?

    B: I (*call, not*) _____ her. I (*write*) _____

        _____ her a letter.

6. A: What (*Laura, talk*) _____ about in her speech tonight?

    B: She (*discuss*) _____ the economy of Southeast Asia.

◇ **PRACTICE 5—GUIDED STUDY:** *Be going to.* (Chart 3-1)

Directions: Pair up with a classmate.
STUDENT A: Ask a question using **BE GOING TO** and the given words.
STUDENT B: Answer the question. Use **BE GOING TO.**

Example: what/do next Monday?
STUDENT A: What are you going to do next Monday?
STUDENT B: I'm going to go to my classes as usual.

Example: watch TV tonight?
STUDENT A: Are you going to watch TV tonight?
STUDENT B: Yes, I'm going to watch TV tonight. OR: No, I'm not going to watch TV tonight.

1. where/go after your last class today?
2. have pizza for dinner tonight?
3. what/do this evening?
4. when/visit your family?
5. play soccer with (. . .)* Saturday?
6. what/do this coming Saturday?
7. look for a new place to live soon?
8. where/live next year?

(*Change roles:* STUDENT A *becomes* STUDENT B *and vice versa.*)

9. what time/go to bed tonight?
10. what/wear tomorrow?
11. wear your raincoat tomorrow?
12. take a trip sometime this year or next?
13. where/go and what/do?
14. how long/stay at this school?
15. talk to your family soon?
16. when/see your family again?

◇ **PRACTICE 6—GUIDED STUDY:** *Be going to.* (Chart 3-1)

Directions: Use the given words to make sentences with **BE GOING TO.** Use your own ideas. Be sure to use a form of **BE GOING TO** in each sentence. Notice the various time expressions that are used to indicate future time.

Example: you/today?
Response: Are you going to eat lunch at McDonald's today?

_____
*The symbol (. . .) means that you should use the name of a person you know.

Example: (. . .)/tonight.
Response: Abdul is going to hang around with his friends tonight.

1. I/in a half an hour.
2. I/after a while.
3. you/today?
4. (. . .)/later today.
5. I/not/tomorrow morning.
6. you/the day after tomorrow?
7. my friends/next Sunday.
8. we/this coming Monday.
9. (. . .)/this week?
10. (. . .) and I/not/this weekend.
11. (. . .) and (. . .)/this year.
12. I/two years from now.
13. my country/in the future.
14. people/in the twenty-first century?

◇ PRACTICE 7—SELFSTUDY: *Will.* (Chart 3–2)

Directions: Complete the dialogues. Use **WILL**.

1. A: (*you, help*) _____ **Will you help** _____ me tomorrow?

   B: Yes, ____ **I will*** ____. OR: No, ____ **I won't** ____.

2. A: (*Paul, lend*) _____ us some money?

   B: Yes, _____. OR: No, _____.

3. A: (*Jane, graduate*) _____ this spring?

   B: Yes, _____. OR: No, _____.

4. A: (*her parents, be*) _____ at the ceremony?

   B: Yes, _____. OR: No, _____.

5. A: (*I, benefit*) _____ from this business deal?

   B: Yes, _____. OR: No, _____.

◇ PRACTICE 8—SELFSTUDY: *Will probably.* (Chart 3–3)

Directions: Complete the sentences with **WILL** or **WON'T**. Also use **PROBABLY**.

1. The clouds are leaving, and the sun is coming out. It _____ **probably won't** _____ rain

   anymore.

2. The weather is cold today. There's no reason to expect the weather to change. It

   _____ **will probably** _____ be cold tomorrow, too.

3. Sam, Sharon, and Carl worked hard on this project. They _____

   turn in the best work. The other students didn't work as hard.

4. Ronald is having a very difficult time in advanced algebra. He didn't understand anything

   that happened in class today, and he _____ understand tomorrow's

   class either.

5. Jan skipped lunch today. She _____ eat as soon as she gets home.

---

*Pronouns are NOT contracted with helping verbs in short answers.
    CORRECT: *Yes, I will.*
    INCORRECT: *Yes, I'll.*

6. I don't like parties. Mike really wants me to come to his birthday party, but I
_____ go. I'd rather stay home.

7. Conditions in the factory have been very bad for a long time. All of the people who work on the assembly line are angry. They _____ vote to go out on strike.

8. We are using up the earth's resources at a rapid rate. We _____ continue to do so★ for years to come.

◇ **PRACTICE 9—GUIDED STUDY:** *Will probably.* (Chart 3–3)

Directions: For each situation, predict something that **WILL PROBABLY** happen and something that **PROBABLY WON'T** happen.

Example: Emily has a test in ten minutes. She didn't study for it at all. (*pass it / fail it*)
Response: She probably won't pass it. She'll probably fail it.

1. It's raining. Greg doesn't have an umbrella. (*get wet / stay outside for a long time*)
2. Mr. Lee works at an aircraft factory. He has a bad cold. (*go to work / stay home today*)
3. Sam didn't sleep at all last night. (*go to bed early tonight / stay up all night again tonight*)
4. Alan has to go to Chicago on business. He hates to fly. (*go by plane / take a bus or a train*)

Use your own words to make predictions with WILL PROBABLY *and* PROBABLY WON'T:

5. (. . .) likes movies. There's a new movie at the local theater.
6. The weather is going to be rainy tomorrow. You like this kind of weather.
7. (. . .) is going to spend five days in New York as a tourist.
8. Many important events are taking place in the world today. What are some of these events? Make predictions about them.

◇ **PRACTICE 10—GUIDED STUDY:** *Be going to and will.* (Chart 3–3)

Directions: For each situation, predict the future. Use **WILL** or **BE GOING TO**. Use **PROBABLY** if you wish. Use the negative if you wish.

Example: people/go to work only four days a week.
→ *People will probably go to work only four days a week.*

1. we/use electric motors in automobiles in the future
2. we/use solar energy to heat buildings in the future
3. clothing styles/change a lot in fifty years
4. today's rock music/popular twenty years from now
5. we/be able to communicate by videophone
6. doctors/be able to replace nearly all vital organs
7. the population of the earth/double in thirty-five years
8. the earth/have enough fresh water to support a population of twelve billion
9. the earth's tropical rain forests/disappear
10. What other predictions can you make about the twenty-first century?

★*Do so* means "do the thing that the speaker/writer just mentioned." In this sentence, *do so* = *use up the earth's resources at a rapid rate.*

Directions: Using the given information about SPEAKER B's plans, complete the sentences with either **BE GOING TO** or **WILL**.*

1. (SPEAKER B *is planning to listen to the news at six.*)

   A: Why did you turn on the radio?

   B: I ___*'m going to*___ listen to the news at six.

2. (SPEAKER B *didn't have a plan to show the other person how to solve the math problem, but she is glad to do it.*)

   A: I can't figure out this math problem. Do you know how to do it?

   B: Yes. Give me your pencil. I ___*'ll*___ show you how to solve it.

3. (SPEAKER B *has made a plan. He is planning to lie down because he doesn't feel well.*)

   A: What's the matter?

   B: I don't feel well. I _____ lie down for a little while. If anyone calls, tell

   them I'll call back later.

   A: Okay. I hope you feel better.

4. (SPEAKER B *did not plan to take the other person home. He is making the offer spontaneously. He thinks of the idea only after the other person talks about missing his bus.*)

   A: Oh no! I wasn't watching the time. I missed my bus.

   B: That's okay. I _____ give you a ride home.

   A: Hey, thanks!

5. (SPEAKER B *has a plan.*)

   A: Why did you borrow money from the bank?

   B: I _____ buy a new pickup.** I've already picked it out.

6. (SPEAKER B *does not have a plan.*)

   A: Mom, can I have a candy bar?

   B: No, but I _____ buy an apple for you. How does that sound?

   A: Okay, I guess.

7. (SPEAKER B *has already made her plans about what to wear. Then* SPEAKER B *makes a spontaneous offer.*)

   A: I can't figure out what to wear to the Harvest Moon Ball. It's formal, isn't it?

   B: Yes. I _____ wear a floor-length gown.

   A: Maybe I should wear my red gown with the big sleeves. But I think it needs cleaning.

   B: I _____ take it to the cleaner's for you when I go downtown this afternoon

   if you'd like.

   A: Gee, thanks. That'll save me a trip.

---

*Usually *be going to* and *will* are interchangeable: you can use either one of them with little or no difference in meaning. Sometimes, however, they are NOT interchangeable. In this exercise, only one of them is correct, not both. See Chart 3-4.

**A *pickup* is a small truck.

Directions: Complete the sentences with either **BE GOING TO** or **WILL**.

1. A: Why are you looking for a screwdriver?

   B: One of the kitchen chairs has a loose screw. I _____ fix it.

2. A: The computer printer isn't working again! What am I going to do?

   B: Calm down. Give Tom a call. He _____ fix it for you. It's probably just a

   loose connection.

3. A: Are you going to the post office soon?

   B: Yeah. Why?

   A: I need to send this letter today.

   B: I _____ mail it for you.

   A: Thanks.

4. A: Why are you carrying that box?

   B: I _____ mail it to my sister. I'm on my way to the post office.

5. A: Let's meet for a beer after work.

   B: Sounds good to me. I _____ meet you at the Blue Goose Bar at six.

6. A: Can you meet me for a beer after work?

   B: I'd like to, but I can't. I _____ stay at the office until seven tonight.

7. A: It's grandfather's eighty-fifth birthday next Sunday. What _____ you

   _____ give him for his birthday?

   B: I _____ give him a walking stick that I made myself.

8. A: I have a note for Joe from Rachel. I don't know what to do with it.

   B: Let me have it. I _____ give it to him. He's in my algebra class.

   A: Thanks. But you have to promise not to read it.

◇ **PRACTICE 13—SELFSTUDY: Time clauses. (Chart 3–5)**

Directions: Combine the two sentences in any order, using the time expression in parentheses.
Underline the time clause in the sentence you write. Pay special attention to the verb tense you use
in the time clause.

1. I'll call Mike tomorrow. I'll tell him the good news. (*when*)
   → ***When I call Mike tomorrow, I'll tell him the good news.***
   OR: ***I'll tell Mike the good news when I call him tomorrow.***
2. Ann will lock all the doors. She will go to bed. (*before*)
3. I'm going to be in London for two days. I'm going to visit the Tate Museum. (*when*)
4. The show will start. The curtain will go up. (*as soon as*)
5. Nick is going to change the oil in his car. He's going to take a bath. (*after*)
6. We'll call you. We'll drive over to pick you up. (*before*)
7. I'll call you. I'll get an answer from the bank about the loan. (*when*)
8. I'll get my paycheck. I'll pay my rent. (*as soon as*)

◇ PRACTICE 14—SELFSTUDY: Time clauses. (Chart 3–5)

Directions: Use the given verbs to complete the sentences. Use the SIMPLE PRESENT and WILL/ WON'T.

1. *take/read*

   I __'ll read__ the textbook before I _____ *take* _____ the final exam.

2. *return/call*

   Mr. Lee _____ his wife as soon as he _____ to the hotel tonight.

3. *be, not /come*

   I _____ home tomorrow when the painters _____ to paint my apartment. Someone else will have to let them in.

4. *prepare/go*

   Before I _____ to my job interview tomorrow, I _____ a list of questions I want to ask about the company.

5. *visit /take*

   When Sandra _____ us this weekend, we _____ her to our favorite seafood restaurant.

6. *find /move/graduate*

   Sara _____ out of her parents' house after she _____ from school next month and _____ a job.

◇ PRACTICE 15—SELFSTUDY: *If*-clauses. (Chart 3–5)

Directions: Use the given verbs to complete the sentences. Use the SIMPLE PRESENT and WILL/WON'T.

1. *not go/ be*

   If it _____ *is* _____ cold and rainy tomorrow morning, I _____ *won't go* _____ jogging.

2. *get /pay*

   If I _____ a job soon, I _____ you the money I owe you.

3. *not go/ be*

   The boss _____ very disappointed if you _____ to the meeting tomorrow.

4. *stop/tell*

   I _____ taking these pills if Dr. Matthews _____ me it's okay.

5. *get /be /eat*

   If Barbara _____ home on time tonight, we _____ dinner at 6:30. If she _____ late, dinner _____ late.

◇ **PRACTICE 16—GUIDED STUDY: Time clauses and *If*-clauses. (Chart 3–5)**

Directions: Combine the ideas in the pairs of sentences. Use **WHEN, AFTER, AS SOON AS**, or **IF**. Pay special attention to verb tenses. <u>Underline</u> the "time clause" or "*if*-clause" in each sentence you write.

Example: I'll see you Sunday afternoon. I'll give you my answer (then).*

 Written: **<u>When I see you Sunday afternoon</u>, I'll give you my answer.**

  OR: **I'll give you my answer <u>when I see you Sunday afternoon</u>.**

1. I'm going to clean up my apartment (first). My friends are going to come over (later).
2. The storm will be over (in an hour or two). I'm going to do some errands (then).
3. (Maybe) you won't learn how to use a computer. (As a result), you will have trouble finding a job.
4. Joe will meet us at the coffee shop. He'll finish his report (soon).
5. Sue will wash and dry the dishes. (Then) she will put them away.
6. They may not leave at seven. (As a result), they won't get to the theater on time.

◇ **PRACTICE 17—SELFSTUDY: Parallel verbs. (Chart 3–6)**

Directions: <u>Underline</u> the first verb in each parallel structure. Circle the word **and**. Then complete the sentence with the PARALLEL FORM OF THE VERB in parentheses.

1. Last night, I <u>was listening</u> to music ⟨and⟩ (*do*) _____ **(was) doing** _____ my homework when Kim stopped by.

2. My classmates <u>are going to meet</u> at Danny's ⟨and⟩ (*study*) **(are going to) study** _____ together tonight.

3. Tomorrow the sun will rise at 6:34 and (*set*) _____ at 8:59.

4. While Paul was carrying brushes and paint and

   (*climb*) _____ a ladder, a bird flew

   down and (*sit*) _____ on his head. Paul

   dropped the paint and (*spill*) _____ it all

   over the ground.

5. Next weekend, Nick is going to meet his friends downtown

   and (*go*) _____ to a soccer game.

6. Anna moves into her apartment on Sunday and (*start*)

   _____ her new job on Monday.

7. My pen slipped out of my hand and (*fall*)

   _____ to the floor.

8. I'm getting up early tomorrow morning and

   (*walk*) _____ to work.

_____
*When you combine the sentences, omit the words in parentheses.

9. When I first arrived in this city and (*start*) _____ going to school here, I knew no one. I was lonely and (*feel*) _____ that I didn't have a friend in the world. One day while I was watching TV alone in my room and (*feel*) _____ sorry for myself, a woman I had met in one of my classes knocked on my door and (*ask*) _____ me if I wanted to accompany her to the student center. That was the beginning of my friendship with Lisa King. Now we see each other every day and usually (*spend*) _____ time talking on the phone, too. This week we're borrowing her brother's car and (*go*) _____ to visit her aunt in the country. Next week we're going to take a bus to Fall City and (*go*) _____ to a football game. I'm really enjoying our friendship.

◇ **PRACTICE 18—SELFSTUDY: Parallel verbs. (Chart 3–6)**

Directions: Complete the sentences with the verbs in parentheses.

1. Fifteen years from now, my wife and I (*retire*) _____**will retire**_____ and (*travel*) _____**(will) travel**_____ all over the world.

2. If I feel tense, I (*close*) _____**close**_____ my eyes and (*think*) _____**think**_____ about nothing at all.

3. A: What is Pete doing in the other room?
   B: He (*watch*) _____ TV and (*study*) _____ for his chemistry exam.

4. Every morning without exception, Mrs. Carter (*take*) _____ her dog for a walk and (*buy*) _____ a newspaper at Charlie's newsstand.

5. Before I (*go*) _____ to your boss and (*tell*) _____ her about your mistake, I want to give you an opportunity to explain it to her yourself.

6. Next month, I (*take*) _____ my vacation and (*forget*) _____ about everything that is connected to my job.

7. Kathy thinks I was the cause of her problems, but I wasn't. Someday she (*discover*) _____ the truth and (*apologize*) _____ to me.

8. Yesterday I (*see*) _____ the man who stole the radio from my car last Friday. I (*run*) _____ after him, (*catch*) _____ him, and (*knock*) _____ him down. A passerby (*go*) _____ to call the police. I (*sit*) _____ on the man while I (*wait*) _____ for them to come. After they (*get*) _____ there and (*understand*) _____ the situation, they (*put*) _____ handcuffs on him and (*take*) _____ him to jail.

◇ **PRACTICE 19—GUIDED STUDY:** Past and future. (Chapters 2 and 3)

Directions: Read Part I. Use the information in Part I to complete Part II with appropriate verbs and tenses. Use **WILL** (not *be going to*) for future time in Part II.

PART I:

(1) Yesterday morning **was** an ordinary morning. I **got** up at 6:30. I **washed** my face and **brushed** my teeth. Then I **put** on my jeans and a sweater. I **went** to the kitchen and **started** the electric coffee maker.

(2) Then I **walked** down my driveway to get the morning newspaper. While I **was walking** to get the paper, I **saw** a deer. It **was eating** the flowers in my garden. After I **watched** the deer for a little while, I **made** some noise to make the deer run away before it **destroyed** my flowers.

(3) As soon as I **got** back to the kitchen, I **poured** myself a cup of coffee and **opened** the morning paper. While I **was reading** the paper, my teenage daughter **came** downstairs. We **talked** about her plans for the day. I **helped** her with her breakfast and **made** a lunch for her to take to school. After we **said** goodbye, I **ate** some fruit and cereal and **finished** reading the paper.

(4) Then I **went** to my office. My office **is** in my home. My office **has** a desk, a computer, a radio, a TV set, a copy machine, and a lot of bookshelves. I **worked** all morning. While I **was working**, the phone **rang** many times. I **talked** to many people. At 11:30, I **went** to the kitchen and **made** a sandwich for lunch. As I said, it **was** an ordinary morning.

PART II:

(1) Tomorrow morning _____***will be***_____ an ordinary morning. I ___***'ll get***_____ up at 6:30. I __***'ll wash***_____ my face and _____***brush***_____ my teeth. Then I _____ probably _____ on my jeans and a sweater. I _____ to the kitchen and _____ the electric coffee maker.

(2) Then I _____ down my driveway to get the morning newspaper. If I _____ a deer in my garden, I _____ it for a while and then _____ some noise to chase it away before it _____ my flowers.

(3) As soon as I _____ back to the kitchen, I _____ myself a cup of coffee and _____ the morning paper. While I'm reading the paper, my teenage daughter _____ downstairs. We _____ about her plans for the day. I _____ her with her breakfast and _____ a lunch for her to take to school. After we _____ goodbye, I _____ some fruit and cereal and _____ reading the morning paper.

(4) Then I _____ to my office. My office _____ in my home. My office _____ a desk, a computer, a radio, a TV set, a copy machine, and a lot of bookshelves. I _____ all morning. While I'm working, the phone _____ many times. I _____ to many people. At 11:30, I _____ to the kitchen and _____ a sandwich for lunch. As I said, tomorrow morning _____ an ordinary morning.

Directions: Complete the sentences with the PRESENT PROGRESSIVE. Use the verbs in the list. Use each verb only one time. Notice the future time expressions in italics.

arrive	*leave*	*speak*	*take*
attend	*meet*	*spend*	✔*travel*
get	*see*	*study*	*visit*

1. Kathy _____**is traveling**_____ to Caracas *next month* to attend a conference.

2. A: Are you expecting guests? Your apartment is so neat!

   B: How did you guess? My parents _____ *tomorrow* for a two-day visit.

3. A: Do you have any plans for lunch today?

   B: I _____ Shannon at the Shamrock Cafe *in an hour*. Want to join us?

4. A: I _____ a bicycle for my son for his birthday *next month*. Do you

   know anything about bikes for kids?

   B: Sure. What do you want to know?

5. Amanda likes to take her two children with her on trips whenever she can, but she

   _____ not _____ them with her to El Paso, Texas, *next week*. It's

   strictly a business trip.

6. A: What are your plans for the rest of the year?

   B: I _____ French in Grenoble, France, *this coming summer*. Then I'll be

   back here in school in the fall.

7. A: Why are you packing your suitcase?

   B: I _____ for Los Angeles *in a couple of hours*.

8. A: My regular doctor, Dr. Jordan, _____ a conference in Las Vegas *next*

   week, so I _____ her partner, Dr. Peterson, when I go for my

   appointment *next Friday*.

9. A: Do we have a test in English class tomorrow?

   B: No. Don't you remember? We're going to have a guest lecturer.

   A: Really? Who? Are you sure we don't have a test?

   B: A professor from the Department of Environmental Sciences _____

   to our class tomorrow morning.

   A: Great. That sounds interesting. And it sure beats having a test.

10. A: Why are you looking for your passport?

    B: I need it because I'm leaving for Taipei next Monday.

    A: Oh? How long will you be away?

    B: A week. I _____ the first few days with my brother, who is going to

    school there. After that I _____ some old friends I went to school

    with in Australia several years ago. They've invited me to be their house guest.

    A: Sounds like a great trip. Hope you find your passport.

◇ PRACTICE 21—SELFSTUDY: The present progressive to express future time. (Chart 3–7)

Directions: Look at Fred's calendar. Then complete the sentences about Fred's plans for the coming week. Use the PRESENT PROGRESSIVE.

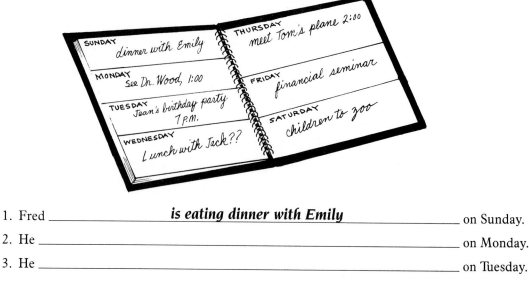

1. Fred _____*is eating dinner with Emily*_____ on Sunday.

2. He _____ on Monday.

3. He _____ on Tuesday.

4. He _____ probably _____ on Wednesday.

5. He _____ on Thursday.

6. He _____ on Friday.

7. He _____ on Saturday.

◇ PRACTICE 22—GUIDED STUDY: The present progressive to express future time. (Chart 3–7)

Directions: Make a calendar of **your plans** for the coming week. Then complete the sentences about these plans. Use the PRESENT PROGRESSIVE.

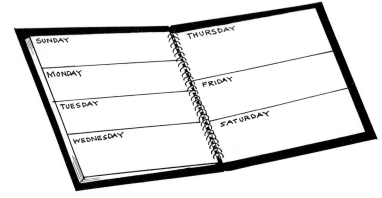

1. I _____ on Sunday.

2. I _____ on Monday.

3. I _____ on Tuesday.

4. I _____ on Wednesday.

5. I _____ on Thursday.

6. I _____ on Friday.

7. I _____ on Saturday.

◇ PRACTICE 23—GUIDED STUDY: The present progressive to express future time. (Chart 3-7)

Directions: Think of a place you would like to visit. Pretend you are going to take a trip there this weekend. Pretend you have already made all of your plans. Write a paragraph in which you describe your trip. Use the PRESENT PROGRESSIVE where appropriate.

Example: This coming weekend, my friend Benito and I are taking a trip. We're going to Nashville, Tennessee. Benito likes country music and wants to go to some shows. I don't know anything about country music, but I'm looking forward to going to Nashville. We're leaving Friday afternoon as soon as Benito gets off work. (Etc.)

Possible questions to answer in your paragraph:
1. Where are you going?
2. When are you leaving?
3. Are you traveling alone?
4. How are you getting there?
5. Where are you staying?
6. Who are you visiting, if anyone?
7. How long are you staying there?
8. When are you getting back?

◇ PRACTICE 24—SELFSTUDY: The simple present to express future time. (Chart 3-8)

Directions: Use any of the verbs in the list to complete the sentences. Use the SIMPLE PRESENT to express future time.

begin	finish	leave
close	get in	open
end	land	start

1. A: What time _____ **does** _____ class _____ **begin (OR: start)** _____ tomorrow morning?

   B: It _____ **begins (OR: starts)** _____ at eight o'clock sharp.

2. A: The coffee shop _____ at seven o'clock tomorrow morning. I'll meet you

   there at 7:15.

   B: Okay. I'll be there.

3. A: What time are you going to go to the airport tonight?

   B: Tom's plane _____ around 7:15, but I think I'll go a little early in case it

   gets in ahead of schedule.

4. A: What time should we go to the theater tonight?

   B: Around 7:30. The movie _____ at 8:00.

   A: What time _____ it _____?

   B: It's a two-hour movie. It _____ at 10:00.

5. A: What time _____ the dry cleaning shop _____ tonight? If I

   don't get there in time, I'll have nothing to wear to the banquet tonight.

   B: It _____ at 6:00. I can pick up your dry cleaning for you.

   A: Hey, thanks! That'll really help!

6. A: What's the hurry?

   B: I've got to take a shower, change clothes, and get to the theater fast. The play
   _____ in forty-five minutes, and I don't want to miss the beginning.

◇ **PRACTICE 25—SELFSTUDY:** *Be about to.* (Chart 3–10)

Directions: Describe the actions that are about to happen in the pictures. Use **BE ABOUT TO**.

1. ___*The chimpanzee is about to eat a banana.*___

2. _____

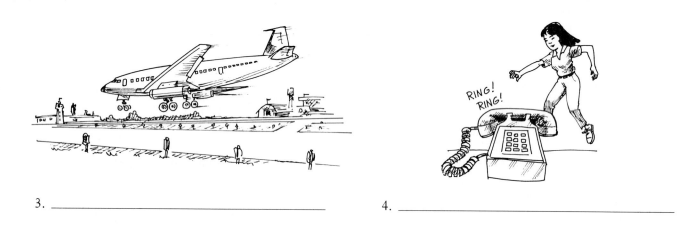

3. _____

4. _____

◇ **PRACTICE 26—SELFSTUDY:** Verb tense review. (Chapters 1, 2 and 3)

Directions: Complete the sentences with a form of the verb in parentheses.

1. A: I'll lend you my bike if I (*need, not*) _____ it tomorrow.

   B: Thanks.

2. A: Everyone in the office (*plan*) _____ to come to the annual company
   picnic tomorrow. (*you, come*) _____?

   B: Of course!

3. A: How (*you, get, usually*) _____ to work?

   B: I (*take*) _____ the commuter train every morning.

4. A few days ago, Janet (*watch*) _____ a drama on TV when the screen suddenly (*become*) _____ blank and the TV set (*stop*) _____ working. She never (*find*) _____ out how the story ended.

5. A: I (*go*) _____ to a lecture on Shakespeare tomorrow evening. Want to join me?

   B: Nah. Brian and I (*go*) _____ to a movie—*Godzilla Eats the Earth*.

6. A: When's Barbara going to call? We have to leave soon.

   B: She (*call, probably*) _____ any minute. I'm sure she'll call us before we (*go*) _____ out to dinner.

7. A: Look! There (*be*) _____ a police car behind us. Its lights (*flash*) _____.

   B: I (*know*) _____! I (*know*) _____! I (*see*) _____ it!

   A: What (*go*) _____ on? (*you, speed*) _____?

   B: No, I'm not. I (*go*) _____ the speed limit.

   A: Ah, look. The police car (*pass*) _____ us. Whew.

8. Sometime in the next twenty-five years, a spaceship with a human crew (*land*) _____ on Mars. At least, that's what I (*think*) _____.

9. I usually (*ride*) _____ my bicycle to work in the morning, but it (*rain*) _____ when I left my house early this morning, so I (*drive*) _____ my car. After I (*arrive*) _____ at work, I (*discover*) _____ that I had left my briefcase at home.

10. A: How do you like your new job?

    B: I don't start it until tomorrow. I (*give*) _____ you an answer next week.

11. A: What (*you, wear*) _____ to Eric's wedding tomorrow?

    B: My blue dress, I guess. How about you?

    A: I (*plan*) _____ to wear my new outfit. I (*buy*) _____ it just a few days ago. It (*be*) _____ a yellow suit with a white blouse. Just a minute. I (*show*) _____ it to you. Wait right here. I (*get*) _____ it from my closet and (*bring*) _____ it out.

12. A: Where's my blue sweater?

    B: Lizzy (*wear*) _____ it today.

    A: She's what? I (*lend, not*) _____ her my sweater.

    B: Oh? Well, Lizzy (*be*) _____ back soon. You can get your sweater back then.

Directions: Complete the sentences with a form of the verb in parentheses.

(1) Two hundred and fifty years ago, people (*make*) _____ their own clothes. They (*have, not*) _____ machines for making clothes. There (*be, not*) _____ any clothing factories. People (*wear*) _____ homemade clothes that were sewn by hand.

(2) Today, very few people (*make*) _____ their own clothes. Clothing (*come*) _____ ready-made from factories. People (*buy*) _____ almost all their clothes from stores.

(3) The modern clothing industry (*be*) _____ international. As a result, people from different countries often (*wear*) _____ similar clothes. For example, people in many different countries throughout the world (*wear*) _____ jeans and T-shirts.

(4) However, regional differences in clothing still (*exist*) _____. For instance, people of the Arabian deserts (*wear*) _____ loose, flowing robes to protect themselves from the heat of the sun. In northern Europe, fur hats (*be*) _____ common in the winter.

(5) In the future, there (*be, probably*) _____ fewer and fewer differences in clothing in the world. People throughout the world (*wear*) _____ clothes from the same factories. (*we all, dress*) _____ almost alike in the future? TV shows and movies about the future often (*show*) _____ everybody in a uniform of some kind. What (*you, think*) _____?

◇ PRACTICE 28—GUIDED STUDY: Verb tense review. (Chapters 1, 2, and 3)

Directions: Complete the sentences with a form of the verb in parentheses.

Dianne, Sara, and Emily all (*1. go*) _____ to college together twenty years ago. They (*2. have*) _____ a wonderful time and (*3. learn*) _____ a lot. Now, the three of them (*4. work*) _____ at the same insurance company. They (*5. eat*) _____ lunch together every day and sometimes (*6. tell*) _____ stories about their school days.

Yesterday, they (*7. remember*) _____ a funny incident at a special banquet during their sophomore year. At this dinner, they (*8. sit*) _____ at the same table as the president of the university. Everything (*9. go*) _____ along fine, but then disaster (*10. strike*) _____. To make a long story short, Sara (*11. spill*) _____ a serving dish full of spaghetti onto the president.

Sara (*12. be*) _____ terribly embarrassed. She (*13. apologize*) _____ profusely and (*14. leave*) _____ the banquet room in tears.

Now, twenty years later, the three women (*15. remember*) _____ every detail,

especially the look on the president's face. When they (*16. tell*) _____ that story at

lunch yesterday, they (*17. laugh*) _____ until tears streamed down their faces.

The spaghetti incident (*18. be, not*) _____ funny when it happened, but it

(*19. be*) _____ funny to the women now. Terrible embarrassments that we suffer

when we (*20. be*) _____ young often seem funny when we (*21. be*) _____

older. As we (*22. get*) _____ older, we (*23. get*) _____ more

tolerant of our own foibles. Right now you (*24. be*) _____ young. When you

(*25. be*) _____ older, you (*26. smile*) _____ with amusement

about some of the seemingly terrible and embarrassing things that happen to you as a young adult.

◇ **PRACTICE 29—GUIDED STUDY: Verb tense review. (Chapters 1, 2, and 3)**

Directions: Complete the sentences with a form of the verb in parentheses.

1. This morning, Bob (*comb*) _____ his hair when the comb (*break*)

   _____. So he (*finish*) _____ combing his hair with his fingers

   and (*rush*) _____ out the door to class.

2. I'm exhausted! When I (*get*) _____ home tonight, I (*read*) _____

   _____ the paper and (*watch*) _____ the news. I (*do, not*) _____

   _____ any work around the house.

3. A: My cousin (*have*) _____ a new cat. She now (*have*) _____

   four cats.

   B: Why (*she, have*) _____ so many?

   A: To catch the mice in her house.

   B: (*you, have*) _____ any cats?

   A: No, and I (*get, not*) _____ any. I (*have, not*) _____

   mice in my house.

4. A: Ouch!

   B: What happened?

   A: I (*cut*) _____ my finger.

   B: It (*bleed*) _____!

   A: I know!

   B: Put pressure on it. I (*get*) _____ some antibiotic and a bandage.

   A: Thanks.

5. A: (*you, take*) _____ the kids to the amusement park tomorrow

   morning?

   B: Yes. It (*open*) _____ at 10:00. If we (*leave*) _____ here at

   9:30, we (*get, probably*) _____ there at 9:55. The kids can be the

   first ones in the park.

6. A: Your phone (*ring*) _____.

   B: I (*know*) _____.

   A: (*you, answer*) _____ it?

   B: No.

   A: (*you, want*) _____ me to get it?

   B: No thanks.

   A: Why (*you, want, not*) _____ to answer your phone?

   B: I (*expect*) _____ another call from the bill collector. I have a bunch of

   bills I haven't paid. I (*want, not*) _____ to talk to her.

   A: Oh.

7. My grandmother used to say, "If adversity (*destroy, not*) _____ you,

   it will strengthen you." In other words, if you (*learn*) _____ to survive bad

   times and bad luck, you will become a stonger person.

8. A: Peter B. Peas is a piece-by-piece pizza eater.

   B: What (*you, say*) _____?

   A: I (*say*) _____, "Peter B. Peas is a piece-by-piece pizza eater." It (*be*)

   _____ a tongue-twister. How fast can *you* say it?

9. A: Okay, let's all open our fortune cookies.

   B: What (*yours, say*) _____?

   A: Mine says, "An unexpected gift (*add*) _____ to your pleasure."

   Great! (*you, plan*) _____ to give me a gift soon?

   B: Not that I know of. Mine says, "Your trust in a friend (*prove*) _____

   well-founded." Good. I (*like*) _____ having trustworthy friends.

C: This one says, "A smile (overcome) _____ a language barrier."
Well, that's good! After this, when I (understand, not) _____
people who (speak) _____ English to me, I (smile, just)
_____ at them!

D: My fortune is this: "Your determination (make) _____ you succeed in
everything."

A: Well, it (look) _____ like all of us (have) _____ good
luck in the future!

10. A: (the sun, keep) _____ burning forever, or (it, burn, eventually)
_____ itself out?

B: It (burn, eventually) _____ itself out, but that
(happen, not) _____ for another five or ten billion years.

◇ **PRACTICE 30—GUIDED STUDY:** Future time. (Chapter 3)

Directions: Do you believe that some people are able to predict the future? Pretend that you have
the ability to see into the future. Choose several people you know (classmates, teachers, family
members, friends) and tell them in writing about their future lives. Discuss such topics as marriage,
children, jobs, contributions to humankind, fame, and exciting adventures. With your words, paint
interesting and fun pictures of their future lives.

◇ **PRACTICE 31—SELFSTUDY:** Prepositions. (Chapter 3)

Directions: Complete the sentences with appropriate PREPOSITIONS.*

1. What are you laughing _____?

2. I can't stop staring _____ Tom's necktie. The colors are wild!

3. A: I don't believe _____ flying saucers. Do you?

   B: I don't know. I think anything is possible.

4. Ted is going to help me _____ my homework tonight.

5. Do you mind if I apply _____ your job after you quit?

6. I'm traveling _____ Indonesia next week to discuss my new business plan _____ our
   contacts in Jakarta.

7. I admire Carmen _____ her courage and honesty in admitting that mistake.

8. A: Where did you get that new car?

   B: I borrowed it _____ my neighbor.

9. A: What are you two arguing _____?

   B: Modern art.

10. A: Where will you go to school next year?

    B: Well, I applied _____ admission at five different universities, but I'm worried that
       none of them will accept me.

Directions: Complete the sentences with appropriate PREPOSIITONS.

1. Dan is always nice _____ everyone.

2. A: How long do you need to keep the Spanish book you borrowed _____ me?

   B: I'd like to keep it until I'm ready _____ the exam next week.

3. A: Why weren't you more polite _____ Alan's friend?

   B: Because he kept staring _____ me all evening. He made me nervous.

4. A: We're going to beat you in the soccer game on Saturday.

   B: No way. Two of your players are equal _____ only one of ours.

   A: Oh yeah? We'll see.

5. Stop pouring! My cup is already full _____ coffee.

6. May I please borrow some money _____ you? I'm thirsty _____ an ice-cream soda, and we're walking right by the ice cream shop.

7. A: Do you believe _____ astrology?

   B: I'm really not familiar _____ it.

8. A: Mike, I really admire you _____ your ability to remember names. Will you help me _____ the introductions?

   B: Sure. Ellen, let me introduce you _____ Pat, Andy, Debbie, Nora, Jack, and Kate.

------

*See Appendix 1 for a list of preposition combinations.

CHAPTER *4*

Nouns and Pronouns

◇ **PRACTICE 1—SELFSTUDY:** Plural nouns. (Charts 4–1 and 4–2)

Directions: These sentences have many mistakes in the use of nouns. <u>Underline</u> each NOUN. Write the correct PLURAL FORM if necessary. Do not change any of the other words in the sentences.

1. <u>Chicago</u> has busy <u>street</u>⁓ and <u>highway</u>⁓.   *streets*   *highways*

2. Box have six side.

3. Big city have many problem.

4. Banana grow in hot, humid area.

5. Insect don't have nose.

6. Lamb are the offspring of sheep.

7. Library keep book on shelf.

8. Parent support their child.

9. Indonesia has several active volcano.

10. Baboon are big monkey. They have large head and sharp tooth. They eat leaf, root, insect,

    and egg.

◇ **PRACTICE 2—SELFSTUDY:** Plural nouns. (Chart 4–1)

Directions: Write the correct SINGULAR or PLURAL form.

SINGULAR	PLURAL	SINGULAR	PLURAL
1. *mouse*	mice	9. duty	_____
2. pocket	*pockets*	10. highway	_____
3. _____	teeth	11. _____	thieves
4. _____	tomatoes	12. belief	_____
5. _____	fish	13. potato	_____
6. _____	women	14. radio	_____
7. branch	_____	15. offspring	_____
8. friend	_____	16. _____	children

SINGULAR	PLURAL		SINGULAR	PLURAL
17. season	_____		21. occurrence	_____
18. custom	_____		22. _____	phenomena
19. business	_____		23. sheep	_____
20. _____	centuries		24. _____	loaves

◇ **PRACTICE 3—GUIDED STUDY:** Plural nouns. (Chart 4–1)

Directions: Practice pronouncing **FINAL -S/-ES** by saying the words in the list aloud.

PRONUNCIATION NOTES: Final *-s/-es* has three different pronunciations: /s/, /z/, and /əz/.

• /s/ is the sound of "s" in "bus." Final *-s* is pronounced /s/ after voiceless sounds: *seats = seat + /s/*. (Examples of voiceless sounds are: /t/, /p/, /k/, /f/.)

• /z/ is the sound of "z" in "buzz." Final *-s* is pronounced /z/ after voiced sounds: *seeds = seed + /z/*. (Examples of voiced sounds are: /d/, /b/, /r/, /l/, /m/, /n/ and all vowel sounds.)

• /əz/ adds a whole syllable to a plural noun. Final *-es* and *-s* are pronounced /əz/ after *-sh, -ch, -s, -z,* and *-ge/dge* sounds:

wishes = wish + /əz/	*sizes = size + /əz/*
matches = match + /əz/	*pages = page + /əz/*
classes = class + /əz/	*judges = judge + /əz/*

---

1. cats = *cat* + /s/
2. heads = *head* + /z/
3. eyes = *eye* + /z/
4. cars = *car* + /z/
5. backs = *back* + /s/
6. words = *word* + /z/
7. boats = *boat* + /s/
8. lips = *lip* + /s/
9. ribs = *rib* + /z/
10. hills = *hill* + /z/

11. dishes = *dish* + /əz/
12. matches = *match* + /əz/
13. eyelashes = *eyelash* + /əz/
14. edges = *edge* + /əz/
15. pages = *page* + /əz/
16. horses = *horse* + /əz/
17. glasses = *glass* + /əz/
18. places = *place* + /əz/
19. prices = *price* + /əz/
20. prizes = *prize* + /əz/

◇ **PRACTICE 4—GUIDED STUDY:** Plural nouns. (Chart 4–1)

Directions: Practice pronouncing **FINAL -S/-ES** by reading the sentences aloud.

1. Our **classrooms** have **tables, chairs,** and **desks**.
   classroom/z/   table/z/ chair/z/   desk/s/

2. **Carrots** and **peas** are **vegetables**.
   carrot/s/   pea/z/   vegetable/z/

3. I was in Alaska for two **weeks** and three **days**.
   week/s/   day/z/

4. **Hospitals**, **businesses**, and **schools** use closed-circuit television.
   hospital/z/ business/ə z/   school/z/

5. There were two **messages** on my answering machine.
                       message/ə z/

6. There are many TV **programs** about **doctors, detectives**, and **cowboys**.
              program/z/   doctor/z/ detective/z/   cowboy/z/

7. **Insects** don't have **ears**. They have **membranes** that can detect **vibrations**.
   insect/s/   ear/z/   membrane/z/   vibration/z/

8. Modern **tools, machines**, and **sources** of power make our **jobs** easier.
   tool/z/ machine/z/   source/ə z/   job/z/

9. **Writers** need to support their **opinions** with **facts** and logical **thoughts**.
   writer/z/   opinion/z/   fact/s/   thought/s/

10. Cotton is used to make **blankets, blouses,   rugs,   gloves**, and **shirts**.
    blanket/s/ blouse/ə z/ rug/z/ glove/z/   shirt/s/

◇ PRACTICE 5—SELFSTUDY: Subjects, verbs, objects, and prepositions. (Charts 4–2 and 4–3)

Directions: Identify the SUBJECTS (**S**), VERBS (**V**), OBJECTS (**O**), and PREPOSITIONAL PHRASES (**PP**)
in the following sentences.

       S   **V**   **O**
1. [Bridges] [cross] [rivers.]
           S   **V**   **PP**
2. [A terrible earthquake] [occurred] [in Turkey.]

3. Airplanes fly above the clouds.

4. Trucks carry large loads.

5. Rivers flow toward the sea.

6. Salespeople treat customers with courtesy.

7. Bacteria can cause diseases.

8. Clouds are floating across the sky.

9. The audience in the theater applauded the performers at the end of the

   show.

10. Helmets protect bicyclists from serious injuries.

◇ PRACTICE 6—SELFSTUDY: Nouns and verbs. (Charts 4–1 → 4–3).

Directions: Some words can be used both as a noun and as a verb. If the word in *italics* is used as a
NOUN, circle **n**. If the word in *italics* is used as a VERB, circle **v**. (**n**. = **noun** and **v**. = **verb**).

1. **n.** (**v.**) People *smile* when they're happy.

2. (**n.**) **v.** Mary has a nice *smile* when she's happy.

3. **n.** **v.** Emily likes her *work*.

4. **n.** **v.** Emily and Mike *work* at the cafeteria.

5. **n.** **v.** The semester will *end* next month.

6. **n.** **v.** I'll go on vacation at the *end* of next month.

7. **n.** **v.** The child wrote her *name* on the wall with a crayon.

8. **n.** **v.** People often *name* their children after relatives.

9. **n.** **v.** I rarely add *salt* to my food.

10. **n.** **v.** Some people *salt* their food before they even taste it.

11. **n.** **v.** Kings and queens *rule* their countries.

12. **n.** **v.** We learned a spelling *rule* in grammar class.

13. **n.** **v.** People usually *store* milk in a refrigerator.

14. **n.** **v.** We went to the *store* to buy some milk.

15. **n.** **v.** Airplanes *land* on runways at the airport.

16. **n.** **v.** The ship reached *land* after seventeen days at sea.

17. **n.** **v.** I took a *train* from New York to Boston.

18. **n.** **v.** I *train* my dogs to sit on command.

19. **n.** **v.** Alex *visits* his aunt every week.

20. **n.** **v.** Alex's aunt enjoys his *visits* every week.

21. **n.** **v.** Marilyn killed the *flies* in the kitchen with a fly swatter.

22. **n.** **v.** Marti *flies* her airplane to an island in Canada at least once a month.

◇ **PRACTICE 7—GUIDED STUDY:**   Nouns and verbs. (Charts 4–1 → 4–3)

Directions: Use each word in **two** different sentences. Use the word as a NOUN (n.) in the first sentence and as a VERB (v.) in the second sentence. Consult your dictionary if necessary to find out the different uses and meanings of a word.

Example: watch
Written: ***n. I am wearing a <u>watch</u>.***
           v. I <u>watched</u> TV after dinner last night.

1. snow   4. phone   7. water
2. paint   5. smoke   8. circle
3. tie   6. face   9. mail

Other common words that are used as both nouns and verbs are listed below. Choose several from the list to make additional sentences. Use your dictionary if necessary.

center/centre,* date, experience, fear, fish, garden, mind, place, plant, promise, question, rain, rock, season, sense, shape, shop, star, tip, trip, value

---

*center = American English.
centre = British English.

◇ **PRACTICE 8—SELFSTUDY:** Adjectives. (Chart 4–4)

Directions: All of the following words are adjectives. For each, write an ADJECTIVE that has the OPPOSITE MEANING.

1. new	_____*old*_____	13. dangerous	_____
2. young	_____*old*_____	14. noisy	_____
3. cold	_____	15. shallow	_____
4. fast	_____	16. sweet	_____
5. sad	_____	17. cheap	_____
6. good	_____	18. dark	_____
7. wet	_____	19. heavy	_____
8. easy	_____	20. public	_____
9. soft	_____	21. left	_____
10. wide	_____	22. wrong	_____
11. clean	_____	23. weak	_____
12. empty	_____	24. long	_____

◇ **PRACTICE 9—SELFSTUDY:** Adjectives and nouns. (Chart 4–4)

Directions: Circle each ADJECTIVE. Draw an arrow to the noun it describes.

1. Paul has a (loud) voice.

2. Sugar is (sweet).

3. The students took an easy test.

4. Air is free.

5. We ate some delicious food at a Mexican restaurant.

6. An encyclopedia contains important facts about a wide variety of subjects.

7. The child was sick.

8. The sick child crawled into his warm bed and sipped hot tea.

◇ **PRACTICE 10—GUIDED STUDY:** Adjectives and nouns. (Chart 4–4)

Directions: Add ADJECTIVES to the sentences. Choose **two** of the three adjectives in each list to add to the given sentences.

Example: hard, heavy, strong   A man lifted the box.
    → *A strong man lifted the heavy box.*

1. *beautiful, safe, red*	Roses are flowers.
2. *dark, cold, dry*	Rain fell from the clouds.
3. *empty, wet, hot*	The waiter poured coffee into my cup.
4. *easy, blue, young*	The girl in the dress was looking for a telephone.

5. *quiet, sharp, soft*   Annie sleeps on a bed in a room.

6. *fresh, clear, hungry*   Mrs. Fox gave the children some fruit.

7. *dirty, modern, delicious* After we finished our dinner, Frank helped me with the dishes.

8. *round, inexperienced, right* When Tom was getting a haircut, the barber accidentally cut Tom's ear with the scissors.

◇ PRACTICE 11—SELFSTUDY: Nouns as adjectives. (Chart 4–5)

Directions: Use the information in *italics* to complete the sentences. Each completion should have a NOUN THAT IS USED AS AN ADJECTIVE in front of another noun.

1. *Articles in newspapers* are called _____ **newspaper articles** _____.

2. *Numbers on pages* are called _____.

3. *Money that is made of paper* is called _____.

4. *Buildings with apartments* are called _____.

5. *Chains for keys* are called _____.

6. *Governments in cities* are called _____.

7. *Ponds for ducks* are called _____.

8. *Pads for shoulders* are called _____.

9. *Knives that people carry in their pockets* are called _____.

10. *Lights that regulate traffic* are called _____.

◇ PRACTICE 12—SELFSTUDY: Nouns. (Charts 4–1 → 4–5)

Directions: These sentences contain many mistakes in noun usage. Make the nouns PLURAL whenever possible and appropriate. Do not change any other words.

                   bottles   *caps*
1. Medicine ~~bottle~~ have childproof ~~cap~~.

2. Airplane seat are narrow and uncomfortable.

3. Science student do laboratory experiment in their class.

4. Housefly are dangerous pest. They carry germ.

5. Computer cannot think. They need human operator.

6. There are approximately 250,000 different kind of flower in the world.

7. Newspaper reporter have high-pressure job.

8. Good telephone manner are important.

9. I bought two theatre ticket for Thursday evening's performance of *A Doll's House*.

10. Our daily life have changed in many way in the past one hundred year. We no longer need to use oil lamp or candle in our house, raise our own chicken, or build daily fire for cooking.

Directions: These sentences contain many mistakes in noun usage. Make the nouns PLURAL whenever possible and appropriate. Do not change any other words.

kinds birds
1. There are around 8,600 ~~kind~~ of ~~bird~~ in the world.

2. Bird hatch from egg.

3. Baby bird stay in their nest for several week or month. Their parent feed them until they can fly.

4. People eat chicken egg. Some animal eat bird egg.

5. Fox and snake are natural enemy of bird. They eat bird and their egg.

6. Some bird eat only seed and plant. Other bird eat mainly insect and earthworm.

7. Weed are unwanted plant. They prevent farm crop and garden flower from growing properly. Bird help farmer by eating weed seed and harmful insect.

8. Rat, rabbit, and mouse can cause huge loss on farm by eating stored crop. Certain big bird like hawk help farmer by hunting these animal.

9. The feather of certain kind of bird are used in pillow and mattress. The soft feather from goose are often used for pillow. Goose feather are also used in winter jacket.

10. The wing feather from goose were used as pen from the sixth century to the nineteenth century, when steel pen were invented.

◇ PRACTICE 14—SELFSTUDY: Personal pronouns. (Chart 4–6)

Directions: Find each PRONOUN. Note how it is used:
- SUBJECT (**S**)
- OBJECT OF A VERB (**O of vb**), or
- OBJECT OF A PREPOSITION (**O of prep**).

                       O of vb
1. The teacher helped [me] with the lesson.

   S   **O of prep**
2. [I] carry a dictionary with [me] at all times.

3. Mr. Fong has a computer. He uses it for many things. It helps him in many ways.

4. Jessica went to Hawaii with Ann and me. We like her, and she likes us. We had a good time with her.

5. Mike had dirty socks. He washed them in the kitchen sink and hung them to dry in front of the window. They dried quickly.

6. Joseph and I are close friends. No bad feelings will ever come between him and me. He and I share a strong bond of friendship.

◇ PRACTICE 15—SELFSTUDY: Personal pronouns. (Chart 4–6)

Directions: Circle each PRONOUN, and draw an arrow to the noun or noun phrase it refers to.

1. [Janet] had [a green apple.] (She) ate (it) after class.

2. Betsy called this morning. John spoke to her.

3. Nick and Rob are at the market. They are buying fresh vegetables.

4. Eric took some phone messages for Karen. They're on a pad of yellow paper in the kitchen.

5. When Louie called, Alice talked to him. He asked her for a date. She accepted.

6. Jane wrote a letter to Mr. and Mrs. Moore. She mailed it to them yesterday. They should get the letter from her on Friday.

◇ PRACTICE 16—SELFSTUDY: Personal pronouns. (Chart 4–6)

Directions: Complete the sentences with **SHE, HE, IT, HER, HIM, THEY,** or **THEM.**

1. I have a grammar book. _____*It*_____ is black.

2. Tom borrowed my books. _____*He*_____ returned _____*them*_____ yesterday.

3. Susan is wearing some new earrings. _____ look good on _____.

4. Don't look directly at the sun. The intensity of its light can injure your eyes. Don't look at _____ directly even if you are wearing sunglasses.

5. Table tennis (also called ping-pong) began in England in the late 1800s. Today _____ is an international sport. My brother and I played _____ a lot when we were teenagers. I beat _____ sometimes, but _____ was a better player and usually won.

6. Do bees sleep at night? Or do _____ work in the hive all night long? You never see _____ after dark. What do _____ do after night falls?

7. The apples were rotten, so we didn't eat _____ even though we were really hungry.

8. The scent of perfume rises. According to one expert, you should put _____ on the soles of your feet.

9. Clean, safe water is fundamental to human health. It is shocking that an estimated 800 million people in the world are still without _____. Unsafe water causes illnesses. _____ contributes to high numbers of deaths in children under five years of age.

10. Magazines are popular. I enjoy reading _____. _____ have news about recent events and discoveries. Recently, I read about "micromachines." _____ are human-made machines that are smaller than a grain of sand. One scientist called _____ "the greatest scientific invention of our time."

◇ **PRACTICE 17—SELFSTUDY: Personal pronouns. (Chart 4–6)**

Directions: Circle the correct PRONOUN.

1. You can ride with Jennifer and   *I,* (*me.*)

2. Did you see Mark?   *He, Him*   was waiting in your office to talk to you.

3. I saw Rob a few minutes ago. I passed Sara and   *he, him*   on the steps of the classroom building.

4. Nick used to work in his father's store, but his father and   *he, him*   had a serious disagreement. Nick left and started his own business.

5. When the doctor came into the room, I asked   *she, her*   a question.

6. The doctor was very helpful. *She, Her* answered all of my questions.

7. Prof. Molina left a message for you and *I, me*. *He, him* needs to see *we, us*.

8. Emily is a good basketball player. I watch Betsy and *she, her* carefully during games. *They, Them* are the best players.

9. One time my little sister and *I, me* were home alone. When our parents returned, they found a valuable vase had been broken. *They, Them* blamed *we, us* for the broken vase, but in truth the cat had broken *it, them*. *We, Us* got in trouble with *they, them* because of the cat.

10. Take these secret documents and destroy *it, them*.

11. Ron invited Mary and *I, me* to have dinner with *he, him*.

12. Maureen likes movies. Ron and *she, her* go to the movies every chance they get.

13. Tom and *I, me* both want to marry Ann. She has to choose between *he and I, him and me*.

◇ PRACTICE 18—SELFSTUDY: Possessive nouns. (Chart 4–7)

Directions: Use the *italicized* noun in the first sentence to write a POSSESSIVE NOUN in the second sentence. Pay special attention to where you put the apostrophe.

1. I have one *friend*. My _____**friend's**_____ name is Paul.

2. I have two *friends*. My _____**friends'**_____ names are Paul and Kevin.

3. I have one *son*. My _____ name is Ryan.

4. I have two *sons*. My _____ names are Ryan and Scott.

5. I have one *baby*. My _____ name is Joy.

6. I have two *babies*. My _____ names are Joy and Erica.

7. I have one *child*. My _____ name is Anna.

8. I have two *children*. My _____ names are Anna and Keith.

9. I know one *person*. This _____ name is Nick.

10. I know several *people*. These _____ names are Nick, Karen and Rita.

11. I have one *teacher*. My _____ name is Ms. West.

12. I have two *teachers*. My _____ names are Ms. West and Mr. Fox.

13. I know a *man*. This _____ name is Alan Burns.

14. I know two *men*. These _____ names are Alan Burns and Joe Lee.

15. We live on the *earth*. The _____ surface is seventy percent water.

◇ PRACTICE 19—SELFSTUDY: Possessive nouns. (Chart 4–7)

Directions: These sentences contain mistakes in the punctuation of possessive nouns. Add APOSTROPHES in the right places.

1. A king's chair is called a throne.

2. Kings' chairs are called thrones.

3. Babies toys are often brightly colored.

4. It's important to make sure a babys toys are safe.

5. Someone called, but because of the static on the phone, I couldn't understand the callers words.

6. A receptionists job is to write down callers names and take messages.

7. Newspapers aren't interested in yesterdays news. They want to report todays events.

8. Each flight has at least two pilots. The pilots seats are in a small area called the cockpit.

9. Rain forests cover five percent of the earths surface but have fifty percent of the different species of plants.

10. Mosquitoes wings move incredibly fast.

11. A mosquitos wings move about one thousand times per second. Its wing movement is the sound we hear when a mosquito is humming in our ears.

12. The average pulse of a human being is seventy beats per minute. A cats heart beats one hundred and thirty times per minute. Elephants have slow heartbeats. Did you know that an elephants heart beats only twenty-five times per minute?

13. When we went to the circus, we saw three elephants. All of us enjoyed watching the elephants tricks. Elephants are quite intelligent animals that can be taught to respond to spoken commands.

14. Elephants like to roll in mud. The mud protects the animals bodies from insects and the sun.

15. When we were walking in the woods, we saw an animals footprints on the muddy path.

◇ **PRACTICE 20—GUIDED STUDY: Possessive nouns. (Chart 4–7)**

Directions: Make the nouns POSSESSIVE if necessary.

       Dan's
1. I met Dan sister yesterday.

2. I met Dan and his sister yesterday. (*no change*)

3. I know Jack roommates.

4. I know Jack well. He's a good friend of mine.

5. I have one roommate. My roommate desk is always messy.

6. You have two roommates. Your roommates desks are always neat.

7. Jo Ann and Betty are sisters.

8. Jo Ann is Betty sister. My sister name is Sonya.

9. My name is Richard. I have two sisters. My sisters names are Jo Ann and Betty.

10. There is an old saying: "A woman work is never done."

11. I read a book about the changes in women roles and men roles in modern society.

12. Jupiter is the largest planet in our solar system. We cannot see Jupiter surface from the earth because thick clouds surround the planet.

13. Mercury is the closest planet to the sun. Mercury atmosphere is extremely hot and dry.

14. Mars★ surface has some of the same characteristics as the earth surface, but Mars could not support life as we know it on earth. The plants and animals that live on the earth could not live on any of the other planets in our solar system.

15. Venus is sometimes called the earth twin because the two planets are almost the same size. But like Mars, Venus surface is extremely hot and dry.

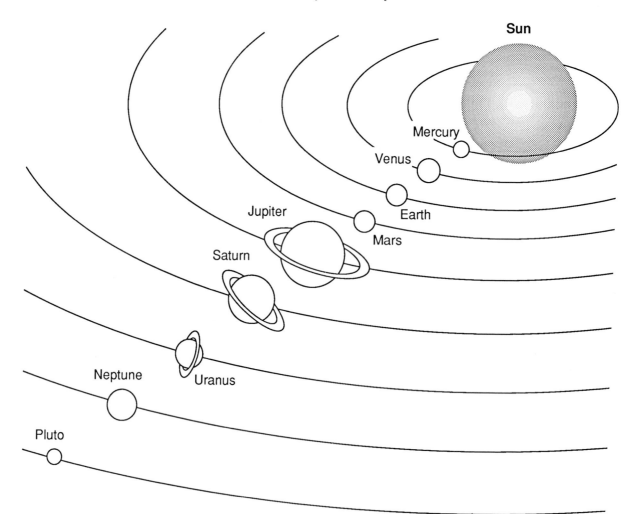

16. The planets English names come from ancient Roman mythology. For example, Mars was the name of the god of war in ancient Rome. Jupiter was the king of the gods. Mercury, who was Jupiter son, was the messenger of the gods. Venus was the goddess of love, beauty, and creativity. Venus son was named Cupid, the god of love and desire.

★When a singular noun ends in -s, there are two possible possessive forms, as in the examples below:

SINGULAR NOUN   POSSESSIVE FORMS
James   I know *James'* brother. OR: I know *James's* brother.
Chris   *Chris'* car is red. OR: *Chris's* car is red.
Carlos   *Carlos'* last name is Rivera. OR: *Carlos's* last name is Rivera.

◇ PRACTICE 21—GUIDED STUDY: Review of nouns + -s/-es. (Charts 4–1 and 4–7)

Directions: Add -S/-ES if necessary. Add an APOSTROPHE to possessive nouns as appropriate.

Examples: **Butterflies**   **David's**
~~Butterfly~~ are beautiful.   Nick is ~~David~~ brother.

1. Most leaf are green.

2. My mother apartment is small.

3. Potato are good for us.

4. Do bird have teeth?

5. Tom last name is Miller.

6. Two thief stole Mr. Lee car.

7. Mountain are high, and valley are low.

8. A good toy holds a child interest for a long time.

9. Children toy need to be strong and safe.

10. All of the actor name are listed on page six of your program.

11. Teacher are interested in young people idea.

12. Almost all monkey have opposable thumb on not only their hand but also their feet. People have thumb only on their hand.

◇ PRACTICE 22—SELFSTUDY: Possessive pronouns and possessive adjectives. (Chart 4–8)

Directions: Complete the sentences with POSSESSIVE PRONOUNS or POSSESSIVE ADJECTIVES that refer to the words in *italics*.

1. A: Can I look at your grammar book?

   B: Why? *You* have _____**your**_____ own* book. You have _____**yours**_____, and I have mine.

2. A: Anna wants to look at your grammar book.

   B: Why? *She* has _____ own book. *She* has _____, and I have mine.

3. A: Tom wants to look at your grammar book.

   B: Why? *He* has _____ own book. *He* has _____, and I have mine.

4. A: Tom and I want to look at your grammar book.

   B: Why? *You* have _____ own books. *You* have _____, and I have mine.

5. A: Tom and Anna want to look at our grammar books.

   B: Why? *They* have _____ own books. *We* have _____ own books. *They* have _____, and *we* have _____.

---
*Own frequently follows a possessive adjective: e.g., *my own, your own, their own*. The word **own** emphasizes that nobody else possesses the exact same thing(s); ownership belongs **only** to me (*my own book*), to you (*your own book*), to them (*their own books*), to us (*our own books*), etc.

PRACTICE 23—GUIDED STUDY: Possessive pronouns and possessive adjectives. (Charts 4-8 and 4-9)

Directions: Complete the sentences with POSSESSIVE PRONOUNS or POSSESSIVE ADJECTIVES that refer to the words in *italics*.

1. *Sara* asked _____ **her** _____ mother for permission to go to a movie.

2. I don't need to borrow your bicycle. *Sara* loaned me _____ **hers** _____.

3. *Ted and I* are roommates. _____ apartment is small.

4. Brian and Louie have a huge apartment, but *we* don't. _____ is small.

5. *You* can find _____ keys in the top drawer of the desk.

6. The keys in the drawer belong to you. *I* have _____ in _____ pocket. *You* should look in the drawer for _____.

7. *Tom and Paul* talked about _____ experiences in the wilderness areas of Canada. I've had a lot of interesting experiences in the wilderness, but nothing to compare with _____.

8. *I* know Eric well. He is a good friend of _____. *You* know him, too, don't you? Isn't he a friend of _____, too?

9. Omar, *my wife and I* would like to introduce you to a good friend of _____. His name is Dan Lightfeather.

PRACTICE 24—SELFSTUDY: Reflexive pronouns. (Chart 4-10)

Directions: Complete the sentences with REFLEXIVE PRONOUNS that refer to the words in italics.

1. *I* enjoyed _____ **myself** _____ at Disney World.

2. *Paul* enjoyed _____.

3. *Paul and I* enjoyed _____.

4. Hi, Emily! Did *you* enjoy _____?

5. Hi, Emily and Dan! Did *you* enjoy _____?

6. *Jessica* enjoyed _____.

7. *Jessica and Paul* enjoyed _____.

PRACTICE 25—SELFSTUDY: Reflexive pronouns. (Chart 4-10)

Directions: Complete the sentences with the words in the list + REFLEXIVE PRONOUNS. Use any appropriate verb tense.

believe in	help	talk to
✔blame	introduce	teach
✔cut	kill	work for
feel sorry for	take care of	wish

1. This accident was my fault. I caused it. I was responsible. In other words, I _____ **blamed** _____ **myself** _____ for the accident.

2. Be careful with that sharp knife! You _____ ***are going to cut yourself*** _____ if you're not careful.

3. It was the first day of class. I sat next to another student and started a conversation about the class and the classroom. After we had talked for a few minutes, I said, "My name is Rita Woo." In other words, I _____ to the other student.

4. When I walked into the room, I heard Joe's voice. He was speaking. I looked around, but the only person I saw and heard was Joe. In other words, Joe _____ _____ when I walked into the room.

5. My wife and I have our own business. We don't have a boss. In other words, we

_____.

6. Mr. and Mrs. Hall own their own business. No one taught them how to run a business. In other words, they _____ everything they needed to know about running a small business.

7. Mr. Baker committed suicide. In other words, he _____.

8. I climbed to the top of the diving tower and walked to the end of the diving board. Before I dived into the pool, I said "good luck" to myself. In other words, I _____ _____ luck.

9. Rebecca is in bed because she has the flu. She isn't at work. Instead, she's resting at home and drinking plenty of fluids. She is being careful about her health. In other words, she

_____.

10. Sometimes we have problems in our lives. Sometimes we fail. But we shouldn't get discouraged and sad. We need to have faith that we can solve our problems and succeed. If we _____, we can accomplish our goals.

11. When I failed to get the new job, I was sad and depressed. In other words, I _____ _____ because I didn't get the job.

12. In a cafeteria, people walk through a section of the restaurant and pick up their food. They are not served by waiters. In other words, in a cafeteria people _____ _____ to the food they want.

◇ PRACTICE 26—SELFSTUDY: Pronouns. (Charts 4–6 → 4–10)

Directions: Circle the correct PRONOUNS.

1. Nick invited *I, me* to go to dinner with *he, him.*

2. Sam and you should be proud of *yourself, yourselves.* The two of you did a good job.

3. The room was almost empty. The only furniture was one table. The table stood by *it, itself* in one corner.

4. The bird returned to *its, it's** nest to feed *its, it's* offspring.

5. Nick has his tennis racket, and Ann has *her, hers, her's.**

6. Where's Eric? I have some good news for Joe and *he, him, his, himself.*

7. Don't listen to Greg. You need to think for *yourself, yourselves*, Jane. It's *you, your, yours* life.

8. We all have *us, our, ours* own ideas about how to live *our, ours, our's** lives.

9. You have your beliefs, and we have *our, ours.*

10. People usually enjoy *themself, themselves, theirselves*** at family gatherings.

11. History repeats *himself, herself, itself.*

12. David didn't need my help. He finished the work by *him, himself, his, his self.*

◇ **PRACTICE 27—GUIDED STUDY:** Pronoun review. (Charts 4–6 → 4–10)

Directions: Complete the sentences with PRONOUNS that refer to the words in *italics.*

1. *Tom* is wearing a bandage on _____**his**_____ arm. _____**He**_____ hurt _____**himself**_____ while _____**he**_____ was repairing the roof. I'll help _____**him**_____ with the roof later.

2. I have *a sister.* _____ name is Kate. _____ and I share a room.

3. *My sister and I* share a room. _____ room is pretty small. _____ have only one desk.

4. Our desk has five drawers. *Kate* puts _____ things in the two drawers on the right.

5. *I* keep _____ stuff in the two drawers on the left. She and _____ share the middle drawer.

6. *Kate* doesn't open my two drawers, and I don't open _____.

7. *I* don't put things in her drawers, and she doesn't put things in _____.

8. *Ms. Lake and Mr. Ramirez* work together at the advertising company. _____ often work on projects by _____, but I work with _____ sometimes. My office is next to _____. _____ office has _____ names on the door, and mine has my name.

9. I have my dictionary, and *Sara* has _____. But *Nick* doesn't have _____.

10. My friend *James* enjoyed _____ at Mike's house yesterday. When I talked to _____ on the phone, _____ told me about _____ day with Mike. _____ and Mike played basketball, ate junk food, and played computer games. I like James a lot. I'm going to spend next Saturday with Mike and _____ at a science fair.

---

*REMINDER: Apostrophes are NOT used with possessive pronouns. Note that *its* = possessive adjective, *it's* = *it is*. Also note that *her's, your's,* and *our's* are **NOT POSSIBLE** in grammatically correct English.

NOTE: *themself* and *theirselves* are not really words—they are **NOT POSSIBLE in grammatically correct English. Only *themselves* is the correct reflexive pronoun form.

11. *Karen* has a bandage on _____ thumb because _____ accidentally cut

_____ with a hatchet while _____ was cutting wood for _____

fireplace.

12. We don't agree with you. *You* have _____ opinion, and *we* have _____ .

◇ **PRACTICE 28—SELFSTUDY:** Singular forms of *other.* (Chart 4–11)

Directions: Complete the sentences with **ANOTHER** or **THE OTHER**.

1. There are two birds in Drawing A. One is an eagle. ___***The other***___ is a chicken.

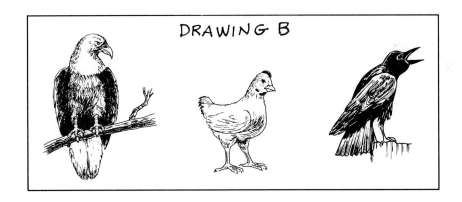

2. There are three birds in Drawing B. One is an eagle.

a. _____ one is a chicken.

b. _____ bird is a crow.

3. There are many kinds of birds in the world. One kind is an eagle.

a. _____ kind is a chicken.

b. _____ kind is a crow.

c. _____ kind is a sea gull.

d. What is the name of _____ kind of bird in the world?

4. There are two women in Picture A. One is Ann. _____ is Sara.

5. There are three men in Picture B. One is Alex. _____ one is Mike.

6. In Picture B, Alex and Mike are smiling. _____ man looks sad.

7. There are three men in Picture B. All three have common first names. One is named Alex.

    a. _____ is named David.

    b. The name of _____ one is Mike.

8. There are many common English names for men. Alex is one.

    a. Mike is _____.

    b. David is _____.

    c. John is _____ common name.

    d. Joe is _____.

    e. What is _____ common English name for a man?

◇ **PRACTICE 29—SELFSTUDY:** Plural forms of *other*. (Chart 4–12)

    Directions: Complete the sentences with **THE OTHER**, **THE OTHERS**, **OTHER**, or **OTHERS**.

1. There are four birds in the picture. One is an eagle, and another one is a crow.

    _____ birds in the picture are chickens.

2. There are four birds in the picture. One is an eagle, and another one is a crow.

    _____ are chickens.

3. Birds have different eating habits. Some birds eat insects.

   a. _____ birds get their food chiefly from plants.

   b. _____ eat only fish.

   c. _____ hunt small animals like mice and rabbits.

   d. _____ birds prefer dead and rotting flesh.

4. There are five English vowels. One is "a." Another is "e."

   a. What are _____ vowels?

   b. _____ are "i", "o", and "u."

5. There are many consonants in English. The letters "b" and "c" are consonants.

   a. What are some _____ consonants?

   b. Some _____ are "d", "f", and "g."

6. Some people are tall, and _____ are short. Some people
   are neither tall nor short.

7. Some people are tall, and _____ people are short.

8. Some animals are huge. _____ are tiny.

9. Some animals are huge. _____ animals are tiny.

10. A: There were ten questions on the test. Seven of them were easy.

    _____ three were really hard.

    B: Any question is easy if you know the answer. Seven of the questions were
    "easy" for you because you had studied for them. _____
    were "hard" only because you hadn't studied for them.

◇ **PRACTICE 30—SELFSTUDY: Summary forms of *other*. (Charts 4–11 → 4–13)**

Directions: Choose the correct completion.

Example: Copper in one kind of metal. Silver is __**A**__.
  A. another   B. the other   C. the others   D. others   E. other

1. Summer is one season. Spring is _____.
   A. another   B. the other   C. the others   D. others   E. other

2. There are four seasons. Summer is one. _____ are winter, fall and spring.
   A. Another   B. The other   C. The others   D. Others   E. Other

3. What's your favorite season? Some people like spring the best. _____ think fall is the nicest
   season.
   A. Another   B. The other   C. The others   D. Others   E. Other

4. My eyes are different colors. One eye is gray and _____ is green.
   A. another   B. the other   C. the others   D. others   E. other

5. One color I like a lot is blue. _____ colors that I think are nice are green and yellow. Purple is
   a pretty color, too.
   A. Another   B. The other   C. The others   D. Others   E. Other

6. There are five letters in the word "fresh." One of the letters is a vowel. _____ are consonants.
   A. Another   B. The other   C. The others   D. Others   E. Other

7. Alex failed his English exam, but his teacher is going to give him _____ chance to pass it.
   A. another   B. the other   C. the others   D. others   E. other

8. Some people drink tea in the morning. _____ have coffee. I prefer fruit juice.
   A. Another   B. The other   C. The others   D. Others   E. Other

9. There are five digits in the number 20,000. One digit is a 2. _____ digits are all zeroes.
   A. Another   B. The other   C. The others   D. Others   E. Other

10. Smith is a common last name in English. _____ common names are Johnson, Jones, and Miller. Others are Anderson, Moore, and Brown.
    A. Another   B. The other   C. The others   D. Others   E. Other

◇ PRACTICE 31—GUIDED STUDY: Summary forms of *other*. (Charts 4–11 → 4–13)

Directions: Complete the sentences with your own words. Use a form of OTHER in the blank and underline it.

Example: I have . . . books on my desk. One is . . . , and _____ is/are . . . .
Written: **I have three books on my desk. One is a grammar book, and <u>the others</u> are my dictionary and a science book.**

1. I have two favorite colors. One is . . . , and _____ is . . . .

2. Some students walk to school. _____ . . . .

3. Ted drank . . . , but he was still thirsty, so . . . _____ one.

4. I speak . . . languages. One is . . . , and _____ is/are . . . .

5. Some people . . . , and _____ . . . .

6. I have . . . (sisters, brothers, and/or cousins). One is . . . , and _____ is/are . . . .

7. One of my teachers is . . . . _____ is/are . . . .

8. . . . and . . . are two common names in my country. _____ are . . . .

9. . . . of the students in my class are from . . . . _____ students are from . . . .

10. There are many popular sports in the world. One is . . . . _____ is . . . . _____ are . . . .

◇ PRACTICE 32—SELFSTUDY: Capitalization. (Chart 4–14)

Directions: Add CAPITAL LETTERS where necessary.

1. Do you know **R**obert **J**ones?

2. Do you know my uncle? (*no change*)

3. I like uncle joe and aunt sara.

4. I'd like you to meet my aunt.

5. susan w. miller is a professor.

6. I am in prof. miller's class.

7. The weather is cold in january.

8. The weather is cold in winter.

9. I have three classes on monday.

10. I would like to visit los angeles.

11. It's a large city in california.

12. I like to visit large cities in foreign countries.

13. There are fifty states in the united states of america.

14. It used to take weeks or months to cross an ocean.

15. Today we can fly across the atlantic ocean in hours.

16. I live on a busy street near the local high school.

17. I live on market street near washington high school.

18. We stayed at a very comfortable hotel.

19. We stayed at the hilton hotel in bangkok.

20. Yoko is japanese, but she can also speak german.

◇ PRACTICE 33—SELFSTUDY: Prepositions. (Chapter 4)

Directions: Complete the sentences with appropriate PREPOSITIONS.*

1. How much did you pay ___*for*___ that beautiful table?

2. A: Did you talk _____ the manager _____ returning that dress?

   B: No. She didn't arrive _____ the store while I was there. I waited _____ her for a

   half an hour and then left.

3. I listened _____ you very carefully, but I didn't understand anything you said.

4. When I graduated _____ college, my mother and father told everyone we knew that I had

   graduated.

5. I paid too much _____ this watch. It's not worth it.

6. A: We don't have all day! How long is it going take for someone to wait _____ us? I'm

   hungry.

   B: We just got here. Be patient. Do you have to complain _____ everything?

7. When did you arrive _____ Mexico City?

8. A: This sauce is delicious! What is it?

   B: Well, it consists _____ tomatoes, garlic, olive oil, and lemon juice all blended

   together.

9. There were ten people at the meeting and ten different opinions. No one agreed _____

   anyone else _____ the best way to solve the club's financial problems.

10. I have to complain _____ the manager. Both the food and the service are terrible.

◇ PRACTICE 34—SELFSTUDY: Prepositions. (Chapters 1, 3, and 4)

Directions: Complete the sentences with appropriate PREPOSITIONS.

1. Everyone is talking _____ the explosion in the high school chemistry lab.

2. Carlos was absent _____ class six times last term.

3. Fruit consists mostly _____ water.

---
*See Appendix 1 for a list of preposition combinations.

4. Our children are very polite _____ adults, but they argue _____ their playmates all the time.

5. Three centimeters is equal _____ approximately one and a half inches.

6. I'm not ready _____ my trip. I haven't packed yet.

7. I borrowed some clothes _____ my best friend.

8. Are you familiar _____ ancient Roman mythology?

9. I discussed my problem _____ my uncle.

10. Someday astronauts will travel _____ another solar system.

11. Jennifer arrived _____ Singapore last Tuesday.

12. Jack's plane arrived _____ the airport in Mexico City two hours ago.

13. I admire you _____ your ability to laugh _____ yourself when you make a silly mistake.

14. A: Why are staring _____ the wall?

    B: I'm not. I'm thinking.

15. A: Are you two arguing _____ each other _____ your in-laws again?

    B: Do you know what his father did?

    C: Oh yeah? Listen _____ what her sister said.

    A: Shh. I don't want to hear any of this. Stop complaining _____ me _____ your relatives. I don't agree _____ either of you.

CHAPTER **5**
Modal Auxiliaries

◇ PRACTICE 1—SELFSTUDY: *To* with modal auxiliaries. (Chart 5–1)

Directions: Add the word **TO** where necessary. Write Ø if **TO** is not necessary.

1. Mr. Alvarez spilled tea on his shirt. He must ____Ø____ change clothes before dinner.

2. Mr. Alverez has ____*to*____ change his shirt before dinner.

3. Everyone should _____ pay attention to local politics.

4. Everyone ought _____ participate in local government.

5. May I _____ borrow your pen?

6. A good book can _____ be a friend for life.

7. Jimmy is yawning and rubbing his eyes. He must _____ be sleepy.

8. You can't _____ open a can without a can opener, can you?

9. I'd like to stay and talk some more, but I've got _____ hurry over to the chemistry
   building for my next class.

10. A: Should I _____ tell the boss about the accounting error in the report?

    B: You have _____ tell him. That error could _____ get the company in trouble.

    A: I know that I ought _____ be honest about it, but I'm afraid he'll get angry. He might
       _____ fire me. Would you _____ go with me to see him?

    B: I think you should _____ do this yourself. You can _____ do it. I'm sure the
       boss will _____ understand.

    A: No, you must _____ go with me. I can't _____ face him alone.

◇ PRACTICE 2—GUIDED STUDY: *To* with modal auxiliaries. (Chart 5–1)

Directions: Add the word **TO** where necessary. Write Ø if **TO** is not necessary.

(1)   Everyone in my family has ____*to*____ contribute to keeping order in our house. My parents

(2) assign chores to my brother, George, and me. We must ____Ø____ do these tasks every day.

(3) Sometimes if one of us is busy and can't _____ do a chore, the other one may _____ take

(4) care of it.

(5)   For example, last Friday it was George's turn to wash the dishes after dinner. He couldn't

(6) _____ stay to do it because he had _____ hurry to school for a basketball game. George

(7) asked me, "Will you _____ do the dishes for me, please? I'll _____ do them for you

(8) tomorrow when it's your turn. I've got _____ get to the school for the game." I reluctantly

(9) agreed to do George's chores and washed the dishes after dinner. But then the next night, George

(10) "forgot" that we had traded days. When I reminded him to wash the dishes, he said, "Who?

(11) Me? It's not *my* turn. You have _____ do the dishes tonight. It's *your* turn."

(12)   I think I'd better _____ write our agreement down when I take my brother George's

(13) chores, and I ought _____ give him a copy of the agreement. George has a short memory,

(14) especially if he has _____ wash dishes or take out the garbage. I should _____ write

(15) everything down. In fact, I might _____ write out a weekly schedule. Then we could

(16) _____ write our names in and change assignments if necessary. That ought _____ solve

(17) the problem. I must _____ remember to do that.

◇ **PRACTICE 3—SELFSTUDY: Expressing ability. (Chart 5–2)**

Directions: Choose one of the words in parentheses to complete each sentence.

1. A _____*zebra*_____ **can't stretch** its neck to reach the tops of trees. (*giraffe, zebra*)

2. A single _____ **can kill** a thousand mice in a year. (*bee, cat*)

3. _____ **can crush** small trees under their huge feet. (*Rabbits, Elephants*)

4. _____ **can climb** trees with ease. (*Monkeys, Chickens*)

5. Did you know that _____ **can survive** seventeen days without any water at all? (*ducks, camels*)

6. One _____ **can produce** as much as 8,500 lbs. (3,860 kgs) of milk in a year. (*cow, bull*)

7. A person **can sit** on a _____ without hurting it. (*horse, cat*)

8. A _____ **can carry** heavy loads on its back. (*donkey, snake*)

9. A _____ **can stay** high up in the trees for weeks, leaping from branch to branch. (*squirrel, polar bear*)

10. Most _____ **can lift** objects that are ten times heavier than their own bodies. (*people, ants*)

◇ **PRACTICE 4—GUIDED STUDY:** Expressing ability. (Chart 5–2)

Directions: Interview a classmate about each item in the list below, then write a report about your classmate's abilities.

Example: read pages that are upside down?
STUDENT A: (Jose), can you read pages that are upside down?
STUDENT B: Yes, I can. Here, I'll show you.
        OR: No, I can't.
        OR: I don't know. I'll try. Turn your book upside down and I'll try to read it.

PART I: STUDENT A interviews STUDENT B:

1. speak more than two languages?

2. play chess?

3. drive a car?

4. read upside down?

5. play any musical instrument?

6. do card tricks?

7. pat the top of your head up and down with one hand and rub your stomach in a circular motion with the other hand at the same time?

PART II: STUDENT B interviews STUDENT A:

8. fold a piece of paper in half more than six times?

9. draw well—for example, draw a picture of me?

10. cook?

11. walk on your hands?

12. play tennis?

13. use a computer?

14. write legibly with both your right hand and your left hand?

◇ **PRACTICE 5—GUIDED STUDY:** Expressing past ability. (Chart 5–2)

Directions: Complete the sentences with **COULD** or **COULDN'T** and your own words.

Example: A year ago I . . . , but now I can.
Written: A year ago I couldn't speak English, but now I can.

1. When I was a baby, I . . . , but now I can.

2. When I was a child, I . . . , but now I can't.

3. When I was thirteen, I . . . , but I couldn't do the same thing when I was three.

4. Five years ago, I . . . , but now I can't.

5. Last year/month/week, I . . . , but now I can.

◇ PRACTICE 6—SELFSTUDY: Expressing ability and possibility. (Charts 5–2 and 5–3)

Directions: Complete the sentences with CAN, CAN'T, MAY, or MAY NOT.

1. I _____**can**_____ play only one musical instrument: the piano. I _____**can't**_____ play a guitar.

2. Dark clouds are gathering in the sky. It _____ rain soon.

3. Michael will be your interpreter during your trip to Korea. He _____ speak Korean fluently.

4. One minute John wants to go to the dinner party. The next minute he doesn't want to go. He can't make up his mind. He _____ go to the dinner party tonight, or he _____.

5. You'd better take a book with you to the airport when you go to meet Danny's plane. It _____ be late because of the snowstorm in Denver.

6. A: What channel is the news special on tonight?

   B: I'm not sure. It _____ be on Channel Seven. Try that one first.

7. Alice is a runner. She likes to compete, but two days ago she broke her ankle when she fell. She _____ run in the race tomorrow.

8. A: Do you remember a famous actor named Basil Rathbone? Is he still making movies?

   B: I think he _____ be dead.

Directions: Complete the sentences with CAN, CAN'T, MIGHT, *or* MIGHT NOT.

9. Jessica hasn't made up her mind about where to go to school. She _____**might**_____ or she _____**might not**_____ attend Duke University. She just doesn't know yet.

10. Ducks _____ swim well, but chickens _____ because they don't have webbed feet.

11. A: What are you going to order?

    B: I dunno.* I _____ have a hamburger or a cheeseburger.

12. A: Carol's in New York now. Is she going to return to school in Chicago in September?

    B: It depends. If she _____ find a job in New York, she'll stay there this fall. Who knows? She _____ stay there through the winter and spring, too. If she likes her job, she _____ want to return to school in Chicago next year at all. We'll have to wait and see.

13. A: Which one of these oranges is sweet? I like only sweet oranges.

    B: How should I know? I _____ tell if an orange is sweet just by looking at it. _____ you? Here. Try this one. It _____ be sweet enough for you. If it isn't, put some sugar on it.

---

*"I dunno" = informal spoken English for "I don't know."

86 ◇ *CHAPTER 5*

Directions: Choose the expression that has the same meaning as the *italicized* verb.

1. Twenty years ago, David *could speak* Arabic fluently. Now he's forgotten a lot.
   (A) was able to speak   B. may/might speak

2. Let's leave for the airport now. Lenny's plane *could arrive* early tonight.
   A. was able to arrive   B. may/might arrive

3. "Where's Alice?"
   "I don't know. She *could be* at the mall."
   A. was able to be   B. may/might be

4. I think I'll take my umbrella. It *could rain* today.
   A. was able to rain   B. may/might rain

5. "What's in this box?"
   "I don't know. It looks like a bottle, but it *could be* a flower vase."
   A. was able to be   B. may/might be

6. When I was a child, we *could swim* in the Duckfoot River, but now it's too polluted.
   Today even the fish get sick.
   A. were able to swim   B. may/might swim

7. "How long will it take you to paint two small rooms?"
   "I'm not sure. If the job isn't complicated, I *could finish* by Thursday."
   A. was able to finish   B. may/might finish

8. When I was a kid, I *could jump* rope really well.
   A. was able to jump   B. may/might jump

◇ PRACTICE 8—GUIDED STUDY: Expressing possibility. (Chart 5–4)

Directions: For each situation, use **COULD** to suggest possible courses of action.

Example: Jack has to go to work early tomorrow. His car is out of gas. His bicycle is broken.
Response: Jack could take the bus to work.
   He could take a gas can to a gas station, fill it up, and carry it home to his car.
   He could try to fix his bicycle.
   He could get up very early and walk to work. Etc.

1. Nancy walked to school today. Now she wants to go home. It's raining hard. She doesn't
   have an umbrella. She doesn't want to get wet.

2. Ann and Carmen want to get some exercise. They have a date to play tennis this morning, but
   the tennis court is covered with snow.

3. Sam just bought a new camera. He has it at home now. He has the instruction manual. It is written in Japanese. He can't read Japanese. He doesn't know how to operate the camera.

4. Dennis likes to travel around the world. He is twenty-two years old. Today he is alone in (*name of a city*). He needs to eat, and he needs to find a place to stay overnight. But while he was asleep on the train last night, someone stole his wallet. He has no money.

◇ PRACTICE 9—GUIDED STUDY: Expressing possibility. (Charts 5–2 → 5–4)

Directions: Complete the sentences with your own words.

Example: I could _____ today. (. . .) could _____ too, but we'll probably _____.
Response: **I could** skip class and go to a movie **today**. Pedro **could** come along **too, but we'll probably** go to class just like we're supposed to.

1. Tonight I could _____. Or I might _____. Of course, I may _____. But I'll probably _____.

2. Next year, I might _____. But I could _____. I may _____. But I'll probably _____.

3. My friend (. . .) may _____ this weekend, but I'm not sure. He/She might _____.
He/She could also _____. But he/she'll probably _____.

4. One hundred years from now, _____ may _____. _____ could _____.
_____ will probably _____.

◇ PRACTICE 10—SELFSTUDY: Polite questions. (Charts 5–5 and 5–6)

Directions: Circle the correct completion.

1. A: This desk is too heavy for me.   *May,* (*Can*) you help me lift it?
   B: Sure. No problem.

2. A: Ms. Milan,   *may, will*   I be excused from class early today? I have a doctor's appointment.
   B: Yes. You may leave early. That would be fine.

3. A: I'm having trouble with this word processor.   *Would, May*   you show me how to set the margins one more time?
   B: Of course.

4. A: Andrew,   *would, could*   I speak to you for a minute?
   B: Sure. What's up?

5. A: I can't meet David's plane tonight.   *Can, May*   you pick him up?
   B: Sorry. I have to work tonight. Call Uncle Frank. Maybe he can pick David up.

6. A: *Could, May*   you please take these letters to the post office before noon?
   B: I'd be happy to, sir. Hmmm. It's almost eleven-thirty.   *May, Will*   I leave for the post office now and then go to lunch early?
   A: That would be fine.

7. A: Marilyn, are you feeling okay?   *Would, Can*   I get you something?
   B: *May, Will*   you get me a glass of water, please?
   A: Right away.

8. A: Darn these medicine bottles! I can't ever get the cap off!

   B: *Would, Could*   I open that for you?

   A: Thanks. I'd really appreciate it.

◇ PRACTICE 11—GUIDED STUDY: Polite questions.   (Charts 5–5 and 5–6)

Directions: Write a dialogue for each situation.   The beginning of each dialogue is given.

Example:
   SITUATION: You're in a restaurant. You want the waiter to refill your coffee cup. You catch
   the waiter's eye and raise your hand slightly. The waiter approaches your table.
   DIALOGUE: *A: Yes? What can I do for you?*

Written: **A: *Yes? What can I do for you?***

   B: *Could I please have some more coffee?*

   A: *Of course. Right away.*

1. SITUATION: You've been waiting in line at a busy bakery. Finally, the person in front of you is
   getting waited on, and the clerk turns toward you.
   DIALOGUE: *A: Next!*

2. SITUATION: You are at work. You feel sick. Your head is pounding, and you have a slight
   fever. You really want to go home. You see your boss, Mr. Jenkins, passing by
   your desk.
   DIALOGUE: *A: Mr. Jenkins?*

3. SITUATION: Your cousin, Willy, is in the next room listening to music. You are talking on the
   telephone. The music is getting louder and louder. Finally, you can no longer
   hear your conversation over the phone. You put the phone down and turn toward
   the door to the next room.
   DIALOGUE: *A: Willy!*

4. SITUATION: The person next to you on the plane has finished reading his newspaper. You
   would like to read it.
   DIALOGUE: *A: Excuse me.*

5. SITUATION: You see a car on the side of the road with the hood raised and an older man
   standing next to it. He looks tired and concerned. You pull over and get out of
   your car to walk over to him.
   DIALOGUE: *A: Do you need some help, sir?*

◇ PRACTICE 12—SELFSTUDY: Expressing advice.   (Chart 5–7)

Directions: Choose the correct completion.

1. Danny doesn't feel well. He _____ see a doctor.
      A. should   B. ought   C. had

2. Danny doesn't feel well. He _____ better see a doctor.
      A. should   B. ought   C. had

3. Danny doesn't feel well. He _____ to see a doctor.
      A. should   B. ought   C. had

4. It's extremely warm in here. We _____ open some windows.
    A. should   B. ought   C. had

5. It's really cold in here. We _____ to close some windows.
    A. should   B. ought   C. had

6. There's a police car behind us. You _____ better slow down!
    A. should   B. ought   C. had

7. People who use public parks _____ clean up after themselves.
    A. should   B. ought   C. had

8. I have no money left in my bank account. I _____ better stop charging things on my credit card.
    A. should   B. ought   C. had

9. It's going to be a formal dinner and dance. You _____ to change clothes.
    A. should   B. ought   C. had

10. This library book is overdue. I _____ better return it today.
    A. should   B. ought   C. had

◇ PRACTICE 13—GUIDED STUDY: Expressing advice. (Chart 5-7)

Directions: Give advice. Use **SHOULD**, **OUGHT TO**, and **HAD BETTER**.

Example: I forgot my dad's birthday. It was yesterday. I feel terrible about it. What should I do?
Possible responses:
        You'd better call him on the phone right away.
        You should send him a card and a little present.
        You ought to write him a long letter and tell him you're sorry.

1. Sam studies, but he doesn't understand his physics class. It's the middle of the term, and he is failing the course. He needs a science course in order to graduate. What should he do?

2. Dan just discovered that he made dinner plans for tonight with two different people. He is supposed to meet his fiancée at one restaurant at 7:00, and he is supposed to meet his boss at a different restaurant across town at 8:00. What should he do?

3. The boss wants me to finish my report before I go on vacation, but I probably don't have time. What should I do?

4. I borrowed Karen's favorite book of poems. It was special to her. A note on the inside cover said "To Karen." The poet's signature was at the bottom of the note. Now I can't find the book. I think I lost it. What am I going to do?

◇ PRACTICE 14—SELFSTUDY: Expressing necessity. (Chart 5-8)

Directions: Choose the correct completion.

1. I _____ to wash the dishes after dinner last night. It was my turn.
    A. have   B. has   C. had   D. must

2. Bye! I'm leaving now. I _____ got to take this package to the post office.
    A. have   B. has   C. had   D. must

3. I know you didn't mean what you said. You _____ think before you speak!
    A. have   B. has   C. had   D. must

4. Yesterday everyone in the office _____ to leave the building for a fire drill. I'm glad it wasn't a real fire.
    A. have   B. has   C. had   D. must

5. Janet _____ to take an educational psychology course next semester. It's a required course.
    A. have   B. has   C. had   D. must

6. Pete, Chris, and Anna _____ to stay after class this afternoon. Professor Irwin wants them to help him grade papers.
    A. have   B. has   C. had   D. must

7. Mr. Silva, you _____ not be late today. The vice-president is coming in, and you're the only one who can answer her questions about the new project.
    A. have   B. has   C. had   D. must

8. Last year our town didn't have many tourists because of the oil spill. Business was bad. My wife and I own a small souvenir shop near the ocean. We _____ to borrow money from the bank last month to save our business.
    A. have   B. has   C. had   D. must

◇ **PRACTICE 15—GUIDED STUDY:** Expressing necessity. (Chart 5–8)

Directions: Use the information in *PART I* to answer the questions in *PART II*. Answer in complete sentences using the verb in *italics*.

PART I: INFORMATION

a. Mr. Lin is nearsighted.

b. Carmen's boss just told her that she's going to Rome next month to an important international conference.

c. Gloria's car is in the garage.

d. Jake's parents are going out to play cards with their friends.

e. The students in this class want to improve their English.

f. Professor Clark got the flu.

PART II: QUESTIONS

1. Who *has to take* the bus to work and why?
    → *Gloria has to take the bus to work because her car is in the garage.*

2. Who *had to cancel* classes and why?

3. Who *must renew* her passport immediately and why?

4. Who *has to wear* glasses and why?

5. Who's *got to stay* home and babysit his little sister tonight and why?

6. Who *has to study* hard and why?

◇ **PRACTICE 16—SELFSTUDY:** Expressing necessity, lack of necessity, and prohibition. (Charts 5–8 and 5–9)

Directions: Complete the sentences with **MUST NOT** or **DON'T HAVE TO**.

1. You _____***must not***_____ drive when you are tired. It's dangerous.

2. I live only a few blocks from my office. I _____***don't have to***_____ drive to work.

3. You _____ play loud music late at night. The neighbors will call the police.

4. This box isn't as heavy as it looks. You _____ help me with it. Thanks anyway for offering to help.

5. Susan, you _____ go to the university. Your father and I think you should, but it's your choice.

6. People _____ spend their money foolishly if they want to stay out of financial trouble.

7. My new telephone has a "memory." I _____ look up phone numbers anymore. All I have to do is push a button next to someone's name.

8. When you first meet someone, you _____ ask personal questions. For example, it's not polite to ask a person's age.

9. The nations of the world _____ stop trying to achieve total world peace.

10. My husband and I grow all of our own vegetables in the summer. We _____ buy any vegetables at the market.

◇ PRACTICE 17—SELFSTUDY: Expressing necessity, lack of necessity, and prohibition. (Charts 5–8 and 5–9)

Directions: Complete each sentence with a form of **HAVE TO** or **MUST**. Use the negative if necessary to make a sensible sentence.

1. Smoking in this building is prohibited. You _____ ***must/have to*** _____ extinguish your cigar.

2. Alan's company pays all of his travel expenses. Alan _____ ***doesn't have to*** _____ pay for his own plane ticket to the business conference in Amman, Jordan.

3. Our company provides free advice on the use of our products. You _____ pay us.

4. Charles could get fired if he misses any more morning meetings. He _____ be late today under any circumstances.

5. Everyone here _____ leave immediately! The building is on fire!

6. Lynn _____ attend the meeting tonight because she isn't working on the project that we're going to discuss. We're going to discuss raising money for the new library. Lynn isn't involved in that.

7. The construction company _____ finish the building by the end of the month. That's the date they promised, and they will lose a lot of money if they are late.

8. Please remember, you _____ call my house between three and four this afternoon. That's when the baby sleeps, and my mother will get upset if we wake him up.

◇ PRACTICE 18—GUIDED STUDY: Expressing advice and necessity. (Charts 5–7 → 5–9)

Directions: Use the given information to discuss the situation. Use expressions like **OUGHT TO, HAS TO, COULD, SHOULD, MIGHT, HAS GOT TO, HAD BETTER**.

Example: Carol is just recovering from the flu and tires easily. She's at work today.
Possible responses:
        Carol should go directly home from work and get plenty of rest.
        She ought to talk to her boss about leaving work early today.

She's got to take care of her health.
She must not get too tired.
She doesn't have to stay at work if she doesn't feel well.

1. Sara is fifteen. She doesn't have a driver's license. She's planning to drive her brother's car to her girlfriend's house. Her brother isn't home. Her parents aren't home.

2. Steve is a biology major. Chemistry is a required course for biology majors. Steve doesn't want to take chemistry. He thinks it's boring. He would rather take a course in art history or creative writing.

3. Matt and Amy are eighteen years old. They are students. Matt doesn't have a job. Amy works part-time as a waitress. Matt and Amy met a month ago. They fell in love. They plan to get married next week.

4. Kate invited a friend to her apartment for dinner at 8:00 tonight. Right now it's 7:20, and Kate is unexpectedly in a long and late business meeting with an important client. It takes her 30 minutes to get home from her office. She hasn't had time to shop for food for tonight's dinner.

5. I know a story about a rabbit named Rabbit and a frog named Frog. Rabbit and Frog are good friends, but Rabbit's family doesn't like Frog, and Frog's family doesn't like Rabbit. Rabbit's family says, "You shouldn't be friends with Frog. He's too different from us. He's green and has big eyes. He looks strange. You should stay with your own kind." And Frog's family says, "How can you be friends with Rabbit? He's big and clumsy. He's covered with hair and has funny ears. Don't bring Rabbit to our house. What will the neighbors think?"

◇ **PRACTICE 19—GUIDED STUDY:** Expressing advice and necessity. (Charts 5–7 → 5–9)

Directions: Read the passage, and then give advice either in a discussion group or in writing.

Mr. and Mrs. Holtz don't know what to do about their fourteen-year-old son, Mark. He's very intelligent but has no interest in school or in learning. His grades are getting worse, but he won't do any homework. Sometimes he skips school without permission, and then he writes an excuse for the school and signs his mother's name.

His older sister, Kathy, is a good student and never causes any problems at home. Mark's parents keep asking him why he can't be more like Kathy. Kathy makes fun of Mark's school grades and tells him he's stupid.

All Mark does when he's home is stay in his room and listen to very loud music. Sometimes he doesn't even come downstairs to eat meals with his family. He argues with his parents whenever they ask him to do chores around the house, like taking out the garbage.

Mr. and Mrs. Holtz can't stay calm when they talk to him. Mrs. Holtz is always yelling at her son. She nags him constantly to do his chores, clean up his room, finish his homework, stand up straight, get a haircut, wash his face, and tie his shoes. Mr. Holtz is always making new rules. Some of the rules are unreasonable. For instance, one rule Mr. Holtz made was that his son could not listen to music after five o'clock. Mark often becomes angry and goes up to his room and slams the door shut.

This family needs a lot of advice. Tell them what changes they should make. What should Mr. and Mrs. Holtz do? What shouldn't they do? What about Kathy? What should she do? And what's Mark got to do to change his life for the better?

Use each of the following words at least once in the advice you give:

a. should	e. ought to
b. shouldn't	f. have to/has to
c. have got to/has got to	g. must
d. had better	

◇ **PRACTICE 20—SELFSTUDY: Making logical conclusions. (Chart 5–10)**

Directions: Complete the following sentences. Use **MUST** or **MUST NOT**.

1. Joe just bought a new car a few weeks ago, and now he's buying a new car for his sister. Joe _____*must*_____ earn a lot of money.

2. I offered Holly something to eat, but she doesn't want anything. She _____*must not*_____ be hungry.

3. My uncle has been working in the hot sun for hours. He's soaked with perspiration. He _____ be thirsty.

4. A: Erica's really bright. She always gets above ninety-five percent (95%) on her math tests.

   B: I'm sure she's bright, but she _____ also study a lot.

5. A: Fido? What's wrong, old boy?

   B: What's the matter with the dog?

   A: He won't eat. He _____ feel well.

6. A: I've called the bank three times, but no one answers the phone. The bank _____ be open today.

   B: It isn't. Today's a holiday, remember?

   A: Oh, of course!

7. A: Listen. Someone is jumping on the floor in the apartment above us. Look. Your chandelier is shaking.

   B: Mr. Silverberg _____ be doing his morning exercises. The same thing happens every morning. Don't worry about it.

◇ **PRACTICE 21—GUIDED STUDY: Making logical conclusions. (Chart 5–10)**

Directions: Make a logical conclusion about each of the following situations. Use **MUST**.

Example: Emily is crying.
Response: She must be unhappy.

1. Debbie has a big smile on her face.
2. Steve is coughing and sneezing.
3. Rick is wearing a gold ring on the fourth finger of his left hand.
4. Sam is shivering.
5. Matt just bought three mouse traps.
6. Kate just bought a box of floppy disks.
7. James is sweating.
8. Robert never hands in his homework on time.
9. Rita rents ten movies every week.
10. Marilyn always gets the highest score on every test her class takes.
11. Brian can lift one end of a compact car by himself.

◇ **PRACTICE 22—SELFSTUDY: Imperative sentences. (Chart 5–11)**

Directions: Pretend that someone says the following sentences to **you**. Which verbs give **you** instructions? <u>Underline</u> the IMPERATIVE VERBS.

1. I'll be right back. <u>Wait</u> here.

2. <u>Don't wait</u> for Rebecca. She's not going to come with us.

3. Read pages thirty-nine to fifty-five before class tomorrow.

4. What are you doing? Don't put those magazines in the trash. I haven't read them yet.

5. Come in and have a seat. I'll be right with you.

6.

DON'T CROSS THIS FIELD UNLESS YOU CAN DO IT IN 9.9 SECONDS. THE BULL CAN DO IT IN 10.

(NO TRESPASSING)

7. Don't just stand there! Do something!

8. A: Call me around eight, okay?

   B: Okay.

9. Here, little Mike. Take this apple to Daddy. That's good. Go ahead. Walk toward Daddy. That's great! Now give him the apple. Wonderful!

10. Capitalize the first word of each sentence. Put a period at the end of a sentence. If the sentence is a question, use a question mark at the end.

◇ **PRACTICE 23—GUIDED STUDY: Imperative sentences. (Chart 5-11)**

Directions: Pretend that someone says the following sentences to **you**. Which verbs give **you** instructions? <u>Underline</u> the IMPERATIVE VERBS.

1. Here's a number puzzle:

   • Write down the number of the month you were born. (For example, write "2" if you were born in February. Write "3" if you were born in March.)

   • Double it.

   • Add 5.

   • Multiply by 50.

   • Add your age.

   • Subtract 250.

   • In the final number, the last two digits on the right will be your age, and the one or two digits on the left will be the month you were born. (Try it! It works.)

2. Here are some ways to handle stress in your life:

   • Get daily physical exercise.

   • Manage your time efficiently. Don't overload your daily schedule.

   • Take time for yourself. Learn to relax. Read, reflect, listen to music, or just do nothing for a period every day.

   • Don't waste time worrying about things you can't change. Recognize the things that you can't change and accept them.

◇ **PRACTICE 24—SELFSTUDY: Making suggestions with *let's* and *why don't*. (Chart 5-12)**

Directions: Complete the sentences, using verbs from the list. The verbs may be used more than once.

ask	fly	pick up	see
call	get	play	stop
fill up	go	save	take

1. A: There's a strong wind today. Let's _____*go*_____ to the top of the hill on Cascade Avenue and _____*fly*_____ our kite.

   B: Sounds like fun. Why don't we _____*see*_____ if Louie wants to come with us?

   A: Okay. I'll call him.

2. A: What should we buy Mom for her birthday?

   B: I don't know. Let's _____ her some perfume or something.

   A: I have a better idea. Why don't we _____ her out for dinner and a movie?

3. A: My toe hurts. Let's not _____ dancing tonight.

   B: Okay. Why don't we _____ chess instead?

4. A: Let's _____ a taxi from the airport to the hotel.

   B: Why don't we _____ a bus and _____ ourselves some money?

5. A: We're almost out of gas. Why don't we _____ at a gas station and

   _____ before we drive the rest of the way to the beach?

   B: Okay. Are you hungry? I am. Let's _____ some hamburgers, too.

   A: Great.

6. A: Let's _____ to a movie at the mall tonight.

   B: I've already seen all the good movies there. What else can we do?

   A: Well, Marika has a car. Why don't we _____ her and _____ if she

   wants to drive us into the city to an ice hockey game?

   B: Okay. What's her number?

◇ **PRACTICE 25—GUIDED STUDY: Making suggestions with *why don't you*. (Chart 5–12)**

Directions: Make suggestions using **WHY DON'T YOU**. STUDENT A should state the problem, and then others should offer suggestions.

Example: I'm at a restaurant with some business clients. I left my wallet at home. I don't have enough money to pay the bill. What am I going to do?

STUDENT A: Okay, here's the situation. I'm at a restaurant with some business customers. I sell computer parts. I need these customers. I need to impress my clients. I have to pay for dinner, but I left my wallet at home. I don't have enough money to pay the bill. I'm really embarrassed. What am I going to do?

STUDENT B: Why don't you call your office and ask someone to bring you some money?

STUDENT C: Why don't you borrow the money from one of your customers?

STUDENT D: Why don't you excuse yourself and go home to get your wallet?

STUDENT E: Why don't you have a private discussion with the manager? Arrange to pay the bill later.

1. I feel like doing something interesting and fun tonight. Any suggestions?

2. I need regular physical exercise. What would you suggest?

3. My pants keep slipping down! I'm always pulling them up.

4. An important assignment is due in Professor Black's history class today. I haven't done it. Class starts in an hour. What am I going to do?

5. I've lost the key to my apartment, so I can't get in. My roommate isn't home. He's at a concert. What am I going to do?

6. My friend and I had an argument. We stopped talking to each other. Now I'm sorry about the argument. I want to be friends again. What should I do?

7. I work hard all day long every day. I never take time to relax and enjoy myself. I need some recreation in my life. What do you think I should do?

8. I'm trying to learn English, but I'm making slow progress. What can I do to learn English faster?

◇ **PRACTICE 26—SELFSTUDY: Stating preferences. (Chart 5–13)**

Directions: Complete the sentences with **PREFER**, **LIKE**, or **WOULD RATHER**.

1. I _____ *prefer* _____ cold weather to hot weather.

2. A: What's you favorite fruit?

   B: I _____ *like* _____ strawberries better than any other fruit.

3. Mary _____ *would rather* _____ save money than enjoy herself.

4. Unfortunately, many children _____ candy to vegetables.

5. A: Why isn't your brother going with us to the movie?

   B: He _____ stay home and read than go out on a Saturday night.

6. A: Does Peter _____ football to baseball?

   B: No. I think he _____ baseball better than football.

   A: Then, why didn't he go to the game yesterday?

   B: Because he _____ watch sports on TV than go to a ball park.

7. I _____ jog in the morning than after work.

8. Heidi enjoys her independence. She is struggling to start her own business, but she

   _____ borrow money from the bank than ask her parents for help.

9. A: Do you want to go to the Japanese restaurant for dinner?

   B: That would be okay, but in truth I _____ Chinese food to Japanese

   food.

   A: Really? I _____ Japanese food better than Chinese food. What shall

   we do?

   B: Let's go to the Italian restaurant.

10. A: Mother, I can't believe you have another cat! Now you have four cats, two dogs, and three

    birds.

    B: I know, dear. I can't help it. I love having animals around.

    A: Honestly, Mother, I sometimes think you _____ animals to people.

    B: Honestly, dear, sometimes I do.

◇ **PRACTICE 27—GUIDED STUDY: Stating preferences. (Chart 5–13)**

Directions: Give a sentence with the same meaning, using the word(s) in parentheses.

Example: Alex would rather swim than jog. (*prefer*)
Response: *Alex prefers swimming to jogging.*

Example: My son likes fish better than beef. (*would rather*)
Response: *My son would rather eat / have fish than beef.*

1. Kim likes salad better than dessert. (*prefer*)
2. In general, Nicole would rather have coffee than tea. (*like*)
3. Bill prefers teaching history to working as a business executive. (*would rather*)
4. When considering a pet, Sam prefers dogs to cats. (*like*)

5. On a long trip, Susie would rather drive than ride in the back seat. (*prefer*)

6. I like studying in a noisy room better than studying in a completely quiet room. (*would rather*)

7. Alex likes music better than sports. (*would rather*)

◇ PRACTICE 28—SELFSTUDY: Cumulative review. (Charts 5-1 → 5-13)

Directions: Each of the following has a short dialogue. Try to imagine a situation in which the dialogue could take place, and then choose the best completion.

Example:
"My horse is sick."
"Oh? What's the matter? You __*B*__ call the vet."
 A. will   B. had better   C. may

1. "Does this pen belong to you?"
"No. It _____ be Susan's. She was sitting at that desk."
 A. must   B. will   C. had better

2. "I need the milk. _____ you get it out of the refrigerator for me?"
"Sure."
 A. May   B. Should   C. Could

3. "Let's go to a movie this evening."
"That sounds like fun, but I can't. I _____ finish a report before I go to bed tonight."
 A. have got to   B. would rather   C. ought to

4. "Hey, Ted. What's up with Ken? Is he upset about something?"
"He's angry because you recommended Ann instead of him for the promotion. You _____ sit down with him and try to explain your reasons. At least that's what I think."
 A. should   B. will   C. can

5. "Does Tom want to go with us to the film festival tonight?"
"No. He _____ go to the wrestling match than the film festival."
 A. could   B. would rather   C. prefers

6. "I did it! I did it! I got my driver's license!"
"Congratulations, Michelle. I'm really proud of you."
"Thanks, Dad. Now _____ I have the car tonight? Please, please!"
"No. You're not ready for that quite yet."
 A. will   B. should   C. may

7. "I just tripped on your carpet and almost fell! There's a hole in it. You _____ fix that before someone gets hurt."
"Yes, Uncle Ben. I should. I will. I'm sorry. Are you all right?"
 A. can   B. ought to   C. may

8. "Are you going to the conference in Atlanta next month?"
"I _____. It's sort of 'iffy' right now. I've applied for travel money, but who knows what my supervisor will do."
 A. will   B. have to   C. might

9. "What shall we do after the meeting this evening?"
"_____ pick Jan up and all go out to dinner together."
 A. Why don't   B. Let's   C. Should

10. "There's a mistake in this report."
"Really? You _____ tell Erica before she gives it to Ms. Allen."
 A. had better   B. may   C. would rather

11. "Have you seen my denim jacket? I _____ find it."
    "Look in the hall closet."
    A. may not   B. won't   C. can't

12. "_____ you hand me that book, please? I can't reach it."
    "Sure. Here it is."
    A. Would   B. Should   C. Must

13. "Bye, Mom! I'm going to go play soccer with my friends."
    "Wait a minute, young man! You _____ do your chores first."
    A. must not   B. must   C. would rather

14. "What do you like the most about your promotion?"
    "I _____ get up at 5:30 in the morning anymore. I can sleep until 7:00."
    A. must not   B. would rather   C. don't have to

15. "Do you think that Scott will quit his job?"
    "I don't know. He _____. He's very angry. We'll just have to wait and see."
    A. must   B. may   C. will

◇ **PRACTICE 29—GUIDED STUDY:** Cumulative review. (Charts 5–1 → 5–13)

Directions: Each of the following has a short dialogue. Try to imagine a situation in which the dialogue could take place, and then choose the best completion.

Example:
   "My horse is sick."
   "Oh? What's the matter? You __*B*__ call the vet."
   A. will   B. had better   C. may

1. "Do you have a minute? I need to talk to you."
   "I _____ leave here in ten minutes. Can we make an appointment for another time?"
   A. have to   B. could   C. may

2. "Yes? _____ I help you?"
   "Yes. Do you have these sandals in a size eight?"
   A. Should   B. Can   C. Will

3. "Let's go bowling Saturday afternoon."
   "Bowling? I _____ play golf than go bowling."
   A. had better   B. should   C. would rather

4. "The hotel supplies towels, you know. You _____ pack a towel in your suitcase."
   "This is my bathrobe, not a towel."
   A. don't have to   B. must not   C. couldn't

5. "I heard that Bill was seriously ill."
   "Really? Well, he _____ be sick anymore. He just left for New York on a business trip."
   A. won't   B. must   C. must not

6. "Dianne found a library book on a bench at Central Park. Someone had left it there."
   "She _____ take it to any library in the city. I'm sure they'll be glad to have it back."
   A. will   B. should   C. would rather

7. "Do you understand how this computer program works?"
   "Sort of, but not really. _____ you explain it to me one more time? Thanks."
   A. Could   B. Should   C. Must

8. "Did you climb to the top of the Statue of Liberty when you were in New York?"
   "No, I didn't. My knee was very sore, so I _____ climb all those stairs."
   A. couldn't   B. might not   C. must not

9. "Rick, _____ you work for me this evening? I'll take your shift tomorrow."
   "Sure. I was going to ask you to work for me tomorrow anyway."
   A. would   B. should   C. must

10. "Beth got another speeding ticket yesterday."
    "Oh? That's not good. She _____ be more careful. She'll end up in serious trouble if she gets any more."
    A. would rather   B. will   C. ought to

11. "Are you going to take the job transfer when the company moves out of town?"
    "I _____ accept their offer if they are willing to pay all of my moving expenses."
    A. must not   B. might   C. maybe

12. "How are we going to take care of your little brother and go to the concert at the same time?"
    "I have an idea. _____ we take him with us?"
    A. Why don't   B. Let's   C. Will

13. "Are you going to admit your mistake to the boss?"
    "Yes. I _____ tell her about it than have her hear about it from someone else."
    A. can   B. should   C. would rather

14. "Meet me at Tony's at five. Please! I _____ talk to you. It's important."
    "Is something wrong?"
    A. could   B. will   C. have got to

15. "What are you children doing? Stop! You _____ play with sharp knives."
    "What?"
    A. mustn't   B. couldn't   C. don't have to

◇ PRACTICE 30—GUIDED STUDY: Review of auxiliary verbs. (Chapters 1 → 5)

Directions: Complete the sentences with any appropriate auxiliary verb in the list.   There may be more than one possible completion.   Also include any words in parentheses.

List of auxiliary verbs:

am	does	is	should
are	did	may	was
can	had better	might	were
could	has to	must	will
do	have to	ought to	would

1. A: Hello?

    B: Hello. This is Gisella Milazzo. ___*May (Could/Can)*___ I speak with Ms. Morgan, please?

2. A: Where's the newspaper?

    B: I (*not*) _____*don't*_____ have it. Ask Kevin.

3. A: _____ you rather go downtown today or tomorrow?

    B: Tomorrow.

4. A: _____ Nick going to be at the meeting tomorrow?

    B: I hope so.

5. A: _____ you talk to Amanda yesterday?

    B: Yes. Why?

6. A: _____ I help you, sir?

    B: Yes. _____ you show me the third watch from the left on the top shelf?

    A: Of course.

7. A: I'm sorry. _____ you repeat that? I couldn't hear you because my dog _____ barking.

 B: I said, "Why is your dog making all that noise?"

8. A: I don't know whether to turn left or right at the next intersection.

 B: I think you _____ pull over and look at the map.

9. A: Hurry up. Kate and Greg _____ waiting for us.

 B: I _____ hurrying!

10. A: Andy can't teach his class tonight.

 B: He _____ teach tonight! He'll be fired if he doesn't show up.

11. A: Stop! (*not*) _____ touch that pan! It's hot! You'll burn yourself.

 B: Relax. I had no intention of touching it.

12. A: What _____ you carrying? _____ you want some help?

 B: It's a heavy box of books. _____ you open the door for me, please?

13. A: Hello?

 B: Hello. _____ I please speak to Sandra Wilson?

 A: I'm sorry. There's no one here by that name. You _____ have the wrong number.

14. A: Stop! You (*not*) _____ pick those flowers! It's against the law to pick flowers in a national park.

 B: Really? I didn't know that.

15. A: Everyone _____ work toward cleaning up the environment.

   B: I agree. Life on earth (*not*) _____

   survive if we continue to poison the

   land, water, and air.

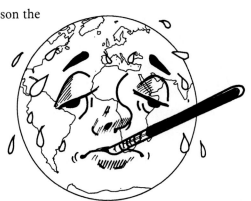

◇ **PRACTICE 31—GUIDED STUDY:**   Cumulative review. (Chapter 5)

> Directions: Following is a passage for you to read. The topic is the process of writing a composition. Read the passage through completely to get the main ideas. Then read it again slowly and choose from the words in *italics*. Which completions seem best to you? Why? Discuss your choices.

Writing a Composition

(1)   "What? Not another composition! I hate writing compositions. I'm not good at it." Do you ever complain about having to write compositions in English class? A lot of students do. You *may, cannot* find it difficult and time-consuming, but you are learning a useful skill. The ability to write clearly *is, must be* important. It *can, must* affect your success in school and in your job. You *may, can* learn to write effectively by practicing. Preparing compositions is one of the best ways to learn the skill of writing clearly.

(2)   The first step in writing a composition is to choose a subject that interests you. You *maybe, should* write about a subject you already know about or *can, have to* find out about through research. Writers *might, should* never pretend to be experts. For example, if you have never bought a car and are not knowledgeable about automobiles, you *should, should not* choose to write an essay on what to look for when buying a used car—unless, of course, you plan to research the subject in books and magazines and make yourself an expert. There is one topic about which you are the most knowledgeable expert in the world, and that topic *is, will be* yourself and your experiences. Many of the most interesting and informative compositions are based simply on a writer's personal experience and observations. The questions you should ask yourself when choosing a topic are "Do I have any expertise in this subject?" and if not,   *"Will, Can* I be able to find information about this subject?"

(3)   After you have a topic and have researched it if necessary, start writing down your thoughts. These notes *must not, do not have to* be in any particular order. You *do not have to, could not* worry about grammar at this time. You *can, may* pay special attention to that later.

(4)   Next you *have to, may* organize your thoughts. You *cannot, might not* say everything possible about a subject in one composition. Therefore, you *may, must* carefully choose the ideas and information you want to include. Look over your notes, think hard about your topic, and find a central idea. Answer these questions: "What *am, do* I want my readers to understand? What *is, does* my main idea? How *can, must* I put this idea into one sentence?" Good writing depends on clear thinking. Writers *should, should not* spend more time thinking than actually writing. After you have a clearly formed main idea, choose relevant information from your notes to include in your composition.

(5)   Before you begin to write the actual composition, you *ought to, can* know exactly what you want to say and how you are going to develop your ideas. Many good writers *prepare, prepared* an outline before they start. An outline is like a road map to keep you headed toward your destination without getting lost or sidetracked.

(6)   There *are, ought to be* many ways to begin a composition. For example, you *might, must* begin with a story that leads up to your main idea. Or you *may, ought to* start with a question that you want your reader to think about and then suggest an answer. *Maybe, May be* you *could, have to* introduce your topic by defining a key word. Simply presenting interesting factual information *is, will be* another common way of beginning a composition. Your goals in your first paragraph *is, are* to catch your reader's attention and then state your main idea clearly and concisely. By the end of the first paragraph, your reader *may, should* understand what you are going to cover in the composition.

(7)   If possible, write the entire first draft of your composition in a single sitting. After you have a first draft, the next step is rewriting. Every composition *could, should* go through several drafts. Rewriting is a natural part of the process of writing. You *will, do not have to* find many things that you *can change, changed* and improve when you reread your first draft. As you revise, you *will, should* be careful to include connecting words such as **then**, **next**, **for example**, **after**, and **therefore**. These words connect one idea to another so that your reader will not get lost. Also pay attention to grammar, punctuation, and spelling as you revise and rewrite. Your dictionary *should, can* be next to you.

(8)   Writing *is, may be* a skill. It improves as you gain experience with the process of choosing a subject, jotting down thoughts, organizing them into a first draft, and then rewriting and polishing. At the end of this process, you *should, should not* have a clear and well-written composition.

◇ PRACTICE 32—SELFSTUDY: Prepositions. (Chapter 5; Appendix 1)

Directions: Complete each sentence with the appropriate preposition.

1. A: Why are you so friendly __*with/to*__ George? I thought you didn't like him.

   B: I'm not crazy _____ his attitude toward his work, but I have to encourage him to do the best he can.

2. A: Do you think it's bad that I drink so much coffee every day?

   B: I believe too much of almost anything is bad _____ you.

3. I don't know why they fired me. It certainly isn't clear _____ me.

4. A: Dad, I got ninety-five percent on my algebra exam!

   B: I'm proud _____ you. I knew you could do it.

5. A: You seem to be interested _____ aerobic exercise and jogging.

   B: I think regular physical exercise is good _____ everyone.

6. That sweater is very similar _____ mine. Did you buy it at the mall?

7. Most children are afraid _____ noises in the middle of the night.

8. A: You were up awfully late last night.

   B: I couldn't sleep. I was hungry _____ something sweet, and I couldn't find anything
      in the kitchen.

9. I have no doubt that I'm doing the right thing. I'm sure _____ it.

10. George Gershwin, an American composer, is most famous _____ *Rhapsody in Blue*, an
    orchestral piece that combines jazz with classical music.

11. A: Why is Gary avoiding you? Is he angry about something?

    B: I don't know. I'm not aware _____ anything I did that could upset him.

12. A: Who is responsible _____ this dog? He's chewing on my desk!

    B: I'm sorry, sir. She followed me from home. I'll take her outside.

13. My car is a lot like yours, but different _____ Margaret's.

CHAPTER 6
Questions

◇ **PRACTICE 1—SELFSTUDY:** Asking "interview" questions. (Charts 6–1 → 6–13)

Directions: In the following, pretend that you are interviewing a member of your class named Anna. Write your name in line (1), and then complete the dialogue with appropriate QUESTIONS.

(1) ME: Hi. My name is _____. Our teacher has asked me to interview you so that I can practice asking questions. Could I ask you a few questions about yourself?

ANNA: Sure.

(2) ME: Well, first of all, ___***what is your name?***_____

ANNA: Anna.

(3) ME: _____

ANNA: Yes, that's my first name.

(4) ME: _____

ANNA: Polanski.

(5) ME: _____

ANNA: P-O-L-A-N-S-K-I.

ME: Let me make sure I have that right. Your first name is Anna, A-N-N-A. And your last name is Polanski, P-O-L-A-N-S-K-I. Right?

ANNA: That's right.

(6) ME: _____

ANNA: Poland.

(7) ME: _____

ANNA: Warsaw.

(8) ME: _____

ANNA: Two weeks ago.

(9) ME: _____

ANNA: Because I wanted to study at this school.

(10) ME: _____

ANNA: Biochemistry.

(11) ME: _____

ANNA: I'm going to stay here for four years or until I graduate.

(12) ME: _____

ANNA: I'm living at my aunt and uncle's house.

(13)   ME: _____
       ANNA: No. Not far.

(14)   ME: _____
       ANNA: Six blocks.

(15)   ME: _____
       ANNA: Sometimes I take the bus, but usually I walk.

(16)   ME: You're lucky. I live far away from the school, so it takes me a long time to get here
             every morning. But that's my only big complaint about living here. Otherwise, I like
             going to this school a lot. _____
       ANNA: Very much.
       ME: Well, thanks for the interview. I think I have enough information for the
             assignment. Nice to meet you.
       ANNA: Nice to meet you, too.

◇ PRACTICE 2—SELFSTUDY: Yes/no questions and short answers. (Charts 6–1 and 6–2)

Directions: Complete Speaker A's QUESTIONS with DO, DOES, IS, or ARE. Complete Speaker B's
SHORT ANSWERS.

1. A: I need a flashlight. _____**Do**_____ you have one?

    B: No, _____**I don't**_____.

2. A: _____ Alaska in North America?

    B: Yes, _____.

3. A: _____ snakes have legs?

    B: No, _____.

4. A: _____ you going to be in class tomorrow?

    B: Yes, _____.

5. A: _____ aspirin relieve pain?

    B: Yes, _____.

6. A: _____ all snakebites poisonous?

    B: No, _____.

7. A: _____ crocodiles lay eggs?

    B: Yes, _____.

8. A: _____ you doing a grammar exercise?

    B: Yes, _____.

9. A: _____ Africa the largest continent?

    B: No, _____. Asia is.

10. A: _____ ants eat other insects?

    B: Yes, _____.

11. A: Mercury is a liquid metal used in thermometers. _____ mercury have a boiling

    point?

    B: Yes, _____. It boils at 356.58°C.

◇ **PRACTICE 3—SELFSTUDY:** Yes/no questions. (Chapters 1, 2, 3, 5, and Chart 6–1)*

Directions: Write the correct QUESTION FORM. The answer to the question is in parentheses.

		helping verb	subject	main verb	rest of sentence
1.	SIMPLE PRESENT	A: *Do*	*you*	*like*	*coffee?*
		B: Yes, I like coffee.			

		helping verb	subject	main verb	rest of sentence
2.	SIMPLE PRESENT	A: _____	_____	_____	_____
		B: Yes, Tom likes coffee.			

		helping verb	subject	main verb	rest of sentence
3.	PRESENT PROGRESSIVE	A: _____	_____	_____	_____
		B: Yes, Ann is watching TV.			

		helping verb	subject	main verb	rest of sentence
4.	PRESENT PROGRESSIVE	A: _____	_____	_____	_____
		B: Yes, I'm having lunch with Rob.			

		helping verb	subject	main verb	rest of sentence
5.	SIMPLE PAST	A: _____	_____	_____	_____
		B: Yes, Sara walked to school.			

		helping verb	subject	main verb	rest of sentence
6.	PAST PROGRESSIVE	A: _____	_____	_____	_____
		B: Yes, Ann was taking a nap.			

		helping verb	subject	main verb	rest of sentence
7.	SIMPLE FUTURE	A: _____	_____	_____	_____
		B: Yes, Ted will come to the meeting.			

		helping verb	subject	main verb	rest of sentence
8.	MODAL: *CAN*	A: _____	_____	_____	_____
		B: Yes, Rita can ride a bicycle.			

		form of *be*	subject		rest of sentence
9.	MAIN VERB *BE* SIMPLE PRESENT	A: _____	_____		_____
		B: Yes, Ann is a good artist.			

		form of *be*	subject		rest of sentence
10.	MAIN VERB *BE* SIMPLE PAST	A: _____	_____		_____
		B: Yes, I was at the wedding.			

Question forms of tenses and modals can be found in the following charts:
Simple present and present progressive: Chart 1–2
Simple past: Chart 2–2
Past progressive: Chart 2–7
Simple future (*will*): Chart 3–2
Modal *can*: Chart 5–2

Directions: Write dialogues between Speakers A and B. Make up QUESTIONS that will fit with the given idea in B's answer.

Example: B: No, I _____. I'm allergic to them.
Written: **A: Do you like cats (dogs/strawberries/etc.)?**
B: No, I don't. I'm allergic to them.

Example: B: Yes, we _____. Would you like to come along with us?
Written: **A: Are you and Yoko going to the festival Saturday?**
B: Yes, we are. Would you like to come along with us?

1. B: No, she _____. It was too expensive.
2. B: Yes, he _____. Yesterday.
3. B: No, I _____. I forgot.
4. B: Yes, we _____. It was delicious.
5. B: Yes, they _____. Don't worry.

6. B: No, I _____. I never learned how to.
7. B: Yes, I _____. What about you?
8. B: Maybe. Let me think about it.
9. B: Probably. She usually does.
10. B: Sure. Sounds like a good idea to me.

◇ PRACTICE 5—SELFSTUDY: Yes/no and information questions. (Charts 6–1 and 6–2)

Directions: Complete the dialogues by writing Speaker A's QUESTION. Write Ø if no word is needed in a space.

(question word)	helping verb	subject	main verb	rest of sentence
1. A: Ø	Did	you	hear	the news yesterday?

B: Yes, I did. (I heard the news yesterday.)

(question word)	helping verb	subject	main verb	rest of sentence
2. A: When	did	you	hear	the news?

B: Yesterday. (I heard the news yesterday.)

(question word)	helping verb	subject	main verb	rest of sentence
3. A: Ø				

B: Yes, he is. (Eric is reading today's paper.)

(question word)	helping verb	subject	main verb	rest of sentence
4. A:				Ø

B: Today's paper. (Eric is reading today's paper.)

(question word)	helping verb	subject	main verb	rest of sentence
5. A:				

B: Yes, I did. (I found my wallet.)

(question word)	helping verb	subject	main verb	rest of sentence
6. A:				

B: On the floor of the car. (I found my wallet on the floor of the car.)

(question word)	helping verb	subject	main verb	rest of sentence
7. A:				

B: Because he enjoys the exercise. (Mr. Li walks to work because he enjoys the exercise.)

(question word)	helping verb	subject	main verb	rest of sentence

8. A: _____ _____ _____ _____ _____
   B: Yes, he does. (Mr. Li walks to work.)

(question word)	helping verb	subject	main verb	rest of sentence

9. A: _____ _____ _____ _____ _____
   B: Yes, she will. (Ms. Cook will return to her office at one o'clock.)

(question word)	helping verb	subject	main verb	rest of sentence

10. A: _____ _____ _____ _____ _____
    B: At one o'clock. (Ms. Cook will return to her office at one o'clock.)

(question word)	form of *be*	subject	rest of sentence

11. A: _____ _____ _____ _____
    B: Yes, it is. (The orange juice is in the refrigerator.)

(question word)	form of *be*	subject	rest of sentence

12. A: _____ _____ _____ _____
    B: In the refrigerator. (The orange juice is in the refrigerator.)

◇ PRACTICE 6—SELFSTUDY: Information questions. (Charts 6–1 and 6–2)

Directions: Make QUESTIONS for the given answers. Use the information in parentheses. Use **WHEN, WHAT TIME, WHERE,** or **WHY.** Pay special attention to the word order in the questions.

1. A: ___*What time (When) do the fireworks start*___ this evening?
   B: 9:30. (The fireworks start at 9:30 this evening.)

2. A: _____ to see the principal?
   B: Because I need to get his signature on this application form. (I'm waiting to see the principal because I need to get his signature on this application form.)

3. A: _____ her new job?
   B: Next Monday morning. (Rachel starts her new job next Monday morning.)

4. A: _____ home for work?
   B: Around 6:00. (I usually leave home for work around 6:00.)

5. A: _____ to the meeting?
   B: Because I fell asleep after dinner and didn't wake up until 9:00. (I didn't get to the meeting because I fell asleep after dinner and didn't wake up until 9:00.)

6. A: _____ razor blades?
   B: At many different kinds of stores. (You can buy razor blades at many different kinds of stores.)

7. A: _____ for home?
   B: Next Saturday. (I'm leaving for home next Saturday.)

8. A: _____ Chinese?
   B: In Germany. (I studied Chinese in Germany.)

   A: _____ Chinese in Germany?
   B: Because there is a good Chinese language school there. (I studied Chinese in Germany because there is a good Chinese language school there.)

   A: _____ to China to study Chinese?
   B: Because I had a scholarship to study in Germany. (I didn't go to China to study Chinese because I had a scholarship to study in Germany.)

9. A: _____ to finish this project?
   B: Next month. (I expect to finish this project next month.)

10. A: _____?
    B: To Mars. (The spaceship will go to Mars.)

◇ **PRACTICE 7—GUIDED STUDY:** Yes/no and information questions. (Charts 6–1 and 6–2)

Directions: Create dialogues between Speakers A and B. In each dialogue:
   A: asks a QUESTION.
   B: gives the SHORT ANSWER that is given below, and then gives a LONG ANSWER.

Example: After midnight.
Dialogue: A: What time did you go to bed last night?
            B: After midnight. I went to bed after midnight last night.

1. The day before yesterday.
2. Yes, I do.
3. Because I had to.
4. At 8:30.
5. Yes, he is.
6. In a supermarket.
7. Tomorrow afternoon.
8. A notebook.
9. No, I can't.
10. Because . . . .
11. Yeah, sure. Why not?
12. I don't know. Maybe.

◇ **PRACTICE 8—GUIDED STUDY:** Asking for the meaning of a word. (Charts 6–2 and 6–3)

Directions: Ask your classmates for the meaning of the *italicized* word in each sentence below. If no one knows the meaning, look it up in a dictionary.

PART I: Ask questions using **"What does . . . mean?"**

1. Captain Cook *explored* many islands in the Pacific Ocean.
   STUDENT A: **What does** "explored" **mean**?
   STUDENT B: "Explored" means "went to a new place and found out about it."
   OR:
   STUDENT A: **What does** "explore" **mean**?
   STUDENT B: "Explore" means "(to) go to a new place and find out about it."★

2. I think Carol's *mad*.
   STUDENT A: **What does** "mad" **mean**?
   STUDENT B: "Mad" can mean "crazy" or "angry."

3. Water is *essential* to all forms of life on earth.

4. Why do soap bubbles *float*?

5. The water on the streets and sidewalks *evaporated* in the morning sun.

6. It's raining. *Perhaps* we should take a taxi.

7. Some fish *bury* themselves in the sand on the ocean bottom and live their entire lives there.

8. He gently put his hand *beneath* the baby's head.

9. I *grabbed* my briefcase and started running for the bus.

10. On the average, how many times a minute do people *blink*?

_____

★Sometimes the infinitive form (**to** + *verb*) is used in definitions of verbs: *"to explore"* means *"to go* to a new place and find out about it."

PART II: Ask for the meaning of nouns.

11. We walked hand in hand through the *orchard*.
    STUDENT A: **What is** an orchard?
    STUDENT B: An orchard is a place where fruit trees grow.
    OR:
    STUDENT A: **What does** ''orchard'' **mean**?
    STUDENT B: ''Orchard'' means ''a place where fruit trees grow.''

12. Sometimes children have *nightmares*.
    STUDENT A: **What are** nightmares?
    STUDENT B: Nightmares are very bad dreams.
    OR:
    STUDENT A: **What does** ''nightmare(s)'' **mean**?
    STUDENT B: ''Nightmare(s)'' means ''very bad dream(s).''

13. Would you like to see the *photographs* from our vacation?

14. While we were eating at the outdoor restaurant, I noticed a *bug* in my soup.

15. Mrs. Hall often wears *pearls*.

16. My daughter is at the university. She wants to be an *archaeologist*.

17. People throughout the world enjoy *fables*.

18. Mark and Olivia went to Hawaii on their *honeymoon*.

19. The *margins* on your composition should be at least one inch wide.*

20. I'm not very good at *small talk*, so I avoid social situations like cocktail parties.

21. If you want to use a computer, you have to learn the *keyboard*.

22. Mr. Weatherbee liked to have *hedges* between his house and his neighbors' houses. He planted the bushes close together so that people couldn't see through them.

◇ **PRACTICE 9—GUIDED STUDY: Questions with *why*. (Chart 6–2)**

Directions: Create dialogues between Speakers A and B. In each dialogue:
   A: says the sentence in the book.
   B: asks **WHY?** or **WHY NOT?** and then asks the full *why*-question.
   A: makes up an answer to the question.

Example: A: I can't go with you tomorrow.
Dialogue: A: I can't go with you tomorrow.
            B: Why not? Why can't you go with me tomorrow?
            A: Because I have to study for a test.**

1. A: I ate two breakfasts this morning.

2. A: I don't like to ride on airplanes.

3. A: I'm going to sell my guitar.

4. A: I didn't go to bed last night.

5. A: I'm happy today.

6. A: I had to call the police last night.

7. A: I can't explain it to you.

8. A: I'm not speaking to my cousin.

---

*One inch = approximately two and a half centimeters.

**See Chart 9–6 for the use of *because*. ''Because I have to study for a test'' is an adverb clause. It is not a complete sentence. In this dialogue, it is the short answer to a question.

◇ PRACTICE 10—SELFSTUDY: Questions with *who, who(m),* and *what.* (Chart 6–3)

Directions: Make questions with **WHO, WHO(M),** and **WHAT.** Write "**S**" if the question word is the subject. Write "**O**" if the question word is the object.

QUESTION   ANSWER

	S	*S*
1.	*Who knows?*	**Someone** knows.
	O	*O*
2.	*Who(m) did you ask?*	I asked **someone**.
3.	_____	**Someone** knocked on the door.
4.	_____	Sara met **someone**.
5.	_____	**Someone** will help us.
6.	_____	I will ask **someone**.
7.	_____	Eric is talking to **someone** on the phone.
8.	_____	**Someone** is knocking on the door.
9.	_____	**Something** surprised them.
10.	_____	Mike learned **something**.
11.	_____	**Something** will change Ann's mind.
12.	_____	Tina can talk about **something**.

◇ PRACTICE 11—SELFSTUDY: *Who, who(m),* and *what.* (Chart 6–3)

Directions: Complete the dialogues by making QUESTIONS. Use the information in the long answer in parentheses to make the question.

1. A: **Who taught you to play chess?** _____
   B: My mother. (My mother taught me to play chess.)

2. A: _____
   B: A bank robbery. (Robert saw a bank robbery.)

3. A: _____
   B: Robert did. (Robert got a good look at the bank robber.)

4. A: _____
   B: A toy for my brother's children. (I'm making a toy for my brother's children.)

5. A: _____
   B: Joe. (That calculator belongs to Joe.)

6. A: _____
   B: A bag of candy. (I have a bag of candy in my pocket.)

7. A: _____
   B: A mouse. (The cat killed a mouse.)

8. A: _____
   B: Curiosity. (Curiosity killed the cat.)*

_____
Curiosity is the desire to learn about something. "Curiosity killed the cat" is an English saying that means we can get into trouble when we want to know too much about something that doesn't really concern us.

9. A: _____
   B: My father. (I got a letter from my father.)

10. A: _____
    B: My sister. (My sister wrote a note on the envelope.)

11. A: _____
    B: Gravity. (Gravity makes an apple fall to the ground from a tree.)

◇ **PRACTICE 12—SELFSTUDY:** *What* + a form of *do.* (Chart 6–4)

Directions: Use the information in parentheses to make QUESTIONS with **WHAT** + A FORM OF **DO** to complete each dialogue. Use the SAME VERB TENSE OR MODAL that is used in the parentheses.

1. A: ***What is Alex doing?***
   B: Watching a movie on TV. (Alex is watching a movie on TV.)

2. A: ***What should I do if someone calls while you're out?***
   B: Just take a message. (You should take a message if someone calls while I'm out.)

3. A: _____
   B: They explore space. (Astronauts explore space.)

4. A: I spilled some juice on the floor. _____
   B: Wipe it up with a paper towel. (You should wipe it up with a paper towel.)

5. A: _____
   B: Play tennis at Waterfall Park. (I'm going to play tennis at Waterfall Park Saturday morning.)

6. A: _____
   B: I see my doctor. (I see my doctor when I get sick.)

7. A: _____
   B: Carry this suitcase. (You can carry this suitcase to help me.)

8. A: _____
   B: She smiled. (Sara smiled when she heard the good news.)

Directions: Use the information in parentheses to make QUESTIONS with **WHAT** + A FORM OF **DO** to complete each dialogue. Use the SAME VERB TENSE OR MODAL that is used in the parentheses.

1. A: _____
   B: I think she plans to look for a job in hotel management. (Emily is going to look for a job in hotel management after she graduates.)

2. A: _____
   B: Can you make twelve photocopies of this report? (You can make twelve photocopies of this report to help me get ready for the meeting.)

3. A: _____
   B: Ran down the stairs and out of the building. (I ran down the stairs and out of the building when the fire alarm sounded.)

4. A: _____
   B: Let's go to the shopping mall, okay? (I would like to go to the shopping mall after school today.)

5. A: _____
   B: Make this coin stand on edge. (I'm trying to make this coin stand on edge.)

6. A: _____
   B: He needs to hand in all of his homework. (Kevin needs to hand in all of his homework if he wants to pass advanced algebra.)

7. A: _____
   B: He's an airplane mechanic. (Nick repairs airplanes for a living.)

8. A: Did you say something to that man over there? Why does he look angry?
   B: I accidentally ran into him and stepped on his foot.

   A: _____
   B: Said something nasty. (He said something nasty when I bumped into him.)

   A: _____
   B: Apologized. (I apologized.)

   A: Then _____
   B: Walked away without saying a word. (Then he walked away without saying a word.)
   A: What an unpleasant person!
   B: I didn't mean to step on his foot. It was just an accident.

◇ PRACTICE 14—GUIDED STUDY: *What* + a form of *do*. (Chart 6–4)

Directions: Create dialogues between Speakers A and B. Speaker A should ask a question that will produce B's given answer. The question should contain **WHAT** + A FORM OF **DO**.

Example: B: Study in the corner of the cafeteria.

Dialogue: A: What are you going to do after class today?
            B: Study in the corner of the cafeteria.

   1. B: Watch TV.

   2. B: Washing his dog.

   3. B: Went home and slept.

   4. B: Writing dialogues.

   5. B: Go to a movie.

   6. B: Get a job on a cruise ship.

◇ **PRACTICE 15—GUIDED STUDY:** *What kind of.* (Chart 6–5)

Directions: Find people who own the following things. Ask them questions using **WHAT KIND OF.**

Example: a camera
First, ask a classmate, friend, or family member: *Do you have a camera?*
If the answer is yes, ask next: *What kind of camera to do you have?*★
Then write the information you have gotten, for example:

→ ***Maria has a 35 millimeter Kodak camera.***

1. a camera	6. a computer
2. a TV	7. a watch
3. a bicycle	8. a dog
4. a car	9. a VCR
5. a refrigerator	10. ???

◇ **PRACTICE 16—SELFSTUDY:** *Which* vs. *what.* (Chart 6–6)

Directions: Complete the questions with **WHICH** or **WHAT.**

1. A: This hat comes in brown and in gray. _____***Which***_____ color do you think your husband would prefer?
   B: Gray, I think.

2. A: I've never been to Mrs. Hall's house. _____***What***_____ color is it?
   B: Gray.

3. A: I have two dictionaries. _____ one do you want?
   B: The Arabic–English dictionary.

4. A: Yes, may I help you?
   B: Please.
   A: _____ are you looking for?
   B: An Arabic–English dictionary.
   A: Right over there in the reference section.
   B: Thanks.

5. A: _____ languages do you speak other than your native language?
   B: Italian and English.
   A: _____ of those two languages do you speak more fluently?
   B: English.

6. A: _____ did you get on your last test?
   B: I don't want to tell you. It was really awful.

7. A: _____ job do you think I should take?
   B: The one at the small computer company. That's the best of the three job offers you've had.

8. A: Here's the remote control if you want to watch TV for a while.
   B: Thanks, I think I will.
   A: Push this button to turn it on.

   B: Okay. And _____ button should I push to change channels?

★If the answer is no, ask another question from the list.

◇ **PRACTICE 17—SELFSTUDY:** *Who vs. whose.* (Chart 6–7)

Directions: Complete the questions with **WHO** or **WHOSE**.

1. A: _____*Who*_____ is driving to the game tonight?
   B: Heidi is.

2. A: _____*Whose*_____ car are we taking to the game?
   B: Heidi's.

3. A: This notebook is mine. _____ is that? Is it yours?
   B: No, it's Sara's.

4. A: There's Ms. Adams. _____ is standing next to her?
   B: Mr. Wilson.

5. A: _____ was the first woman doctor in the United States?
   B: Elizabeth Blackwell, in 1849.

6. A: _____ suitcase did you borrow for your trip?
   B: Andy's.

7. A: _____ motorcycle ran into the telephone pole?
   B: Bill's.

8. A: Okay! _____ forgot to put the ice cream back in the freezer?
   B: I don't know. Don't look at me. It wasn't me.

◇ **PRACTICE 18—GUIDED STUDY:** Asking questions. (Charts 6–1 → 6–7)

Directions: Pair up with a classmate.

STUDENT A: Choose any one of the possible answers below and ask a question that would produce that answer.

STUDENT B: Decide which of the answers STUDENT A has in mind and answer his/her question. Pay special attention to the form of STUDENT A's question. Correct any errors.

(If you don't have a classmate to pair up with, write dialogues in which the given phrases are the answers to questions.)

Example:

STUDENT A: What's Maria's favorite color?

STUDENT B: *(Student B reviews the list of possible answers below and chooses the appropriate one.)* Pink.

POSSIBLE ANSWERS

Sure! Thanks!

Call the insurance company.

Next week.

A rat.

George.

Cooking dinner.

Turkey.

Probably.

The teacher's.

Not that one. The other one.

A Panasonic or a Sony.

Pink.

No, a friend of mine gave them to me a few days ago.

◇ **PRACTICE 19—SELFSTUDY:** Using *how.* (Chart 6–8)

Directions: Complete the sentences with any of the words in the given list.

busy	*fresh*	*safe*	*soon*
expensive	*hot*	*serious*	*well*

1. A: How _____**hot**_____ does it get in Chicago in the summer?

   B: Very _____**hot**_____. It can get over 100°. (100°F = 37.8°C)

2. A: How _____ will dinner be ready? I'm really hungry.

   B: In just a few more minutes.

3. A: Look at that beautiful vase! Let's get it.

   B: How _____ is it?

   A: Oh my gosh! Never mind. We can't afford it.

4. A: Sorry to interrupt, Ted, but I need some help. How _____ are you today? Do you have time to read over this report?

   B: Well, I'm always _____, but I'll make time to read it.

5. A: How _____ is Toshi about becoming an astronomer?

   B: He's very _____. He already knows more about the stars and planets than his high school teachers.

6. A: How _____ is a car with an airbag?

   B: Well, there have been bad accidents where both drivers walked away without injuries because of airbags.

7. A: Tomatoes for sale! Hey, lady! Wanna* buy some tomatoes? Tomatoes for sale!

   B: Hmmm. They look pretty good. How _____ are they?

   A: Whaddaya* mean "How _____ are they?" Would I sell something that wasn't _____? They were picked from the field just this morning.

---

*"Wanna" and "whaddaya" aren't usually written as words. They represent spoken English:

   "wanna" = "want to" (*Wanna buy some tomatoes?* = *Do you want to buy some tomatoes?*)

   "whaddaya" = "what do you" (*Whaddaya mean?* = *What do you mean?*).

8. A: Do you know Jack Young?

   B: Yes.

   A: Oh? How _____ do you know him?

   B: Very _____. He's one of my closest friends. Why?

   A: He's applied for a job at my store.

◇ **PRACTICE 20—SELFSTUDY:** Using *how far* and *how long* (Charts 6-10 and 6-12)

Directions: Complete the questions with **FAR** or **LONG**.

1. A: How _____*far*_____ is it to the nearest police station?
   B: Four blocks.

2. A: How _____*long*_____ does it take you to get to work?
   B: Forty-five minutes.

3. A: How _____ is it to your office from home?
   B: About twenty miles.

4. A: How _____ is it from here to the airport?
   B: Ten kilometers.

5. A: How _____ does it take to get to the airport?
   B: Fifteen minutes.

6. A: How _____ above sea level is Denver, Colorado?
   B: One mile. That's why it's called the Mile High City.

7. A: How _____ does it take to fly from Chicago to Denver?
   B: Around three hours.

8. A: How _____ did it take you to build your own boat?
   B: Four years.

9. A: How _____ did you walk?
   B: Two miles.

10. A: How _____ did you walk?
    B: Two hours.

◇ **PRACTICE 21—SELFSTUDY:** Using *how*. (Charts 6-8 → 6-12)

Directions: Complete the questions with **OFTEN, FAR, LONG,** or **MANY**.

1. A: How _____*often*_____ do you eat out at a restaurant?
   B: About once a week.

2. A: How _____ did you sleep last night?
   B: Six hours.

3. A: How _____ hours did you sleep last night?
   B: Six.

4. A: How _____ did you walk yesterday?
   B: About four miles.

5. A: How _____ miles did you walk yesterday?
   B: About four.

6. A: How _____ kilometers did you walk yesterday?
   B: About six.

7. A: How _____ did your father teach at the university?
    B: Forty-four years.

8. A: How _____ years did your father teach at the university?
    B: Forty-four.

9. A: How _____ do you play softball in the summer?
    B: Sometimes three or four times a week.

10. A: How _____ times a week do you play softball in the summer?
    B: Sometimes three or four times a week.

11. A: How _____ does it take to get a haircut at Bertha's Beauty Boutique?
    B: Half an hour.

12. A: How _____ do you get a haircut?
    B: About every six weeks, I'd guess.

13. A: How _____ is it from the earth to the moon?
    B: Approximately 239,000 miles or 385,000 kilometers.

14. A: How _____ times a day do you brush your teeth?
    B: At least three.

15. A: How _____ does a snake shed its skin?
    B: From once a year to more than six times a year, depending on the kind of snake.

16. A: How _____ is it from your desk to the door?
    B: I'd say about four regular steps or two giant steps.

17. A: How _____ does it take to get over a cold?
    B: As they say, a cold is three days coming, three days here, and three days going.

◇ **PRACTICE 22—GUIDED STUDY:** Using *how*. (Charts 6–8 → 6–13)

Directions: Make questions for the given answers. Use **HOW** in each question.

Example: It's very important.
Written: **How important is good health?**

1. Very expensive.

2. I took a taxi.

3. Four hours.

4. He's nineteen.

5. In five minutes.

6. With a knife.

7. Every day.

8. Three blocks.

9. Fine.

10. With two t's.

11. It gets below zero.

12. Her grades are excellent.

◇ **PRACTICE 23—SELFSTUDY: Cumulative review. (Charts 6–1 → 6–13)**

Directions: Using the information in parentheses, make QUESTIONS for the given answers.

1. A: ***When are you going to buy a new bicycle?***
   B: Next week. (I'm going to buy a new bicycle next week.)

2. A: ***How are you going to pay for it?***
   B: With my credit card. (I'm going to pay for it with my credit card.)

3. A: _____
   B: Ten years. (I had my old bike for ten years.)

4. A: _____
   B: Four or five times a week. (I ride my bike four or five times a week.)

5. A: _____
   B: I usually ride my bike. (I usually get to work by riding my bike.)

6. A: _____
   B: Yes. (I'm going to ride my bike to work tomorrow.)

7. A: _____
   B: I decided I would rather walk. (I didn't ride my bike to work today because I decided I would rather walk.)

8. A: _____
   B: Two weeks ago. (Jason got his new bike two weeks ago.)

9. A: _____
   B: Billy. (Billy broke Jason's new bike.)

10. A: _____
    B: Jason's new bike. (Billy broke Jason's new bike.)

11. A: _____
    B: Jason's new bike. (Jason's new bike is broken.)

12. A: _____
    B: He ran into a brick wall. (Billy broke Jason's bike by running into a brick wall.)

13. A: _____
    B: Yes, it does. (My bike has a comfortable seat.)

14. A: _____
    B: A ten-speed. (I have a ten-speed bicycle.)

15. A: _____
    B: The blue one. (The blue bicycle is mine, not the red one.)

16. A: _____
    B: Inside my apartment. (I keep my bicycle inside my apartment at night.)

17. A: _____
    B: David. (That bike belongs to David.)

18. A: _____
    B: Suzanne's. (I borrowed Suzanne's bike.)

19. A: _____
    B: In the park. (Rita is in the park.)

20. A: _____
    B: Riding her bike. (She's riding her bike.)

21. A: _____
    B: 25 miles. (Rita rode her bike 25 miles* yesterday.)

22. A: _____
    B: B-I-C-Y-C-L-E. (You spell "bicycle" B-I-C-Y-C-L-E.)

◇ PRACTICE 24—GUIDED STUDY: Cumulative review. (Charts 6–1 → 6–13)

Directions: Complete the dialogues by writing QUESTIONS for the given answers. Use the information in parentheses to form the questions.

1. A: *__When will the clean clothes be dry?__*
   B: In about an hour. (The clean clothes will be dry in about an hour.)

2. A: _____
   B: I went to a baseball game. (I went to a baseball game Saturday afternoon.)

3. A: _____
   B: The small paperback. (I bought the small paperback dictionary, not the large one with the hard cover.)

4. A: _____
   B: Four hours. (It took me four hours to clean my apartment before my parents came to visit.)

5. A: _____
   B: Stand on a chair. (You can reach the top shelf by standing on a chair.)

6. A: _____
   B: Whole wheat bread. (I like whole wheat bread the best.)

7. A: _____
   B: Because I was in the middle of dinner with my family. (I didn't answer the phone when it rang because I was in the middle of dinner with my family.)

8. A: _____
   B: Maria and her sister. (I'm going to the show with Maria and her sister.)

_____
*25 miles = 40.225 kilometers.

9. A: _____

   B: Eric. (Eric repaired the radio.)

10. A: _____

   B: It's not bad. It rarely gets below zero. (It rarely gets below zero in my hometown in the
   winter.)

11. A: _____

   B: He's playing tennis. (Jack is playing tennis.)

12. A: _____

   B: Anna. (He is playing tennis with Anna.)

13. A: _____

   B: Serving the ball. (Anna is serving the ball.)

14. A: _____

   B: A tennis ball. (She is throwing a tennis ball in the air.)

15. A: _____

   B: Rackets. (Anna and Jack are holding rackets.)

16. A: _____

   B: A net. (A net is between them.)

17. A: _____

   B: On a tennis court. (They are on a tennis court.)

18. A: _____

   B: For an hour and a half. (They have been playing for an hour and a half.)

19. A: _____

   B: Jack. (Jack is winning right now.)

20. A: _____

   B: Anna. (Anna won the last game.)

◇ PRACTICE 25—GUIDED STUDY: Cumulative review. (Charts 6-1 → 6-13)

Directions: Make dialogues from the given words. Include both Speaker A and Speaker B.

Example: . . . usually get up?
Written: **A: *What time do you usually get up?***
       B: 6:30.

1. . . . should I meet you?
2. . . . fruit do you like best?
3. . . . is south of the United States?
4. . . . times a week do you . . . ?
5. . . . do tomorrow?
6. . . . is it from . . . to . . . ?

7. . . . killed . . . ?
8. . . . you breathing hard?
9. . . . do for a living?
10. . . . spell "happened"?
11. . . . take to get to our hotel from the airport?
12. . . . didn't you call me when . . . ?

◇ PRACTICE 26—GUIDED STUDY: Cumulative review. (Charts 6-1 → 6-13)

Directions: In small groups (or by yourself), make up questions about some or all of the following topics. What would you like to know about these topics? What are you curious about? Share your questions with your classmates. Maybe some of them can answer some of your questions.

Example: tigers
Questions: How long do tigers usually live? Where do they live? What do they eat? Do they kill and eat people? How big is a tiger? Is it bigger than a lion? Can a tiger climb a tree? Do tigers live alone or in groups? Do they have natural enemies? Are human beings their only enemy? Will tigers become extinct soon? How many tigers are there in the world today? How many tigers were there one hundred years ago?

TOPICS:

1. world geography
2. the universe
3. the weather

4. dinosaurs
5. birds
6. (a topic of your own choosing)

◇ PRACTICE 27—GUIDED STUDY: *What about* and *how about.* (Chart 6-14)

Directions: Complete the dialogues with your own words.

1. A: _____?
   B: Nine or nine-thirty.
   A: That's too late for me. How about _____?
   B: Okay.

2. A: _____?
   B: No, Tuesday's not good for me.
   A: Then what about _____?
   B: Okay. That's fine.

3. A: There's room in the car for one more person. Do you think _____ would like
      to go to _____ with us?
   B: _____ can't go with us because _____.
   A: Then how about _____?
   B: _____.

4. A: Do you like fish?

    B: Yes, very much. How about _____?

    A: Yes, I like fish a lot. In fact, I think I'll order fish for dinner tonight. That sounds good.

    What about _____?

    B: No, I think I'll have _____.

◇ PRACTICE 28—SELFSTUDY: Tag questions. (Chart 6–15)

Directions: Complete the TAG QUESTIONS with the correct verb.

1. SIMPLE PRESENT

    a. You **like** strong coffee, _____*don't*_____ you?

    b. David **goes** to Ames High School, _____ he?

    c. Kate and Sara **live** on Tree Road, _____ they?

    d. Jane **has** the keys to the storeroom, _____ she?

    e. Jane**'s** in her office, _____ she?

    f. You**'re** a member of this class, _____ you?

    g. Jack **doesn't** have a car, _____ he?

    h. Ann **isn't** from California, _____ she?

2. SIMPLE PAST

    a. Paul **went** to Florida, _____ he?

    b. You **didn't talk** to the boss, _____ you?

    c. Tom's parents **weren't** at home, _____ they?

    d. That **was** Pat's idea, _____ it?

3. PRESENT PROGRESSIVE, *BE GOING TO*, and PAST PROGRESSIVE

    a. You**'re studying** hard, _____ you?

    b. Tom **isn't working** at the bank, _____ he?

    c. It **isn't going to rain** today, _____ it?

    d. Susan and Kevin **were waiting** for us, _____ they?

    e. It **wasn't raining**, _____ it?

4. MODAL AUXILIARIES

    a. You **can answer** these questions, _____ you?

    b. Kate **won't tell** anyone our secret, _____ she?

    c. Sam **should come** to the meeting, _____ he?

    d. Alice **would like** to come with us, _____ she?

    e. I **don't have to come** to the meeting, _____ I?

    f. Steve **had to leave** early, _____ he?

◇ **PRACTICE 29—SELFSTUDY:** Tag questions. (Chart 6–15)

Directions: Add TAG QUESTIONS.

1. Mr. Adams was born in England, _____ ***wasn't he*** _____?
2. Flies can fly upside down, _____?
3. All birds lay eggs, _____?
4. Mike isn't married, _____?
5. You would rather have a roommate than live alone, _____?
6. These gloves are yours, _____?
7. That's Brian's algebra book, _____?
8. Fire can't melt a diamond, _____?
9. You should call your mom today, _____?
10. Ms. Boxlight will be here tomorrow, _____?
11. Tony Wah lives in Los Angeles, _____?
12. You didn't forget to finish your homework, _____?
13. Tomorrow isn't a holiday, _____?
14. I don't have to be at the meeting, _____?
15. This isn't your book, _____?
16. Jack and Elizabeth were in class yesterday, _____?
17. Jennifer won't be here for dinner tonight, _____?
18. Lightning can kill swimmers when it strikes water. It kills the fish in the water, too,

    _____?

◇ **PRACTICE 30—GUIDED STUDY:** Tag questions. (Chart 6–15)

Directions: Make sentences with TAG QUESTIONS. Your sentences should express your opinion. In the example, the speaker believes that Li is a common name in China.

Example: I think that Li (is/isn't) a common name in China.
Question: Li is a common name in China, isn't it?

1. I think that Athens (is/isn't) the capital of Italy.
2. I think that Athens (is/isn't) the capital of Greece.
3. I think that plants (can/can't) grow in deserts.
4. I think that deserts (are/aren't) complete wastelands.
5. I think that cactuses (thrive/don't thrive) in deserts.
6. I think that dinosaurs (weighed/didn't weigh) more than elephants.
7. I think that blue whales (are/aren't) larger than dinosaurs.
8. I think that whales (lay/don't lay) eggs.
9. I think that turtles (lay/don't lay) eggs.
10. I think that Abraham Lincoln (was/wasn't) the first president of the United States.
11. I think that we (will/won't) have a test on Chapter 6.
12. I think that . . . .

◇ **PRACTICE 31—GUIDED STUDY: Asking questions. (Chapter 6)**

Directions: Pair up with a classmate or any other partner. Together create a long dialogue for the given situation. One of you is Speaker A and the other is Speaker B. The beginning of the dialogue is given.

1. SITUATION: The dialogue takes place on the telephone.
   Speaker A: You are a travel agent.
   Speaker B: You want to take a trip.

   DIALOGUE: *A: Hello, Worldwide Travel Agency. May I help you?*
   B: Yes, I need to make arrangements to go to (think of a place) . . . .
   A: Etc.
   B: Etc.

2. SITUATION: The dialogue takes place at a police station.
   Speaker A: You are a police officer.
   Speaker B: You are the suspect of a crime.

   DIALOGUE: *A: Where were you at eleven o'clock on Tuesday night, the 16th of this month?*
   B: I'm not sure I remember. Why do you want to know, Officer?
   Etc.

3. SITUATION: The dialogue takes place in an office.
   Speaker A: You are the owner of a small company.
   Speaker B: You are interviewing for a job in Speaker A's company.

   DIALOGUE: *A: Come in, come in. I'm (. . .). Glad to meet you.*
   B: How do you do? I'm (. . .). I'm pleased to meet you.
   A: Have a seat, (. . .).
   B: Thank you.
   A: So you're interested in working at (make up the name of a company)?
   Etc.

◇ **PRACTICE 32—SELFSTUDY: Prepositions. (Chapter 6; Appendix 1)**

Directions: Complete each sentence with the appropriate preposition.

1. Ask Ann to help you. She knows something ___*about*___ geometry.

2. Something's the matter _____ Dan. He's crying.

3. Do whatever you want. It doesn't matter _____ me.

4. Look _____ those clouds. It's going to rain.

5. Are you looking forward _____ your trip to Israel?

6. A: Does this watch belong _____ you?

   B: Yes. Where did you find it? I searched _____ it everywhere.

7. I woke up frightened after I dreamed _____ falling off the roof of a building.

8. Tomorrow I'm going to ask my father _____ a ride to school.

9. Tomorrow I'm going to ask my father _____ his work. I don't know much _____ his new job, and I want to ask him about it.

10. Please empty that bowl of fruit and separate the fresh apples _____ the old apples.

CHAPTER *7*

The Present Perfect and the Past Perfect

◇ **PRACTICE 1—SELFSTUDY:** Forms of the present perfect. (Charts 7–1 → 7–3)

Directions: Complete the dialogues with the given verbs and any words in parentheses. Use the PRESENT PERFECT.

1. *eat* A: (*you, ever*) _____**Have you ever eaten**_____ pepperoni pizza?

       B: Yes, I ___**have**___. I ___**have eaten**___ pepperoni pizza many times. OR:

           No, I ___**haven't**___. I (*never*) ___**have never eaten**___ pepperoni pizza.

2. *talk* A: (*you, ever*) _____ to a famous person?

       B: Yes, I _____. I _____ to a lot of famous people. OR:

           No, I _____. I (*never*) _____ to a famous person.

3. *rent* A: (*Erica, ever*) _____ a car?

       B: Yes, she _____. She _____ a car many times. OR:

           No, she _____. She (*never*) _____ a car.

4. *see* A: (*you, ever*) _____ a shooting star?

       B: Yes, I _____. I _____ a lot of shooting stars. OR:

           No, I _____. I (*never*) _____ a shooting star.

5. *catch* A: (*Joe, ever*) _____ a big fish?

       B: Yes, he _____. He _____ lots of big fish. OR:

           No, he _____. He (*never*) _____ a big fish.

6. *have* A: (*you, ever*) _____ a bad sunburn?

       B: Yes, I _____. I _____ a bad sunburn several times. OR:

           No, I _____. I (*never*) _____ a bad sunburn.

◇ **PRACTICE 2—SELFSTUDY:** The present perfect. (Charts 7–1 → 7–3)

Directions: Complete the sentences with the PRESENT PERFECT of the verbs in the list and any words in parentheses. Use each verb only one time.

eat	look	save	✔use
give	play	sleep	wear
improve	rise	speak	win

1. People _____**have used**_____ sheep's wool to make clothing for centuries.

2. The night is over. It's daytime now. The sun _____.

3. I (never) _____ golf, but I'd like to. It looks like fun.

4. Our team is great. They _____ all of their games so far this year. They haven't lost a single game.

5. Amy must be mad at me. She (not) _____ one word to me all evening. I wonder what I did to make her angry.

6. The cat must be sick. He (not) _____ any food for two days. We'd better call the vet.

7. Our teacher _____ us a lot of tests and quizzes since the beginning of the term.

8. We put a little money in our savings account every month. We want to buy a car, but we (not) _____ enough money yet. We'll have enough in a few more months.

9. (you, ever) _____ outdoors for an entire night? I mean without a tent, with nothing between you and the stars?

10. My aunt puts on a wig whenever she goes out, but I (never) _____ a wig in my whole life.

11. Paul's health _____ a lot since he started eating the right kinds of food, exercising regularly, and handling the stress in his life. He's never felt better.

12. I can't find my keys. I _____ everywhere—in all my pockets, in my briefcase, in my desk. They're gone.

◇ **PRACTICE 3—SELFSTUDY:** The present perfect vs. the simple past. (Chart 7–4)

Directions: Complete the sentences with the SIMPLE PAST or the PRESENT PERFECT.

1. A: When are you going to call Jane?
   B: I (call, already) _____**have already called**_____ her. I (call) _____**called**_____ her a half an hour ago.

2. A: When are you going to begin working at the candy store?
   B: I (begin, already) _____ working there. I (begin) _____ yesterday morning.

3. A: Are you going to eat lunch soon?

   B: I (eat, already) _____. I (eat) _____ lunch an

   hour ago.

4. A: When are you going to get a new computer?

   B: I (buy, already) _____ one. I (buy) _____ it

   last week.

5. A: When is Steve going to leave for the concert?

   B: He (leave, already) _____. He (leave) _____

   an hour ago.

6. A: Will you please lock the door?

   B: I (lock, already) _____ it. I (lock) _____ it

   when I got home.

◇ **PRACTICE 4—SELFSTUDY:** Irregular verbs. (Charts 2–3, 2–4, and 7–4)

Directions: This is a review of IRREGULAR VERBS. Complete the sentences with the SIMPLE PAST and the PRESENT PERFECT of the given verbs.

1. *begin*   I _____**began**_____ a new diet and exercise program last week. I

   _____**have begun**_____ lots of new diet and exercise programs in my lifetime.

2. *bend*   I _____ down to pick up my young son from his crib this morning.

   I _____ down to pick him up many times since he was born.

3. *broadcast* The radio _____ news about the terrible earthquake in Iran

   last week. The radio _____ news about Iran every day

   since the earthquake occurred.

4. *catch*   I _____ a cold last week. I _____ a lot of

   colds in my lifetime.

5. *come*   A tourist _____ into Mr. Nasser's jewelry store after lunch. A lot of

   tourists _____ into his store since he opened it last year.

6. *cut*   I _____ some flowers from my garden yesterday. I

   _____ lots of flowers from my garden so far this summer.

7. *dig*   The workers _____ a hole to fix the leak in the water pipe. They

   _____ many holes to fix water leaks since the earthquake.

8. *draw*   The artist _____ a picture of a sunset yesterday. She

   _____ many pictures of sunsets in her lifetime.

9. *feed*   I _____ birds at the park yesterday. I _____

   birds at the park every day since I lost my job.

10. *fight*   We _____ a war last year. We _____ several

   wars since we became an independent country.

11. *forget*   I _____ to turn off the stove after dinner. I _____

to turn off the stove a lot of times in my lifetime.

12. *hide*   The children _____ in the basement yesterday. They _____

_____ in the basement often since they discovered a secret place there.

13. *hit*   The baseball player _____ the ball out of the stadium yesterday. He

_____ a lot of homeruns since he joined our team.

14. *hold*   My husband _____ the door open for me when we entered the

restaurant. He _____ a door open for me many times since

we met each other.

15. *keep*   During the discussion yesterday, I _____ my opinion to myself. I

_____ my opinions to myself a lot of times in my lifetime.

16. *lead*   Mary _____ the group discussion at the conference. She _____

_____ group discussions many times since she started going to

conferences.

17. *lose*   Eddie _____ money at the racetrack yesterday. He _____

_____ money at the racetrack lots of times in his lifetime.

18. *meet*   I _____ two new people in my class yesterday. I _____

a lot of new people since I started going to school here.

19. *ride*   I _____ the bus to work yesterday. I _____

the bus to work many times since I got a job downtown.

20. *ring*   The doorbell _____ a few minutes ago. The doorbell _____

_____ three times so far today.

21. *see*   I _____ a good movie yesterday. I _____ a lot

                              of good movies in my lifetime.

22. *steal*   The fox _____ a chicken from the farmer's yard last night. The fox

                              _____ three chickens so far this month.

23. *stick*   I _____ a stamp on the corner of the envelope. I _____

                              _____ lots of stamps on envelopes in my lifetime.

24. *sweep*   I _____ the floor of my apartment yesterday. I _____

                              _____ the floor of my apartment lots of times since I moved in.

25. *take*   I _____ a test yesterday. I _____ lots of tests

                              in my life as a student.

26. *upset*   The Smith children _____ Mr. Jordan when they broke his

                              window. Because they are careless and noisy, they _____ Mr.

                              Jordan many times since they moved in next door.

27. *withdraw*   I _____ some money from my bank account yesterday. I

                              _____ more than three hundred dollars from my bank

                              account so far this month.

28. *write*   I _____ a letter to a friend last night. I _____

                              lots of letters to my friends in my lifetime.

◇ PRACTICE 5—GUIDED STUDY: Irregular verbs.   (Charts 2–3, 2–4, and 7–4)

Directions: This is a review of IRREGULAR VERBS. Complete the sentences with the SIMPLE PAST or the PRESENT PERFECT of the given verbs.

1. *go*   a. I _____ **have gone** _____ to every play at the local theater so far this year.

          b. My whole family _____ **went** _____ to the play last weekend.

2. *give*   a. Jane _____ **gave** _____ me a ride home from work today.

          b. (*she, ever*) _____ **Has she ever given** _____ you a ride home since she started

             working in your department?

3. *fall*   a. I _____ down many times in my lifetime, but never hard

             enough to really hurt myself or break a bone.

          b. Mike _____ down many times during football practice

             yesterday.

4. *break*   a. (*you, ever*) _____ a bone in your body?

          b. I _____ my leg when I was ten years old. I jumped off the

             roof of my house.

5. *shake*   a. In my entire lifetime, I (*never*) _____ hands with a famous

             movie star.

          b. In 1990, I _____ hands with a famous soccer player.

6. *hear* a. I _____ you practicing your trumpet late last night.

b. In fact, I _____ you practicing every night for two weeks.

7. *fly* a. Mike is a commercial airline pilot. Yesterday he _____ from Tokyo to Los Angeles.

b. Mike _____ to many places in the world since he became a pilot.

8. *wear* a. Carol really likes her new leather jacket. She _____ it every day since she bought it.

b. She _____ her new leather jacket to the opera last night.

9. *build* a. (*you, ever*) _____ a piece of furniture?

b. My daughter _____ a table in her woodworking class at the high school last year.

10. *teach* a. Ms. Kent _____ math at the local high school since 1982.

b. She _____ in Hungary last year on an exchange program.

11. *find* a. In your lifetime, (*you, ever*) _____ something really valuable?

b. My sister _____ a very expensive diamond ring in the park last year.

12. *drive* a. After I took Danny to school, I _____ straight to work.

b. I'm an experienced driver, but I (*never*) _____ a bus or a big truck.

13. *sing* a. I _____ a duet with my mother at the art benefit last night.

   b. We _____ together ever since I was a small child.

14. *run* a. I (*never*) _____ in a marathon race, and I don't intend to.

   b. I'm out of breath because I _____ all the way over here.

15. *tell* a. Last night, my brother _____ me a secret.

   b. He _____ me lots of secrets in his lifetime.

16. *stand* a. When I visited the U.N. last summer, I _____ in the main gallery and felt a great sense of history.

   b. Many great world leaders _____ there over the years.

17. *spend* a. I _____ all of my money at the mall yesterday.

   b. I don't have my rent money this month. I (*already*) _____ it on other things.

18. *make* a. I consider myself fortunate because I _____ many good friends in my lifetime.

   b. I _____ a terrible mistake last night. I forgot that my friend had invited me to his apartment for dinner.

19. *rise* a. The price of flour _____ a lot since 1990.

   b. When his name was announced, Jack _____ from his seat and walked to the podium to receive his award.

20. *feel* a. I _____ terrible yesterday, so I stayed in bed.

   b. I _____ terrible for a week now. I'd better see a doctor.

◇ **PRACTICE 6—SELFSTUDY:** *Since* vs. *for.* (Chart 7–5)

   Directions: Complete the sentences with **SINCE** or **FOR**.

   1. David has worked for the power company _____*since*_____ 1990.

   2. His brother has worked for the power company _____*for*_____ five years.

   3. I have known Peter Gow _____ September.

   4. I've known his sister _____ three months.

   5. Jonas has walked with a limp _____ many years.

   6. He's had a bad leg _____ he was in the war.

   7. Rachel hasn't been in class _____ last Tuesday.

   8. She hasn't been in class _____ three days.

   9. I've had a toothache _____ yesterday morning.

   10. I've had this toothache _____ thirty-six hours.

   11. My vision has improved _____ I got new reading glasses.

   12. I've had a cold _____ almost a week.

   13. Jake hasn't worked _____ last summer when the factory closed down.

   14. I attended Jefferson Elementary School _____ six years.

◇ **PRACTICE 7—SELFSTUDY:** Sentences with *since*-clauses. (Chart 7–5)

Directions: Complete the sentences with the words in parentheses.

1. I (*know*) _____**have known**_____ Mark Miller since we (*be*) _____**were**_____ in college.

2. Jeremy (*change*) _____ his major three times since he (*start*) _____ school.

3. Ever since* I (*be*) _____ a child, I (*be*) _____ afraid of snakes.

4. I can't wait to get home to my own bed. I (*sleep, not*) _____ well since I (*leave*) _____ home three days ago.

5. Ever since Danny (*meet*) _____ Nicole, he (*be, not*) _____ able to think about anything or anyone else. He's in love.

6. Otto (*have*) _____ a lot of problems with his car ever since he (*buy*) _____ it. It's a lemon.

7. A: What (*you, eat*) _____ since you (*get*) _____ up this morning?

   B: I (*eat*) _____ a banana and some yogurt. That's all.

8. I'm eighteen. I have a job and am in school. My life is going okay now, but I (*have*) _____ a miserable home life when I (*be*) _____ a young child. Ever since I (*leave*) _____ home at the age of fifteen, I (*take*) _____ care of myself. I (*have*) _____ some hard times, but I (*learn*) _____ how to stand on my own two feet.

◇ **PRACTICE 8—GUIDED STUDY:** *Since* vs. *for.* (Chart 7–5)

Directions: Write sentences *about yourself* using **SINCE**, **FOR**, or **NEVER** with the PRESENT PERFECT.

Example: have (a particular kind of watch)
Written: **I've had my Seiko quartz watch for two years. OR:**
            I've had my Seiko quartz watch since my eighteenth birthday.

Example: smoke cigars/cigarettes/a pipe
Written: **I've never smoked cigarettes. OR:**
            I've smoked cigarettes since I was seventeen.

1. know (a particular person)
2. live in (this city)
3. study English
4. be in this class/at this school/with this company
5. have long hair/short hair/a mustache
6. wear glasses/contact lenses
7. have (a particular article of clothing)
8. be interested in (a particular subject)
9. be married
10. have a driver's license

_____
*Ever since has the same meaning as *since.*

◇ **PRACTICE 9—GUIDED STUDY: Verb tense review. (Chapters 1, 2, 3, and 7)**

Directions: Following is a conversation between two people: Ann and Ben. Complete the sentences with the words in parentheses.

(1) BEN: I (*need*) _____ **need** _____ to earn some extra money for my school expenses. Got any ideas?

(2) ANN: (*you, have, ever*) _____ a job at a restaurant?

(3) BEN: Yes, I _____ **have** _____. I (*work*) _____ at several restaurants since I (*start*) _____ going to college.

ANN: When was the last time you worked at a restaurant?

(4) BEN: I (*have*) _____ a job as a dishwasher last fall.

ANN: Where?

BEN: At the Bistro Cafe.

(5) ANN: How long (*you, work*) _____ there?

BEN: For two months.

(6) ANN: (*you, enjoy*) _____ your job as a dishwasher at the Bistro?

(7) BEN: No, I _____. It (*be*) _____ hard work for low pay.

(8) ANN: Where (*you, work*) _____ right now?

(9) BEN: I (*have, not*) _____ a job right now.

(10) ANN: (*you, want*) _____ a part-time or full-time job?

(11) BEN: I (*plan*) _____ to look for a part-time job, maybe twenty hours a week.

(12) ANN: I (*go*) _____ to Al's Place tomorrow to see about a job. The restaurant (*look*) _____ for help. Why don't you come along with me?

(13) BEN: Thanks. I think I (*do*) _____ that. I (*look, never*) _____ _____ for a job at Al's Place before. Maybe the pay will be better than at the Bistro.

(14) ANN: I (*know, not*) _____. We (*find*) _____ out when we (*go*) _____ there tomorrow.

◇ **PRACTICE 10—SELFSTUDY: The present perfect progressive. (Charts 7–6 and 7–7)**

Directions: Use the given information to complete the dialogues between Speaker A and Speaker B. Use the PRESENT PERFECT PROGRESSIVE.

1. Eric is studying. He started to **study** at seven o'clock. It is now nine o'clock.

   A: How long _____ **has Eric been studying** _____?

   B: He _____ **'s been studying** _____ for _____ **two hours** _____.

2. Kathy is working at the computer. She began to **work** at the computer at two o'clock. It is now three o'clock.

   A: How long _____ **has Kathy been working at the computer** _____?

   B: She _____ **'s been working** _____ since _____ **two o'clock** _____.

3. It began to **rain** two days ago. It is still raining.

   A: How long _____?

   B: It _____ for _____.

4. Liz is reading. She began to **read** at ten o'clock. It is now ten-thirty.

   A: How long _____?

   B: She_____ for _____.

5. Boris began to **study** English in 1990. He is still studying English.

   A: How long _____?

   B: He_____ since _____.

6. Three months ago, Nicole started to **work** at the Silk Road Clothing Store.

   A: How long _____?

   B: She_____ for _____.

7. Ms. Rice started to **teach** at this school in September 1992.

   A: How long _____?

   B: She_____ since _____.

8. Mr. Fisher is **driving** a Chevy. He bought it twelve years ago.

   A: How long _____?

   B: He _____ for _____.

9. Mrs. Taylor is **waiting** to see her doctor. She arrived at the waiting room at two o'clock. It is now three-thirty.

   A: How long _____?

   B: She_____ for _____.

10. Ted and Erica started to **play** tennis at two o'clock. It's now four-thirty.

    A: How long _____?

    B: They_____ since _____.

◇ PRACTICE 11—SELFSTUDY: The present perfect progressive. (Charts 7–6 and 7–7)

Directions: Choose the correct verb form.

1. Where have you been? I __*B*__ for you for over an hour!
   A. am waiting   B. have been waiting

2. I'm exhausted! I _____ for the last eight hours without a break.
   A. am working   B. have been working

3. Shhh! Susan _____. Let's not make any noise. We don't want to wake her up.
   A. is sleeping   B. has been sleeping

4. Annie, go upstairs and wake your brother up. He _____ for over ten hours. He has chores to do.
   A. is sleeping   B. has been sleeping

5. Erin has never gone camping. She _____ in a tent.
   A. has never slept   B. has never been sleeping

6. This is a great shirt! I _____ it at least a dozen times, and it still looks like new.
   A. have washed   B. have been washing

7. Aren't you about finished with the dishes? You _____ dishes for thirty minutes or more. How long can it take to wash dishes?
   A. have washed   B. have been washing

8. We _____ to the Steak House restaurant many times. The food is excellent.
   A. have gone   B. have been going

◇ **PRACTICE 12—GUIDED STUDY: Verb tenses. (Charts 7–2 → 7–7)**

Directions: Make sentences about your life using the given time expressions. Use the SIMPLE PAST, PRESENT PERFECT, or PRESENT PERFECT PROGRESSIVE.

Example: for the last two weeks
Written: **I've had a cold for the last two weeks.**

1. since I was a child   6. never
2. for a long time   7. since last Tuesday
3. two years ago   8. for a number of years★
4. so far today   9. a week ago today
5. many times in my lifetime   10. for the last ten minutes

◇ **PRACTICE 13—GUIDED STUDY: Verb forms. (Chapters 1, 2, 3, and 7)**

Directions: Complete the sentences with the words in parentheses.

Dear Adam,

(1)   Hi! How are you? Remember me? Just a joke! I (*write, not*) _____

(2) to you for at least six months, but that's not long enough for you to forget me! I think about

(3) writing to you often, but I (*be, not*) _____ a good correspondent for the

(4) last few months. You (*hear, not*) _____ from me for such a long time

(5) because I (*be*) _____ really busy. For the last few months, I (*work*)

(6) _____ full-time at a shoe store and (*go*) _____ to school

(7) at the local community college to study business and computers. When I (*write*) _____

(8) to you six months ago—last April, I think—I (*go*) _____ to the university

(9) full-time and (*study*) _____ anthropology. A lot of things (*happen*)

(10) _____ since then.

(11)   At the end of the spring semester last June, my grades (*be*) _____ terrible. As

(12) a result, I (*lose*) _____ my scholarship and my parents' support. I really (*mess*)

(13) _____ up when I (*get*) _____ those bad grades. When I (*show*)

(14) _____ my grade report to my parents, they (*refuse*) _____ to help

(15) me with my living expenses at school anymore. They (*feel*) _____ that I was

(16) wasting my time and their money, so they (*tell*) _____ me to get a job. So last

_____
★*a number of years = many years.*

(17) June, I (*start*) _____ working at a shoe store: Imperial Shoes at Southcenter Mall.

(18) It (*be, not*) _____ a bad job, but it (*be, not*) _____ wonderful

(19) either. Every day, I (*fetch*) _____ shoes from the back room for people to try on,

(20) boxes and boxes of shoes, all day long.

(21) I (*meet*) _____ some pretty weird people since I (*start*) _____

(22) this job. A couple of weeks ago, a middle-aged man (*come*) _____ into the store.

(23) He (*want*) _____ to try on some black leather loafers. I (*bring*) _____

(24) the loafers, and he (*put*) _____ them on. While he (*walk*) _____

(25) around to see if they fit okay, he (*pull*) _____ from his pocket a little white

(26) mouse with pink eyes and (*start*) _____ talking to it. He (*look*) _____

(27) right at the mouse and (*say*) _____, "George, (*you, like*) _____

(28) this pair of shoes?" When the mouse (*twitch*) _____ its nose, the man (*say*)

(29) _____, "Yes, so do I." Then he (*turn*) _____ to me and (*say*)

(30) _____, "We'll take them." Can you believe that!?

(31) Most of the people I meet are nice—and normal. My favorite customers (*be*) _____

(32) people who (*know*) _____ what they want when they (*enter*) _____

(33) the store. They (*come*) _____ in, (*point*) _____ at one pair of shoes,

(34) politely (*tell*) _____ me their size, (*try*) _____ the shoes on, and

(35) then (*buy*) _____ them, just like that. They (*agonize, not*) _____

(36) _____ for a long time over which pair to buy.

(37) I (*learn*) _____ one important thing from working at the shoe

(38) store: I (*want, not*) _____ to sell shoes as a career. I (*need*)

(39) _____ a good education that (*prepare*) _____ me for a job that I can

(40) enjoy for the rest of my life. And even though I love studying anthropology, I (*decide*)

(41) _____ that a degree in business and computers will provide the best

(42) career opportunities.

(43) I (*want, always*) _____ to be independent, and now I (*be*)

(44) _____. I (*have*) _____ to pay every penny of my tuition and living

(45) expenses now. Ever since I (*lose*) _____ my scholarship and (*make*)

(46) _____ my parents mad, I (*be*) _____ completely on my own.

(47) I'm glad to report that my grades at present (*be*) _____ excellent, and right now I

(48) (*enjoy, really*) _____ my work with computers. In the future, I (*continue*)

(49) _____ to take courses in anthropology whenever I can fit them into my

(50) schedule, and I (*study*) _____ anthropology on my own for the rest of

(51) my life, but I (*pursue*) _____ a career in business. Maybe there is some

(52) way I can combine anthropology, business, and computers. Who knows?

(53) There, I (*tell*) _____ you everything I can think of that is at all

(54) important in my life at the moment. I think I (*grow*) _____ up a lot during

(55) the last six months. I (*understand*) _____ that my education is

(56) important. Losing my scholarship (*make*) _____ my life more difficult, but I

(57) (*feel*) _____ that I (*take, finally*) _____ charge of

(58) my life. It's a good feeling.

(59)   Please write. I'd love to hear from you.

(60)   Jessica

◇ **PRACTICE 14—GUIDED STUDY: Verb forms. (Charts 7-4 and 7-5)**

Directions: Think of a friend you haven't spoken to or written to since the beginning of this term.
Write this friend a letter about your activities from the start of this school term to the present time.
Begin your letter as follows:

> *Dear (. . .),*
> *I'm sorry I haven't written for such a long time. Lots of things have happened since I last*
> *wrote to you.*

◇ **PRACTICE 15—SELFSTUDY: Midsentence adverbs. (Chart 7-8)**

PART I: Placement of MIDSENTENCE ADVERBS IN STATEMENTS.

Directions: *Choose the correct place to add* **ALWAYS** *to the following sentences.*

1. Kate _____**Ø**_____ *is* _____**always**_____ late.

2. Mike _____**always**_____ *finishes* _____**Ø**_____ his work on time.

3. Gina _____ *finished* _____ her work early.

4. Nick _____ *will* _____ *finish* his work on time.

5. Rick _____ *has* _____ *helped* me with my work.

6. Bill _____ *helped* _____ me with my work.

7. They _____ *are* _____ helpful.

8. They _____ *help* _____ me when I need it.

9. They _____ *have* _____ *helped* me.

10. Sara _____ *can* _____ *help* you if you ask her to.

Directions: *Choose the correct place to add* **USUALLY** *to the following sentences.*

11. They _____ *are* _____ very helpful.

12. They _____ *help* _____ me when I need it.

13. They _____ *have* _____ *helped* me.

14. Sara _____ *can* _____ *help* you if you ask her to.

PART II: Placement of MIDSENTENCE ADVERBS in QUESTIONS.

Directions: *Choose the correct place to add* **USUALLY** *to the following sentences.*

15. *Do* _____ you _____ *work* hard?

16. *Is* _____ Mike _____ at home in the evenings?

17. *Did* _____ your mom _____ *read* to you at bedtime?

18. *Were* _____ you _____ in bed by nine?

19. *Can* _____ students _____ *understand* Prof. Milano's lectures?

Directions: *Choose the correct place to add* **EVER** *to the following sentences.*

20. *Do* _____ you _____ *work* hard?

21. *Is* _____ Mike _____ at home in the evenings?

22. *Did* _____ your mom _____ *read* to you at bedtime?

23. *Were* _____ you _____ in bed by nine?

24. *Can* _____ students _____ *understand* Prof. Milano's lectures?

PART III: Placement of MIDSENTENCE ADVERBS in NEGATIVE SENTENCES.

Directions: *Choose the correct place to add* **PROBABLY** *to the following sentences.*

25. Janet _____ *won't* _____ *attend* a meeting.

26. Frank _____ *isn't* _____ in his office.

27. Emily _____ *doesn't* _____ *know* the answer.

28. Brian _____ *hasn't* _____ *finished* his homework yet.

Directions: *Choose the correct place to add* **EVER** *to the following sentences.*

29. Janet _____ *won't* _____ *give* me a straight answer.

30. Frank _____ *isn't* _____ in his office.

Directions: *Choose the correct place to add* **ALWAYS** *to the following sentences.*

31. Emily _____ *doesn't* _____ *know* the right answer in class.

32. Brian _____ *hasn't* _____ *finished* his homework on time.

◇ **PRACTICE 16—GUIDED STUDY: Frequency adverbs. (Chart 7–8)**

Directions: Choose the appropriate FREQUENCY ADVERB to give a sentence with the same meaning. Put the frequency adverb in the correct place.

1. Alice drives to work every day without exception. (*always, generally*)

   → Alice _____**always drives**_____ to work.

2. Jake is tired all of the time. (*always, frequently*)

   → Jake _____**is always**_____ tired.

3. Scott goes swimming at the beach only once a year. (*sometimes, rarely*)

   → Scott _____ swimming at the beach.

4. Have you met David French at any time in your life? (*just, ever*)

   → Have you _____ David French?

5. Karen isn't late for work at any time. (*generally, never*)

   → Karen _____ late for work.

6. Eric is late for work about once a month. (*usually, sometimes*)

   → Eric _____ late for work.

7. Danny is absent from a lot of classes because of illness. (*occasionally, frequently*)

→ Danny _____ absent because of illness.

8. Kathy is a happy, optimistic person most of the time. (*generally, always*)

→ Kathy _____ a happy, optimistic person.

9. It seems to me that very, very few of my wishes come true. (*seldom, occasionally*)

→ My wishes _____ true.

10. Polar bears are huge white bears that live along the northern coasts of Canada, Greenland, and Russia. For the most part, polar bears hunt seals for food. (*generally, rarely*)

→ Polar bears _____ seals for food.

11. Very few polar bears have ever killed a human being. (*often, rarely*)

→ Polar bears _____ human beings.

12. Human beings have killed large numbers of polar bears for their pelts. (*frequently, always*)

→ Human beings _____ polar bears for their pelts.

13. Wild polar bears can live to be thirty-three years old. Polar bears in captivity in zoos may live a little longer. (*usually, seldom*)

→ Polar bears _____ past thirty-five years of age.

◇ **PRACTICE 17—SELFSTUDY:** *Already, still, yet, anymore.* **(Chart 7–9)**

Directions: Choose the correct completion.

1. I haven't finished my composition yet. I'm __***B***__ working on it.
   A. already   B. still   C. yet   D. anymore

2. *Top Rock Videos* used to be my favorite TV show, but I stopped watching it a couple of years ago. I don't watch it _____.
   A. already   B. still   C. yet   D. anymore

3. I don't have to take any more math classes. I've _____ taken all the required courses.
   A. already   B. still   C. yet   D. anymore

4. I used to nearly choke on an airplane because of all the smoke in the cabin. But smoking is now forbidden by law on all domestic flights. You can't smoke in an airplane _____.

    A. already   B. still   C. yet   D. anymore

5. I'm not quite ready to leave. I haven't finished packing my suitcase _____.

    A. already   B. still   C. yet   D. anymore

6. "Don't you have a class at two?"

    "Yeah, why?"

    "Look at your watch."

    "Oh my gosh, it's _____ past two! Bye!"

    A. already   B. still   C. yet   D. anymore

7. Don't sit there! I painted that chair yesterday and the paint isn't completely dry _____.

    A. already   B. still   C. yet   D. anymore

8. 1448 South 45th Street is Joe's old address. He doesn't live there _____.

    A. already   B. still   C. yet   D. anymore

9. Mr. Wood is eighty-eight years old, but he _____ goes into his office every day.

    A. already   B. still   C. yet   D. anymore

10. "Are you going to drive to Woodville with us for the street festival Saturday?"

    "I don't know. I might. I haven't made up my mind _____."

    A. already   B. still   C. yet   D. anymore

◇ **PRACTICE 18—GUIDED STUDY:** Adverb placement. (Charts 7–8 and 7–9)

Directions: Complete the sentences with your own words.

Example: I . . . not . . . because I've already . . . .

Possible responses:

        I'm not hungry because I've already eaten.

        I'm not going to go to the movie because I've already seen it.

        I don't have to take the English test because I've already taken it.

1. I used to . . . , but . . . anymore.

2. I can't . . . because I haven't . . . yet.

3. Are . . . still . . . ?

4. . . . because I've already . . . .

5. She didn't . . . because she probably hasn't . . . .

6. I still . . . , but . . . yet.

7. Dan doesn't . . . because he has already . . . .

8. I can . . . because I've finally . . . .

9. Ann . . . ago. She still . . . .

10. I don't . . . anymore, but . . . still . . . .

◇ **PRACTICE 19—SELFSTUDY:** The past perfect. (Chart 7–10)

Directions: Identify which action took place first (**1st**) in the past and which action took place second (**2nd**).

1. The tennis player **jumped** in the air for joy. She **had won** the match.

    a. __**1st**__ The tennis player won the match.

    b. __**2nd**__ The tennis player jumped in the air.

2. Before I went to bed, I **checked** the front door. My roommate **had** already **locked** it.

    a. ____**2nd**___ I checked the door.

    b. ____**1st**___ My roommate locked the door.

3. I **looked** for Bob, but he **had left** the building.

    a. _____ Bob left the building.

    b. _____ I looked for Bob.

4. I **laughed** when I saw my son. He **had emptied** a bowl of noodles on top of his head.

    a. _____ I laughed.

    b. _____ My son emptied a bowl of noodles on his head.

5. Oliver **arrived** at the airport on time, but he couldn't get on the plane. He **had left** his ticket at home.

    a. _____ Oliver left his ticket at home.

    b. _____ Oliver arrived at the airport.

6. I **handed** Betsy today's newspaper, but she didn't want it. She **had read** it during her lunch hour.

    a. _____ I handed Betsy the newspaper.

    b. _____ Betsy read the newspaper.

7. After Carl arrived in New York, he **called** his mother. He **had promised** to call her as soon as he got in.

    a. _____ Carl made a promise to his mother.

    b. _____ Carl called his mother.

8. Stella was alone in a strange city. She walked down the avenue slowly, looking in shop windows. Suddenly, she **turned** her head and **looked** behind her. Someone **had called** her name.

    a. _____ Stella turned her head and looked behind her.

    b. _____ Someone called her name.

Directions: Complete the sentences with the PRESENT PERFECT or the PAST PERFECT form of the verb in parentheses.

1. A: Oh no! We're too late. The train (*leave, already*) _____**has already left**_____ .

   B: That's okay. We'll catch the next train to Athens.

2. Last Thursday, we went to the station to catch a train to Athens, but we were too late. The train (*leave, already*) _____**had already left**_____ .

3. A: Go back to sleep. It's only six o'clock in the morning.

   B: I am not sleepy. I (*sleep, already*) _____ for seven hours. I'm going to get up.

4. I woke up at six, but I couldn't get back to sleep. I wasn't sleepy. I (*sleep, already*) _____ for seven hours.

5. A: I'll introduce you to Professor Newton at the meeting tonight.

   B: You don't need to. I (*meet, already*) _____ him.

6. Jack offered to introduce me to Professor Newton, but it wasn't necessary. I (*meet, already*) _____ him.

7. A: Do you want to go to the movie tonight?

   B: What are you going to see?

   A: *Distant Drums*.

   B: I (*see, already*) _____ it. Thanks anyway.

8. I didn't go to the movie with Erin last Tuesday night. I (*see, already*) _____ it.

9. A: Jane? Jane! Is that you? How are you? I haven't seen you for ages!

   B: Excuse me? Are you talking to me?

   A: Oh. You're not Jane. I'm sorry. It is clear that I (*make*) _____ a mistake. Please excuse me.

10. Yesterday I approached a stranger who looked like Jane Moore and started talking to her. But she wasn't Jane. It was clear that I (*make*) _____ a mistake. I was really embarrassed.

◇ PRACTICE 21—SELFSTUDY: The past progressive vs. the past perfect. (Chart 7–10)

Directions: Choose the correct completion.

1. Amanda didn't need to study the multiplication tables in fifth grade. She __**B**__ them.
       A. was learning   B. had already learned

2. I enjoyed visiting Tommy's class. It was an arithmetic class. The students __**A**__ their multiplication tables.
       A. were learning   B. had already learned

3. While I _____ up the mountain, I got tired. But I didn't stop until I reached the top.
       A. was walking   B. had walked

4. I was very tired when I got to the top of the mountain. I ____ a long distance.
    A. was walking   B. had walked

5. I knocked. No one answered. I turned the handle and pulled sharply on the door, but it did not open. Someone ____ it.
    A. was locking   B. had locked

6. "Where were you when the earthquake occurred?"
"In my office. I ____ to my assistant. We were working on a report."
    A. was talking   B. had already talked

7. "Ahmed's house was destroyed in the earthquake."
"I know! It's lucky that he and his family ____ for his parents' home before the earthquake struck."
    A. were leaving   B. had already left

8. We drove two hundred miles to see the circus in Kansas City. When we got there, we couldn't find the circus. It had left town. We ____ all the way to Kansas City for nothing.
    A. were driving   B. had driven

◇ **PRACTICE 22—SELFSTUDY:** **The present perfect, past progressive, and past perfect. (Chart 7–10)**

Directions: Complete the sentences with the correct forms of the words in parentheses. Use the PRESENT PERFECT, PAST PROGRESSIVE, or PAST PERFECT.

1. When I went to bed, I turned on the radio. While I (*sleep*) _____, somebody turned it off.

2. You're from Jakarta? I (*be, never*) _____ there. I'd like to go there someday.

3. I started to tell Rodney the news, but he stopped me. He (*already, hear*) _____ _____ it.

4. When Gina went to bed, it was snowing. It (*snow, still*) _____ when she woke up in the morning.

5. Rita called me on the phone to tell me the good news. She (*pass*) _____ _____ her final exam in English.

6. I couldn't think. The people around me (*make*) _____ too much noise. Finally, I gave up and left to try to find a quiet place to work.

7. Are you still waiting for David? (*he, come, not*) _____ yet? He's really late, isn't he?

8. Otto was in the hospital last week. He (*be, never*) _____ a patient in a hospital before. It was a new experience for him.

9. A couple of weeks ago Mr. Fox, our office manager, surprised all of us. When he walked into the office, he (*wear*) _____ a bright red jacket. Everyone stopped and stared. Mr. Fox is a conservative dresser. Before that time, he (*wear, never*) _____ anything but a blue or gray suit. And he (*wear, not*) _____ that jacket again since that time. He wore it only once.

Directions: Choose the correct completion.

1. My mother began to drive cars when she was fourteen. Now she is eighty-nine, and she still
   drives. She _____ cars for seventy-five years.
       A. has been driving   B. drives   C. drove   D. was driving

2. In every culture, people _____ jewelry since prehistoric times.
       A. wear   B. wore   C. have worn   D. had worn

3. It's hard for many young people to find jobs today. As a result, many young adults in their
   twenties and even early thirties _____ with their parents.
       A. have still lived   B. are still living   C. still lived   D. were still living

4. Australian koala bears are interesting
   animals. They _____ practically their
   entire lives in trees without ever coming
   down to the ground.
       A. are spending
       B. have been spending
       C. spent
       D. spend

5. If you continue to work hard and try your best, I _____ you. But if you stop working,
   I'm through.
       A. will help   B. am helping   C. help   D. have helped

6. It's raining hard. It _____ an hour ago and _____ yet.
       A. starts . . . doesn't stop   C. has started . . . didn't stop
       B. started . . . hasn't stopped   D. was starting . . . isn't stopping

7. Alex's bags are almost ready for his trip. He _____ for Syria later this afternoon.
       A. leave   B. left   C. has left   D. is leaving

8. I heard a slight noise, so I walked to the front door to investigate. I looked down at the floor
   and saw a piece of paper. Someone _____ a note under the door to my apartment.
       A. has pushed   B. is pushing   C. had pushed   D. pushed

9. I walked slowly through the market. People _____ all kinds of fruits and vegetables. I studied
   the prices carefully before I decided what to buy.
       A. have sold   B. sell   C. had sold   D. were selling

10. The first advertisement on radio was broadcast in 1922. Since that time, companies _____ tens
    of billions of dollars to advertise their products on radio and television.
        A. are spending   B. have spent   C. spent   D. spend

◇ PRACTICE 24—GUIDED STUDY: Verb tense review. (Chapters 1, 2, 3, and 7)

Directions: Choose the correct completion.

1. Were you at the race yesterday? I _____ you there.
       A. haven't seen   B. didn't see   C. wasn't seeing   D. don't see

2. Nicky, please don't interrupt me. I _____ to Grandma on the phone. Go play with your
   trucks.
       A. talk   B. have talked   C. am talking   D. have been talking

3. Now listen carefully. When Aunt Martha _____ tomorrow, give her a big hug.
       A. arrives   B. will arrive   C. arrived   D. is going to arrive

4. I _____ my glasses three times so far this year. One time I dropped them on a cement floor. Another time I sat on them. And this time I stepped on them.

    A. broke   B. was breaking   C. have broken   D. have been breaking

5. Kate reached to the floor and picked up her glasses. They were broken. She _____ on them.

    A. stepped   B. had stepped   C. was stepping   D. has stepped

6. Sarah gets angry easily. She _____ a bad temper ever since she was a child.

    A. has   B. will have   C. had   D. has had

7. Now, whenever Sarah starts to lose her temper, she _____ a deep breath and _____ to ten.

    A. takes . . . counts   C. took . . . counted

    B. has taken . . . counted   D. is taking . . . counting

8. I unlocked my door and walked into my apartment. I was surprised to see my nephew there. He _____ in the middle of the front room. He _____ in through an open window in the bathroom. I demanded to know why he was in my apartment.

    A. stood . . . was coming   C. was standing . . . came

    B. stood . . . came   D. was standing . . . had come

9. Ever since I told Ted about my illness, he _____ me. Why are people like that?

    A. is avoiding   B. avoided   C. avoids   D. has been avoiding

10. The phone rang, so I _____ it up and _____ hello.

    A. picked . . . had said   C. was picking . . . said

    B. picked . . . said   D. was picking . . . had said

◇ **PRACTICE 25—SELFSTUDY: Prepositions. (Chapter 7; Appendix 1)**

Directions: Complete each sentence with the appropriate preposition.

1. Please don't argue. I insist ___**on**___ lending you the money for your vacation.

2. That thin coat you're wearing won't protect you _____ the bitter, cold wind.

3. A: What's the matter? Don't you approve _____ my behavior?

    B: No, I don't. I think you are rude.

4. A: Can I depend _____ you to pick up my mother at the airport tomorrow?

    B: Of course you can!

5. A: The police arrested a thief in my uncle's store yesterday.

    B: What's going to happen _____ him? Will he go to jail?

6. My friend Ken apologized _____ me _____ forgetting to pick me up in his car after the movie last night. I forgave him _____ leaving me outside the theater in the rain, but I'm not going to rely _____ him for transportation in the future.

7. A: Thank you _____ helping me move to my new apartment last weekend.

    B: You're welcome.

8. It isn't fair to compare Mr. Carlson _____ Ms. Anders. They're both good teachers, but they have different teaching methods.

9. I've had a bad cold for a week and just can't get rid _____ it.

10. Excuse me _____ interrupting you, but I have a call on the other line. Could I get back to you in a second?

CHAPTER *8*
Count/Noncount Nouns and Articles

◇ **PRACTICE 1—SELFSTUDY:** Count and noncount nouns. (Charts 8–1 and 8–2)

Directions: Identify count and noncount nouns.
- Write the word **ONE** in the blank if possible.
  NOTE: *One* is a number. It is used with singular count nouns.
- If it is not correct to use the word *one*, write a slash (/) in the blank.
  NOTE: *One* cannot be used with noncount nouns. A *noncount noun* is called a "noncount noun" because you can't "count" it with numbers *one, two, three,* etc.

1. I have ___/___ **furniture** in my apartment.	*furniture* →	count	(noncount)
2. I have ___one___ **table** in my apartment.	*table* →	(count)	noncount
3. Rita is wearing _____ **ring** on her left hand.	*ring* →	count	noncount
4. Rita is wearing _____ **jewelry** on her left hand.	*jewelry* →	count	noncount
5. 'I have _____ **homework** to do tonight.	*homework* →	count	noncount
6. I have _____ **assignment** to do.	*assignment* →	count	noncount
7. I have _____ **job** to finish.	*job* →	count	noncount
8. I have _____ **work** to do.	*work* →	count	noncount
9. I asked _____ **question**.	*question* →	count	noncount
10. I was looking for _____ **information**.	*information* →	count	noncount
11. I learned _____ new **word** today.	*word* →	count	noncount
12. I learn _____ new **vocabulary** every day.	*vocabulary* →	count	noncount

◇ **PRACTICE 2—SELFSTUDY:** Count and noncount nouns: *a/an* and *some*.
(Charts 8–1 and 8–2)

Directions: Complete the sentences with **A/AN** (for count nouns) or **SOME** (for noncount nouns).

1. I bought ___some___ **furniture** for my apartment.

2. I bought ___a___ **table** for my apartment.

3. Rita is wearing _____ **ring** on her left hand.

4. Rita is wearing _____ **jewelry** on her left hand.

5. I have _____ **homework** to do tonight.

6. I have _____ **assignment** to do.

7. I have _____ **job** to finish.

8. I have _____ **work** to do.

9. I asked _____ **question**.

10. I was looking for _____ **information**.

11. I learned _____ new **word** today.

12. I learn _____ new **vocabulary** every day.

◇ PRACTICE 3—SELFSTUDY: Count and noncount nouns: adding *-s*. (Charts 8–1 and 8–2)

Directions: Add **-s** if possible. Otherwise, write a slash (/) in the blank.

1. I bought **some furniture** / for my apartment.

2. I bought **some table**____ for my apartment.

3. Rita is wearing **some ring** ____ on her left hand.

4. Rita is wearing **some jewelry**____ on her left hand.

5. I have **some homework** ____ to do tonight.

6. I have **some assignment**____ to do.

7. I have **some job**____ to finish.

8. I have **some work** ____ to do.

9. I asked **some question** ____.

10. I was looking for **some information** ____.

11. I learned **some new word** ____ today.

12. I learn **some new vocabulary**____ every day.

◇ PRACTICE 4—SELFSTUDY: Count and noncount nouns: using *two*. (Charts 8-1 and 8-2)

Directions: Change **SOME** to **TWO** if possible. Otherwise, write nothing.

1. I bought **some furniture** for my apartment. (*no change*)

2. I bought ~~some~~ *two* **tables** for my apartment.

3. Rita is wearing **some rings** on her left hand.

4. Rita is wearing **some jewelry** on her left hand.

5. I have **some homework** to do tonight.

6. I have **some assignments** to do.

7. I have **some jobs** to finish.

8. I have **some work** to do.

9. I asked **some questions**.

10. I was looking for **some information**.

11. I learned **some new words** today.

12. I learn **some new vocabulary** every day.

◇ **PRACTICE 5—SELFSTUDY:** Count and noncount nouns: using *a lot of*. (Charts 8–1 and 8–2)

Directions: Change **SOME** to **A LOT OF** if possible. Otherwise, write nothing.

1. I bought ~~some~~ **furniture** for my apartment.   *a lot of*

2. I bought ~~some~~ **tables** for my apartment.   *a lot of*

3. Rita is wearing **some rings** on her left hand.

4. Rita is wearing **some jewelry** on her left hand.

5. I have **some homework** to do tonight.

6. I have **some assignments** to do.

7. I have **some jobs** to finish.

8. I have **some work** to do.

9. I asked **some questions**.

10. I was looking for **some information**.

11. I learned **some** new **words** today.

12. I learn **some** new **vocabulary** every day.

◇ **PRACTICE 6—SELFSTUDY:** Count and noncount nouns: using *too many* and *too much*.
(Charts 8–1 and 8–2)

Directions: Complete the sentences with **MANY** or **MUCH**.

1. I bought too ____*much*____ **furniture** for my apartment.

2. I bought too ____*many*____ **tables** for my apartment.

3. Rita is wearing too _____ **rings** on her left hand.

4. Rita is wearing too _____ **jewelry** on her left hand.

5. I can't go to a movie tonight. I have too _____
   homework to do.

6. I have too _____ **assignments** to do.
   I can't finish all of them.

7. I have too _____ **jobs** to finish. I can't do all of them.

8. I have too _____ **work** to do. I can't finish all of it.

9. The child asked too _____ **questions**. I couldn't answer all of them.

10. I can't remember everything I read in the encyclopedia. There is too _____
    information for me to remember all of it.

11. Sam's writing is wordy. He uses too _____ **words** when he writes.

12. The teacher asked us to learn too _____ new **vocabulary**. I couldn't remember all the
    new words.

◇ PRACTICE 7—SELFSTUDY: Count and noncount nouns: using *a few* and *a little*.
(Charts 8–1 and 8–2)

Directions: Complete the sentences with **A FEW** or **A LITTLE**.

1. I bought _____*a little*_____ **furniture** for my apartment.

2. I bought _____*a few*_____ **tables** for my apartment.

3. Rita is wearing _____ **rings** on her left hand.

4. Rita is wearing _____ **jewelry** on her left hand.

5. I have _____ **homework** to do tonight.

6. I have _____ **assignments** to do.

7. I have _____ **jobs** to finish.

8. I have _____ **work** to do.

9. I asked _____ **questions**.

10. I was looking for _____ **information**.

11. I learned _____ new **words** today.

12. I learn _____ new **vocabulary** every day.

◇ PRACTICE 8—SELFSTUDY: *A* vs. *an*: singular count nouns. (Charts 8–1 and 8–2)

Directions: Write **A** or **AN** in the blanks.

1. _____ game   13. _____ eye

2. _____ rock   14. _____ new car

3. _____ store   15. _____ old car

4. _____ army   16. _____ used car

5. _____ egg   17. _____ uncle

6. _____ island   18. _____ house

7. _____ ocean   19. _____ honest mistake

8. _____ umbrella   20. _____ hospital

9. _____ university★   21. _____ hand

10. _____ horse   22. _____ aunt

11. _____ hour★★   23. _____ ant

12. _____ star   24. _____ neighbor

★*A university, a unit, a uniform, a union*: these nouns begin with a consonant sound, so *a* (not *an*) is used. *An uncle, an umbrella, an umpire, an urge*: these nouns begin with a vowel sound, so *an* (not *a*) is used.

★★If the ''h'' is silent, *an* is used: *an hour, an honor, an honest person.* Usually the ''h'' is pronounced and *a* is used: *a holiday, a hotel, a hero, a high point, a home*, etc.

Directions: Complete the sentences with SOME or A/AN.

1. I wrote _____*a*_____ **letter**.

2. I got _____*some*_____ **mail**.

3. We bought _____ **equipment** for our camping trip.

4. You need _____ **tool** to cut wood.

5. I ate _____ **food**.

6. I had _____ **apple**.

7. I wore _____ old **clothing**.

8. I wore _____ old **shirt**.

9. Jim asked me for _____ **advice**.

10. I gave Jim _____ **suggestion**.

11. I read _____ interesting **story** in the paper.

12. The paper has _____ interesting **news** today.

13. I read _____ **poem** after dinner.

14. I read _____ **poetry** after dinner.

15. I know _____ **song** from India.

16. I know _____ Indian **music**.

17. I learned _____ new **idiom**.

18. I learned _____ new **slang**.

◇ PRACTICE 10—SELFSTUDY: Count and noncount nouns. (Charts 8–1 → 8–3)

Directions: Add final -S/-ES if possible. Otherwise, write a slash (/) in the blank.

1. I'm learning a lot of **grammar** _/_.

2. We're studying count and noncount **noun** _s_.

3. Olga knows several **language**____.

4. Olga has learned a lot of **English** ____.

5. Sara doesn't like to wear **makeup**____.

6. We enjoyed the **scenery**____ in the countryside.

7. Colorado has high **mountain** ____.

8. City streets usually have a lot of **traffic**____.

9. The streets are full of **automobile**____.

10. I had **sand** ____ in my shoes from walking on the beach.

11. The air was full of **dust** ____ from the wind storm.

12. Florida is famous for its white sand **beach** ____.

13. I've learned a lot of **slang** ____ from my new friends.

14. I made a lot of **mistake**____ on my last composition.

15. I have some important **information** ____ for you.

16. I have some important **fact** ___ for you.

17. My favorite team has won a lot of **game** ___ this year.

18. Thailand and India have a lot of hot **weather** ___.

19. We heard a lot of **thunder** ___ during the storm.

20. I drink a lot of **water** ___ when the weather is hot.

21. Both of my **parent** ___ have very good **health** ___.

22. A **circle** ___ has 360 **degree** ___.

23. **Professor** ___ have a lot of **knowledge** ___ about their fields of study.

24. Everyone in my **family** ___ wished me a lot a **luck** ___.

25. I thanked my two **neighbor** ___ for their **help** ___.

26. Sometimes **factory** ___* cause **pollution** ___.

27. Parents take **pride** ___ in the success of their **children** ___.**

28. I admire **people** ___ who use their **intelligence** ___ to the fullest extent.

◇ **PRACTICE 11—GUIDED STUDY:** Count and noncount nouns. (Charts 4–1 and 8–1 → 8–3)

Directions: Add final -S/-ES as necessary. Do not make any other changes. The number in parentheses at the end of each section is the number of nouns that need final -s/-es.

       Plants   *things*
1. Plant are the oldest living thing on earth. (2) = (2 nouns need final -s/-es)

2. Scientist divide living thing into two group: plant and animal. Generally speaking, plant stay in one place, but animal move around. (7)

3. Flower, grass, and tree grow every place where people live. Plant also grow in desert, in ocean, on mountaintop, and in polar region. (7)

4. Plant are useful to people. We eat them. We use them for clothing. We build house from them. Plant are also important to our health. We get many kind of beneficial drug from plant. In addition, plant provide beauty and enjoyment to all our life. (8)

5. Crop are plant that people grow for food. Nature can ruin crop. Bad weather—such as too much rain or too little rain—can destroy field of corn or wheat. Natural disaster such as flood and storm have caused farmer many problem since people first began to grow their own food. (9)

6. Food is a necessity for all living thing. All animal and plant need to eat. Most plant take what they need through their root and their leaf. The majority of insect live solely on plant. Many bird have a diet of worm and insect. Reptile eat small animal, egg, and insect. (15)

---

*See Chart 4–1 for variations in the spelling of words with a final -s.
**Some nouns have irregular plurals. See Chart 4–1.

◇ **PRACTICE 12—GUIDED STUDY: Count and noncount nouns. (Charts 8–1 → 8–3)**

Directions: Choose one or more of the given topics. MAKE A LIST of the things you see. Use expressions of quantity when appropriate.

Example: I'm sitting in my office. These are the things I see:
- *two windows*
- *three desk lamps*
- *a lot of books—around 200 books about English grammar*
- *office equipment—a Macintosh computer, a printer, a photocopy machine*
- *typical office supplies—a stapler, paper clips, pens, pencils, a ruler, disks*
- *some photographs—three pictures of my daughter, one of my husband, one of my parents, two photos of my editors, and several pictures of good friends*
- *Etc.*

1. Sit in any room of your choosing. List the things you see (including things other people are wearing if you wish).

2. Look out a window. List the things and people you see.

3. Go to a place outdoors (a park, a zoo, a city street) and list what you see.

4. Travel in your imagination to a room you lived in when you were a child. List everything you can remember about that room.

◇ **PRACTICE 13—SELFSTUDY: *How many* and *how much.* (Charts 8–1 → 8–3; 4–1; and 6–2)**

Directions: Complete the questions with MANY or MUCH. Add final -S/-ES if necessary to make a noun plural. (Some of the count nouns have irregular plural forms.) If a verb is needed, choose the correct one from the parentheses. If final -S/-ES is not necessary, put a slash (/) in the blank.

1. How ___*many*___ letter__*s*__ (is, ⟨are⟩) there in the English alphabet?[1]

2. How ___*much*___ mail ___/___ did you get yesterday?

3. How ___*many*___ man _*men*_ (has, ⟨have⟩) a full beard at least once in their life?

4. How ___*many*___ famil~~y~~ *ies* (is, ⟨are⟩) there in your apartment building?

5. How _____ word _____ (is, are) there in this sentence?

6. How _____ sentence_____ (is, are) there in this exercise?

7. How _____ chalk _____ (is, are) there in the classroom?

8. How _____ **English** _____ does Stefan know?

9. How _____ English **literature**_____ have you studied?

10. How _____ English **word** _____ do you know?

11. How _____ **gasoline**_____ does it take to fill the tank in your car?

    (*British*: How _____ **petrol** _____ does it take to fill the tank?)

12. How _____ **homework** _____ did the teacher assign?

13. How _____ **grandchild** _____ does Mrs. Cunningham have?

14. How _____ **page**_____ (is, are) there in this book?

15. How _____ **library**_____ (is, are) there in the U.S.?[2]

_____

[1] Answer: twenty-six (26) = There are twenty-six letters in the English alphabet.

[2] Answer: approximately fifteen thousand (15,000).

16. How _____ **bone**_____ (*is, are*) there in the human body?[3]

17. How _____ **tooth** _____ does the average person have?[4]

18. How _____ **water**_____ do you drink every day?

19. How _____ **cup** _____ of tea do you usually drink in an average day?

20. How _____ **tea** _____ do you usually drink in an average day?

21. How _____ **glass** _____ of water do you drink every day?

22. How _____ **fun** _____ did you have at the amusement park?

23. How _____ **education** _____ does Ms. Martinez have?

24. How _____ **soap** _____ should I use in the dishwasher?

25. How _____ **island** _____ (*is, are*) there in Indonesia?[5]

26. How _____ **people**_____ (*was, were*) there on earth 2,000 years ago?[6]

27. How _____ **human being** _____ (*is are*) there in the world today?[7]

28. How _____ **people**_____ will there be by the year 2030?[8]

29. How _____ **zero** _____ (*is, are*) there in a billion?[9]

30. How _____ **butterfly**_____ can you see in one hour on a summer day in a flower garden?

◇ **PRACTICE 14—SELFSTUDY:** A *few* vs. a *little*. (Charts 8–1 → 8–3)

Directions: Complete the sentences with **A FEW** or **A LITTLE**. Add a final **-S** to the noun if necessary. Otherwise, write a slash (/) in the blank.

1. Let's listen to _____*a little*_____ **music** _/_ during dinner.

2. Let's sing _____*a few*_____ **song** _s_ around the campfire.

3. We all need _____ **help**____ at times.

4. Ingrid is from Sweden, but she knows _____ **English**____.

5. I need _____ more **apple**____ to make a pie.

6. I like _____ **honey**____ in my coffee.

7. I have a problem. Could you give me _____ **advice**____?

8. I need _____ **suggestion** ____.

9. He asked _____ **question** ____.

10. We talked to _____ **people**____ on the plane.

11. Please give me _____ more **minute**____.

12. Ann opened the curtains to let in _____ **light** ____ from outdoors.

13. I have _____ **homework** ____ to do tonight.

[3]Answer: two hundred and six (206).
[4]Answer: thirty-two (32).
[5]Answer: more than thirteen thousand seven hundred (13,700).
[6]Answer: approximately two hundred and fifty million (250,000,000).
[7]Answer: around six billion (6,000,000,000).
[8]Answer: estimated at more than twelve billion (12,000,000,000).
[9]Answer: nine (9).

◇ **PRACTICE 15—SELFSTUDY:** *How many* and *how much.* (Charts 8–1 → 8–4; 4–1; and 6–2)

Directions: Make questions with **HOW MANY** or **HOW MUCH**. Use the information in parentheses to form Speaker A's question.

1. A: How _**How many children do the Millers have?**_____
   B: Three. (The Millers have three children.)

2. A: How _**How much money does Jake make?**_____
   B: A lot. (Jake makes a lot of money.)

3. A: How _____
   B: Eleven. (There are eleven players on a soccer team.)

4. A: How _____
   B: Just a little. (I have just a little homework tonight.)

5. A: How _____
   B: 5,280. (There are 5,280 feet in a mile.)*

6. A: How _____
   B: 1,000. (There are 1,000 meters/metres in a kilometer/kilometre.)

7. A: How _____
   B: Three. (I took three suitcases on the plane to Florida.)

8. A: How _____
   B: A lot. (I took a lot of suntan oil with me.)

9. A: How _____
   B: Two pairs. (I took two pairs of sandals.)

10. A: How _____
    B: One tube. (I took one tube of toothpaste.)

11. A: How _____
    B: Just a short time, only two hours. (The flight took two hours.)

12. A: How _____
    B: Three. (I've been in Florida three times.)

13. A: How _____
    B: A lot. (There are a lot of apples in the two baskets.)

14. A: How _____
    B: A lot. (There is a lot of fruit in the two baskets.)

*1 foot = 30 centimeters/centimetres; 1 mile = 1.6 kilometers/kilometres.

◇ **PRACTICE 16—SELFSTUDY:** Units of measure with noncount nouns. (Chart 8–5)

Directions: What units of measure are usually used with the following nouns? More than one unit of measure can be used with some of the nouns.

PART I: You are going to the store. What are you going to buy? Choose from these units of measure:

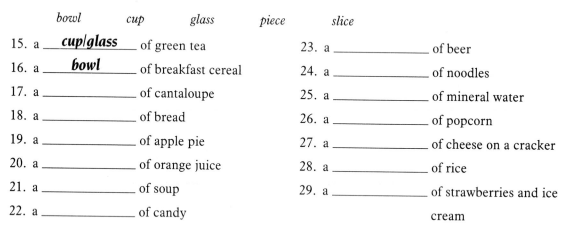

       bag   *bottle*   *box*   *can (tin)★*   *jar*

1. a ___*can/jar*___ of olives
2. a ___*box*___ of breakfast cereal
3. a _____ of mineral water
4. a _____ of jam or jelly
5. a _____ of tuna fish
6. a _____ of crackers
7. a _____ of soup

8. a _____ of sugar
9. a _____ of wine
10. a _____ of corn
11. a _____ of peas
12. a _____ of flour
13. a _____ of soda pop★★
14. a _____ of paint

PART II: You are hungry and thirsty. What are you going to have? Choose from these units of measure:

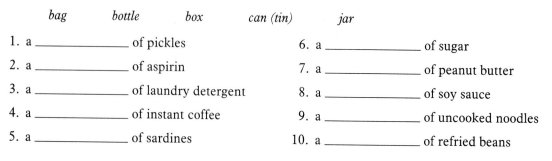

       bowl   *cup*   *glass*   *piece*   *slice*

15. a ___*cup/glass*___ of green tea
16. a ___*bowl*___ of breakfast cereal
17. a _____ of cantaloupe
18. a _____ of bread
19. a _____ of apple pie
20. a _____ of orange juice
21. a _____ of soup
22. a _____ of candy

23. a _____ of beer
24. a _____ of noodles
25. a _____ of mineral water
26. a _____ of popcorn
27. a _____ of cheese on a cracker
28. a _____ of rice
29. a _____ of strawberries and ice cream

◇ **PRACTICE 17—GUIDED STUDY:** Units of measure with noncount nouns. (Chart 8–5)

Directions: What units of measure are usually used with the following nouns? More than one unit of measure can be used with some of the nouns.

You are going to the store. What are you going to buy? Choose from these units of measure:

       bag   *bottle*   *box*   *can (tin)*   *jar*

1. a _____ of pickles
2. a _____ of aspirin
3. a _____ of laundry detergent
4. a _____ of instant coffee
5. a _____ of sardines

6. a _____ of sugar
7. a _____ of peanut butter
8. a _____ of soy sauce
9. a _____ of uncooked noodles
10. a _____ of refried beans

★*a can = a tin* in British English.

★★*Soda pop* refers to sweet carbonated beverages (also called "soft drinks"). This kind of drink is called "soda" in some parts of the United States, but "pop" in other parts of the country.

◇ PRACTICE 18—GUIDED STUDY: *How many* and *how much.*
(Charts 8–1 → 8–3; 4–1; and 6–2)

Directions: Pair up with another student.

PART I: Pretend you are going on a trip. Make a list of ten or so things you are going to take. Exchange your list with your partner. Using your partner's list, ask **HOW MANY** or **HOW MUCH** of each item she/he is going to take on her/his trip.

Example: STUDENT A's list: **suitcases, money, a passport, shoes** (etc.)
STUDENT B: How many suitcases are you going to take?
STUDENT A: Two.
STUDENT B: How much money?
STUDENT A: Three hundred dollars.
STUDENT B: How many passports?
STUDENT A: Just one, of course.
STUDENT B: How many pairs of shoes?
STUDENT A: Etc.

PART II: Look at the shopping list.

STUDENT A: Ask your partner **HOW MANY** or **HOW MUCH** of each item he/she is going to buy.
STUDENT B: Make up a reasonable answer.

SHOPPING LIST
coffee
chicken or steak
potatoes
rice
shoes
toothpaste
bath soap
light bulbs
notebook paper
(rolls of) film
bread
mustard

PART III: Pretend you are going on a shopping trip. Make a list of ten or so things you are going to buy. Exchange your list with your partner. Using your partner's list, ask questions using **HOW MANY, HOW MUCH, WHAT KIND OF,** or any other question that occurs to you.

◇ PRACTICE 19—GUIDED STUDY: Count and noncount nouns. (Charts 8–1 → 8–3)

Directions: In several paragraphs, describe the perfect meal. Use your imagination. If you use the name of a dish that your reader is probably unfamiliar with, describe it in parentheses.

Example:

I'm going to imagine for you the perfect meal. I am on a terrace high on a hillside in Nepal. When I look out, I see snow-capped mountains in the distance. The valley below is hazy and beautiful. I'm with my friends Olga and Roberto. The table has a white tablecloth and a vase of blue flowers. I'm going to eat all of my favorite kinds of food.
First the waiter is going to bring escargots. (Escargots are snails cooked in butter and seasoned with garlic and other herbs). Etc.

◇ PRACTICE 20—SELFSTUDY: Noncount abstractions. (Chart 8–3)

Directions: Complete the sentence in COLUMN A with words from COLUMN B. The completed sentences will be common sayings in English.

COLUMN A

1. Ignorance is __D__

2. Honesty is _____

3. Time is _____

4. Laughter is _____

5. Beauty is _____

6. Knowledge is _____

7. Experience is _____

COLUMN B

A. the best teacher.

B. the best medicine.

C. power.

✔D. bliss.★

E. in the eye of the beholder.

F. money.

G. the best policy.

◇ PRACTICE 21—GUIDED STUDY: Noncount abstractions. (Chart 8–3)

Directions: In groups (or by yourself), complete the lists with ABSTRACT NOUNS.

a. Name six good qualities you admire in a person.

1. ____*patience*____   4. _____

2. _____   5. _____

3. _____   6. _____

b. Name five bad qualities people can have.

1. ____*greed*____   4. _____

2. _____   5. _____

3. _____

c. What conditions, goals, and values is it important for a country to have?

1. ____*prosperity*____   4. _____

2. _____   5. _____

3. _____

d. Certain bad conditions exist in the world. What are they?

1. ____*hunger*____   4. _____

2. _____   5. _____

3. _____

After you finish the lists, answer this question: How many of the nouns in your lists can be made plural with a final -s/-es? Add -s/-es to the nouns if possible.

_____

★"Ignorance is bliss" is a saying. It means: If you know about problems, you have to worry about them and solve them. If you don't know about problems, you can avoid them and be happy (*bliss* = *happiness*). Many people do not believe that this saying is true. What do you think?

◇ PRACTICE 22—SELFSTUDY: Using *a* or *ø* for generalizations. (Chart 8-6)

Directions: Write **A** or **Ø** in the blank before each singular noun. Then write a sentence with the plural form of the noun if possible.

SINGULAR SUBJECTS

1. __A__ bird has feathers.
2. __Ø__ corn is nutritious.
3. _____ milk is white.
4. _____ flower is beautiful.
5. _____ water is a clear liquid.
6. _____ horse is strong.
7. _____ jewelry is expensive.
8. _____ honey comes from bees.
9. _____ shirt has sleeves.
10. _____ soap produces bubbles.

PLURAL SUBJECTS

1. ___*Birds have feathers.*___
2. ___*(none possible)*___
3. _____
4. _____
5. _____
6. _____
7. _____
8. _____
9. _____
10. _____

◇ PRACTICE 23—SELFSTUDY: Using *a* or *some*. (Chart 8–6)

Directions: Write **A** or **SOME** in the blank before each singular noun. Then write a sentence with the plural form of the noun if possible.

SINGULAR OBJECTS

1. I saw ___*a*___ bird.
2. I ate ___*some*___ corn.
3. Would you like _____ milk?
4. I picked _____ flower.
5. I drank _____ water.
6. I fed grass to _____ horse.
7. Pat is wearing _____ jewelry.
8. I bought _____ honey.
9. Tom bought _____ new shirt.
10. I need _____ soap to wash the dishes.

PLURAL OBJECTS

1. ___*I saw some birds.*___
2. ___*(none possible)*___
3. _____
4. _____
5. _____
6. _____
7. _____
8. _____
9. _____
10. _____

◇ PRACTICE 24—SELFSTUDY: *A/an* vs. *the*: singular count nouns. (Chart 8–6)

Directions: Complete the sentences with **A/AN** or **THE**.

1. A: ___*A*___ dog makes a good pet.

   B: I agree.

2. A: Did you feed ___*the*___ dog?

   B: Yes, I did.

3. A: Let's listen to _____ radio.

   B: Okay. I'll turn it on.

4. A: Does your car have _____ radio?

   B: Yes, and _____ tape player.

5. My dorm room has _____ desk, _____ bed, _____ chest of drawers, and two chairs.

6. A: Jessica, where's the stapler?

   B: On _____ desk. If it's not there, look in _____ top drawer.

7. A: Sara, put your bike in _____ basement before dark.

   B: Okay, Dad.

8. Our apartment building has _____ basement. Sara keeps her bike there at night.

9. Every sentence has _____ subject and _____ verb.

10. Look at this sentence: *Jack lives in Miami.* What is _____ subject and what is _____ verb?

11. A: I can't see you at four. I'll be in _____ meeting then. How about four-thirty?

    B: Fine.

12. A: What time does _____ meeting start Tuesday?

    B: Eight.

13. Jack's car ran out of gas. He had to walk _____ long distance to find _____ telephone and call his brother for help.

14. _____ distance from _____ sun to _____ earth is 93,000,000 miles.

15. A: Jake, _____ telephone is ringing. Can you get it?

    B: Sure.

16. A: I have _____ question.

    B: Okay. What do you want to know?

17. A: Ms. Ming, you have to help me!

    B: Calm down. What's _____ problem?

18. A: I wrote _____ poem. Would you like to read it?

    B: Sure. What's it about?

19. A: Was _____ lecture interesting?

    B: Yes. _____ speaker gave _____ interesting talk.

20. A: Where should we go for _____ cup of coffee after class?

    B: Let's go to _____ cafe around _____ corner from the First National Bank.

◇ **PRACTICE 25 —SELFSTUDY:** ø vs. *the*: plural count nouns and noncount nouns. **(Chart 8–6)**

Directions: Write Ø or **THE** in the blanks.

1. A: _____Ø_____ dogs make good pets.

   B: I agree.

2. A: Did you feed _____**the**_____ dogs?

   B: Yes, I did.

3. A: _____Ø_____ fruit is good for you.

   B: I agree.

4. A: _____**The**_____ fruit in this bowl is ripe.

   B: Good. I think I'll have a piece.

5. As every parent knows, _____ children require a lot of time and attention.

6. A: Frank, where are _____ children?

   B: Next door at the Jacksons.

7. _____ paper is made from _____ trees or other plants.

8. _____ paper in my notebook is lined.

9. A: Mom, please pass _____ potatoes.

   B: Here you are. Anything else? Want some more chicken, too?

10. _____ potatoes are _____ vegetables.

11. _____ nurses are trained to care for sick and injured people.

12. When I was in Memorial Hospital, _____ nurses were wonderful.

13. _____ frogs are _____ small animals without _____ tails that live on

    land or in water. _____ turtles also live on land or in water, but they have

    _____ tails and _____ hard shells.

14. A: Nicole, what are those animals doing in here!?

    B: We're playing. _____ frogs belong to Jason. _____ turtles are mine.

15. There are many kinds of _____ books. We use _____ textbooks and _____ workbooks in school. We use _____ dictionaries and _____ encyclopedias for reference. For _____ entertainment, we read _____ novels and _____ poetry.

16. _____ books on this desk are mine.

17. All of our food comes from _____ plants. Some food, such as _____ fruit and _____ vegetables, comes directly from _____ plants. Other food, such as _____ meat, comes indirectly from _____ plants.

18. I'm not very good at keeping houseplants alive. _____ plants in my apartment have to be tough. They survive in spite of me.

19. A: What do you want to be when you grow up?

    B: _____ engineer.

    A: Really? Why?

    B: Because _____ engineers build _____ bridges.

    A: That's right. And where do they build bridges?

    B: Across _____ rivers, across _____ valleys, across _____ highways, across _____ railroad tracks, and across _____ other places I can't think of right now.

20. There was a bad earthquake in my city. I couldn't drive from my side of the city to the other side because _____ bridges across the river were unsafe. All of them had been damaged in the quake.

◇ PRACTICE 26—SELFSTUDY: Using *the* for second mention. (Chart 8–6)

Directions: Write A/AN, SOME, or THE in the blanks.

1. I had ____*a*____ banana and ____*an*____ apple. I gave ____*the*____ banana to Mary. I ate ____*the*____ apple.

2. I had ____*some*____ bananas and ____*some*____ apples. I gave ____*the*____ bananas to Mary. I ate ____*the*____ apples.

3. I drank ____*some*____ coffee and ____*some*____ milk. ____*The*____ coffee was hot. _____ milk was cold.

4. I have _____ desk and _____ bed in my room. _____ desk is hard. _____ bed is hard, too, even though it's supposed to be soft.

5. I forgot to bring my things with me to class yesterday, so I borrowed _____ pen and _____ paper from Joe. I returned _____ pen, but I used _____ paper for my homework.

6. I bought _____ bag of flour and _____ sugar to make _____ cookies. _____ sugar was okay, but I had to return _____ flour. When I opened _____ flour, I found _____ little bugs in it. I took it back to the people at the store and showed them _____ little bugs. They gave me _____ new bag of flour. _____ new bag didn't have any bugs in it.

7. Yesterday while I was walking to work, I saw _____ birds in _____ tree. I also saw _____ cat under _____ tree. _____ birds didn't pay any attention to _____ cat, but _____ cat was watching _____ birds intently.

8. Once upon a time, _____ princess fell in love with _____ prince. _____ princess wanted to marry _____ prince, who lived in a distant land. She summoned _____ messenger to take _____ things to _____ prince to show him her love. _____ messenger took _____ jewels and _____ robe made of yellow and red silk to _____ prince. _____ princess anxiously awaited _____ messenger's return. She hoped that _____ prince would send her _____ tokens of his love. But when _____ messenger returned, he brought back _____ jewels and _____ beautiful silk robe that _____ princess had sent. Why? Why? she wondered. Then _____ messenger told her: _____ prince already had _____ wife.

◇ PRACTICE 27—GUIDED STUDY: Using *the* for second mention. (Chart 8–6)

Directions: Write A/AN, SOME, or THE in the blanks.

(1)   One day last month while I was driving through the countryside, I saw _____ man

(2) and _____ truck next to _____ covered bridge. _____ bridge crossed

(3) _____ small river. I stopped and asked _____ man, "What's the matter? Can I be

(4) of help?"

(5)   "Well," said _____ man, "my truck is about a half inch* too tall. Or _____

(6) top of _____ bridge is a half inch too short. Either way, my truck won't fit under

(7) _____ bridge."

(8)   "Hmmm. There must be _____ solution to this problem," I said.

(9)   "I don't know. I guess I'll have to turn around and take another route."

(10)   After a few moments of thought, I said, "Aha! I have _____ solution!"

(11)   "What is it?" said _____ man.

(12)   "Let a little air out of your tires. Then _____ truck won't be too tall and you can

(13) cross _____ bridge over _____ river."

(14)   "Hey, that's _____ great idea. Let's try it!" So _____ man let a little air out

(15) of _____ tires and was able to cross _____ river and be on his way.

◇ PRACTICE 28—SELFSTUDY: Summary: *A/an* vs. Ø vs. *the*. (Chart 8–6)

Directions: Write A/AN, Ø, or THE in the blanks.

1. A: What would you like for breakfast?

   B: ___*An*___ egg and some toast.

   A: How would you like ___*the*___ egg?

   B: Fried, sunny side up.

---

*One-half inch = 1.27 centimeters.

2. _____Ø_____ eggs are nutritious.

3. It is _____ scientific fact: _____ steam rises when _____ water boils.

4. A: I'm looking for _____ tape player. Where is it?

   B: It's on one of _____ shelves next to my desk.

   A: Ah! There it is. Thanks.

   B: You're welcome.

   A: Hmmm. I don't think it works. Maybe _____ batteries are dead.

5. _____ chalk is _____ necessity in a classroom.

6. A: Where'd _____ plumber go? _____ sink's still leaking!

   B: Relax. He went to shut off _____ water supply to _____ house. He'll fix

   _____ leak when he gets back.

7. _____ water is essential to human life, but don't drink _____ water in the Flat

   River. It'll kill you! _____ pollution in that river is terrible.

8. A: How did you get here? Did you walk?

   B: No, I took _____ taxi.

9. A: We're ready to go, kids. Get in _____ car.

   B: Just _____ minute! We forgot something.

   A: Marge, can you get _____ kids in _____ car, please?

   B: Just _____ minute, Harry. They're coming.

10. _____ newspapers are _____ important source of _____ information.

11. _____ sun is _____ star. We need _____ sun for _____ heat,

    _____ light, and _____ energy.

12. _____ ducks are my favorite farm animals.

13. A: Where's _____ letter I wrote to Ted?

    B: It's gone. _____ strong wind blew it on _____ floor, and _____ dog

    tore it up. I threw _____ scraps in _____ wastebasket.

14. _____ efficient transportation system is _____ essential part of a healthy

    economy.

15. A: Did you set _____ alarm?

    B: Yes.

    A: Did you lock _____ door?

    B: Yes.

    A: Did you check _____ stove?

    B: Yes.

    A: Did you close all _____ windows?

    B: Yes.

    A: Then let's turn out _____ lights.

    B: Goodnight, dear.

16. Karen is _____ exceptionally talented person.

17. A: Can I have some money, Dad?

    B: What for?

    A: I want to go to the movies with my friends and hang around the mall.

    B: What you need is a job! _____ money doesn't grow on _____ trees, you
    know.

18. A doctor cures _____ sick people. _____ farmer grows _____ crops.
    _____ architect designs _____ buildings. _____ artist creates
    _____ new ways of looking at _____ world and _____ life.

19. _____ earthquakes are _____ relatively rare events in central Africa.

20. My city experienced _____ earthquake recently. I was riding my bicycle when
    _____ earthquake occurred. _____ ground beneath me trembled so hard that
    it shook me off my bike.

◇ **PRACTICE 29—GUIDED STUDY: Summary: *A/an* vs. *ø* vs. *the*. (Chart 8–6)**

Directions: Complete the sentences with **A/AN**, **Ø**, or **THE**.

1. _____ good food keeps us healthy and adds _____ pleasure to our lives.

2. A: What is your favorite food?

    B: _____ ice cream—it's cold, sweet, and smooth.

3. _____ pizza originated in Italy. It is a pie with _____ cheese, _____
   tomatoes, and other things on top. _____ "pizza" is _____ Italian word for
   _____ "pie."

4. A: Hey, Nick. Pass _____ pizza. I want another piece.

    B: There're only two pieces left. You take _____ big piece, and I'll take _____
    small one.

5. We had _____ steamed rice, _____ fish, and _____ vegetables for lunch
   yesterday. _____ rice was cooked just right. _____ fish was very tasty.
   _____ vegetables were fresh.

6. A: Well, are you ready to leave?

   B: Let me take just one last sip of coffee. I've really enjoyed this meal.

   A: I agree. _____ food was excellent—especially _____ fish. And _____ service was exceptionally good. Let's leave _____ waitress _____ good tip.

   B: I usually tip around fifteen percent, sometimes eighteen percent.

7. Only one of _____ continents in _____ world is uninhabited. Which one?

8. Last week, I took _____ easy exam. It was in my economics class. I had _____ right answers for all of _____ questions on _____ exam. My score was 100%.

9. Generally speaking, anyone who goes to _____ job interview should wear _____ nice clothes.

10. A mouse has _____ long, thin, almost hairless tail. _____ rats also have _____ long, skinny tails.

11. Years ago, people used _____ wood or _____ coal for _____ heat, but now most people use _____ gas, _____ oil, or _____ electricity.

12. _____ good book is _____ friend for _____ life.

13. _____ gold is _____ excellent conductor of _____ electricity. It is used in many of the electrical circuits on _____ spaceship.

14. A: Where's Alice?

    B: She's in _____ kitchen making _____ sandwich.

15. In ancient times, people did not use _____ coins for money. Instead they used _____ shells, _____ beads, or _____ salt. The first coins were made around 2600 years ago. Today, most money is made from _____ paper.

16. Ted, pass _____ salt, please. And _____ pepper. Thanks.

17. _____ different countries have _____ different geography. Italy is located on _____ peninsula. Japan is _____ island nation.

18. There are some wonderful small markets in my neighborhood. You can always get _____ fresh fish at Mr. Rico's fish market.

19. A: I saw _____ good program on TV last night.

    B: Oh? What was it?

    A: It was _____ documentary about wildlife in Alaska. It was really interesting. Did you see it, too?

    B: No, I watched _____ old movie. It wasn't very good. I wish I'd known about _____ documentary. I would have watched it.

20. _____ modern people, just like their ancestors, are curious about _____ universe. Where did _____ moon come from? Does _____ life exist on other planets? What is _____ star? How large is _____ universe? How long will _____ sun continue to burn?

Directions: Complete the sentences with **ONE** or **IT**.

1. A: Do you need a pen?

   B: No. I already have _____ *one* _____.

2. A: Where is my pen?

   B: Mike has _____ *it* _____.

3. A: Do you have a car?

   B: No. I don't have enough money to get _____.

4. A: Does Erica like her new car?

   B: Does she like _____? She loves _____!

5. A: Do you have a bicycle?

   B: Yes.

   A: Can I use _____ this afternoon?

6. A: Does Tom have a bicycle?

   B: No, but I think Eric has _____.

7. A: Do you see an empty table?

   B: Yes. I see _____ over there in the corner.

8. A: This table is empty.

   B: Let's take _____.

9. A: Do you have a dictionary?

   B: No, but I think Yoko has _____.

10. A: Where's my dictionary?

    B: I don't know. I haven't seen _____.

◇ PRACTICE 31—GUIDED STUDY: Object pronouns: *one* vs. *it.* (Charts 8–7 and 8–8)

Directions: Complete the sentences with **ONE** or **IT**.

1. A: Where's my pencil?

   B: Jason has _____.

2. A: I need a pencil.

   B: Jason has an extra _____. Ask him.

3. I don't have a small calculator. I need to buy _____ for my math class.

4. A: Do you have a small calculator?

   B: Yes.

   A: May I borrow _____ for a minute?

5. A: Are you going to take a sandwich along with you for lunch?

   B: No. I'll get _____ at the deli around the corner from the office.

6. I made a sandwich for James's lunch, but he forgot to take _____ to school.

7. Westville Hospital is the name of our new hospital. We built _____ two years ago.

8. Our village doesn't have a hospital. We hope to build _____ in the next five years.

9. When I moved into my new apartment, I wanted to hang my paintings on the wall. I didn't have a hammer, so I went to the hardware store and bought _____.

10. My friend Ralph helped me hang my paintings on the wall. When I handed him the hammer, he dropped _____ on his toe.

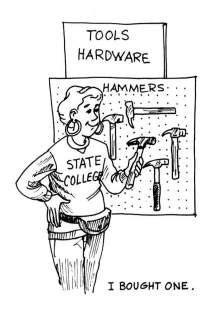

I BOUGHT ONE.

RALPH DROPPED IT.

◇ **PRACTICE 32—SELFSTUDY:** *Some/any* vs. *it/them.* (Charts 8–7 and 8–8)

Directions: Select the appropriate completion from the *italicized* words.

1. A: Where did you get all of this new furniture?

   B: I bought *some,* (*it.*)

2. A: Does Jones Department Store sell bedroom furniture?

   B: No, but you can find *some, it* at Charlie's Bargain Warehouse.

3. A: What are you eating?

   B: Cheese. Would you like *some, it*? There's plenty.

4. A: Here's the cheese you wanted me to buy.

   B: Thanks. Put *some, it* in the refrigerator, please.

5. A: Where did you get these magazines?

   B: I got *some, them* at the newstand on Pyle Street.

6. A: Do you read a lot of magazines?

   B: Not usually, but I often pick *some, them* up at the airport before I get on a flight. I always read magazines when I fly.

7. A: How about some hot tea?

   B: Thanks, but I don't want *any, it* right now.

8. A: Here's some hot tea. Would you like some sugar or lemon?

   B: No, but I'd like to put a little milk in *some, it*.

◇ **PRACTICE 33—GUIDED STUDY:** *Some/any* vs. *it/them.* (Charts 8–7 and 8–8)

Directions: Select the appropriate completion from the *italicized* words.

1. A: Where are the scissors—the ones with the orange handles?

   B: I put   *some, it, them*   in the top drawer.

2. A: Do you have any scissors?

   B: No, but I think Aunt Ella has   *some, it, them*.   Ask her.

3. A: Do you have any dog shampoo?

   B: No, but I think Aunt Ella has   *some, it, them*.   Ask her.

4. A: What are those?

   B: What do you mean? They're scissors, of course.

   A: Where did you get   *some, it, them*?

   B: I borrowed   *some, it, them*   from Aunt Ella.

5. A: What's that?

   B: It's shampoo especially for dogs. It kills fleas.

   A: Where did you get   *some, it, them*?

   B: I borrowed   *some, it, them*   from Aunt Ella. My dog has fleas. I'm going to give her a bath
      and kill   *some, it, them*.

   A: Look at the label. Read   *some, it, them*.   What does it say?

   B: It says ''Flea Shampoo'' on the label.

   A: That means you're supposed to give the fleas a bath, not the dog!

   B: Oh sure! Ha-ha. Stop joking around and help me give the dog a bath.

6. A: I'm going to the post office this afternoon.

   B: Really? Could you take these letters with you and mail   *some, it, them*   for me? Thanks.

7. A: Is the mail here?

   B: Yes.

   A: Did I get   *any, it, them*?

8. A: Take this letter and give *some, it, them* to Alison.

   B: Okay.

9. A: Could you save those newspapers for me? I'd like to read *some, it, them* later.

   B: Sure.

   A: I especially want to read the local paper. Be sure to save *some, it, them* for me.

   B: Don't worry.

10. A: Does your son Kevin like to read books?

    B: He hasn't read *any, it, them* in a long time.

    A: Maybe you should buy *some, it, them* for him. Children like to have their own books.

    B: I bought him a book for his last birthday. He never read *some, it, them*.

◇ **PRACTICE 34—SELFSTUDY: Prepositions. (Chapter 8; Appendix1)**

Directions: Complete each sentence with the appropriate preposition.

1. The twins may look alike, but Robby's behavior is very different ____**from**____ Tim's.

2. I'm sorry _____ my behavior last night. I was pretty upset and was just feeling

   sorry _____ myself. I didn't mean anything I said.

3. I spoke _____ my brother _____ your problem, and he said that there

   was nothing he could do to help you.

4. All right, children, here is your math problem: add ten _____ twelve, subtract two

   _____ that total; divide ten _____ that answer; and multiply the result

   _____ five. What is the final answer?

5. I feel pretty good about my final examination in English. I'm hoping _____ a good

   grade, and I'm anxious to get my paper back.

6. Please try to concentrate _____ my explanation. I can't repeat it.

7. A: Did you hear _____ the plans to build a new hotel in the middle of town? It's

      wonderful!

   B: Yes, I heard, but I disagree _____ you. I think it's terrible! It means the town

      will be full of tourists all the time.

8. A: Have you heard _____ your friend in Thailand recently?

   B: Yes. She's having a difficult time. She's not accustomed _____ hot weather.

9. A: I must tell you _____ a crazy thing that happened last night. Have you heard?

   B: What? What happened?

   A: A hundred monkeys escaped _____ the zoo.

   B: You've got to be kidding! How did that happen?

Directions: Complete each sentence with the appropriate preposition.

1. I'm ready _____ the test. I studied hard.

2. It's important for you to believe _____ your own abilities. Tell yourself, "I can do it!"

3. _____ the past, people traveled from Europe _____ North and South America only by boat.

4. I applied _____ a job at a florist's. I like to arrange flowers.

5. I will not discuss this _____ you. It's private information.

6. It's not polite to laugh _____ other people's mistakes.

7. Carol's house is full _____ people. Is she having a party?

8. Listen _____ me!

9. Jack arrived _____ the bus stop just after the bus had left.

10. I arrived _____ this city _____ September third.

11. Your grades are wonderful. Your mother and I are very proud _____ you.

12. I'm looking forward _____ my holiday in Spain.

13. Canada belongs _____ the United Nations.

14. The army protected the president _____ his enemies. The rebels attacked the presidential palace. They tried to get rid _____ the president by force.

15. A: What are you doing under the sink?

    B: I'm looking _____ my ring. It went down the drain, and I've taken the pipe out.

16. A: Did you hear _____ my promotion?

    B: Yes. They told me to report to you _____ noon tomorrow.

17. I'm a little afraid _____ flying, so when I was buying an airplane ticket, I asked _____ a seat near the front because I thought it was safer near the main door. The person behind me insisted _____ having a seat near the back, because he thought it was safer there. The next person paid _____ his ticket only after they assured him that he could have a seat over the wing, which he felt was the safest location on the airplane. It's very confusing. _____ the future, I think I'll just sit wherever they put me.

18. The people of the Hawaiian islands are famous _____ their warm hospitality. When we visited the islands, everyone we met was extremely nice _____ us.

19. A: Barbara is telling Ben something _____ you. I think she's complaining _____ you. Is she angry _____ you?

    B: I borrowed some money _____ her a long time ago, and I never paid her back. I'd better try to see her _____ the morning and give her the money I owe her. I'd also better apologize _____ her _____ waiting so long.

20. My chemistry examination consisted _____ all of the things I didn't understand during the semester. I couldn't concentrate _____ it at all. I'm sure that I didn't pass.

Index

★The abbreviation "*fn.*" means "footnote." A footnote is found at the bottom of a chart or a page.
Footnotes contain additional information.

Present perfect progressive, 136–138
Present progressive, 2–3, 5–6, 9–17, 29, 32
   for future time, 51–53
Present time, 2–17 (SEE ALSO Tenses)
Probably, 43–44
Progressive vs. nonprogressive verbs, 11 (SEE
    ALSO Tenses)
Prohibition, 91–92
Pronouns:
   nonspecific objects (*some, any, one*), 170–172
   personal (*I, them*), 68–69, 75–76
   possessive (*mine, theirs*), 73–76
   reflexive (*myself, themselves*), 74–75, 76*fn.*
Pronunciation:
   -ed, 24, 25*fn.*
   -s/-es, 62
Punctuation:
   apostrophe, 72–73, 76*fn.*
   quotation marks, 35*fn.*

Q

Question forms:
   present perfect (*have you done?*), 128
   present progressive (*are you doing?*), 5
   simple future (*will you do?*), 40–41
   simple past (*did you do?*), 20, 40–41
   simple present (*do you do?*), 4, 40–41
Questions:
   information, 109–124
   polite, 88–89
   review of, 121–124, 127
   short answers to, 12, 20, 107
     contractions with pronouns, 43*fn.*
   tag, 125–126
   yes/no, 107–109, 111
Quotation marks, 35*fn.*

R

Reflexive pronouns, 74–75, 76*fn.*

S

-S/-es:
   with plural nouns, 62, 73, 150, 153–156
   pronunciation, 62
   with possessive nouns, 70–71
   with simple present verbs, 4–5
   spelling, 154
Short answers to questions, 12, 20, 107
Should, 89–90, 92–93
Simple future, 40, 43–50, 59
Simple past, 19–27, 30–32, 34–38, 40–41, 50
   vs. present perfect, 129–133
Simple present, 2–8, 11–12, 14–17, 27, 32,
    40–41
   for future time, 53
Simple sentence structure, 63

Since and ***for***, 134–135
Singular and plural:
   nouns (*-s/-es*), 61–62, 66–67
   nouns used as adjectives, 66
   personal pronouns, 68–69
   possessive nouns, 70–71
   present tense verbs (*-s/-es*), 4–6
Some, 149–150, 153, 161, 164–166
   as object pronoun vs. *it /them*, 171–172
Spelling:
   -ed, 26
   -ing, 26
   -s/-es, 4–5
Stative verbs (nonprogressive verbs), 11
Still, 142
Subject pronouns, personal, 68–69, 75–76
Subjects, verbs, objects, prepositions, 63
Suggestions, 96–97

T

Tag questions, 125–126
Tenses:
   past perfect (*had done*), 143–146
   past progressive (*were doing*), 28–32, 34,
     145–146
   present perfect (*have done*), 128–135, 145–146
   present perfect progressive (*have been doing*),
     136–138
   present progressive (*are doing*), 2–3, 5–6,
     9–17, 29, 32
    for future time, 51–53
   review of, 34–37, 54–59, 136, 138–140, 147
   simple future (*will do*), 40, 43–50, 59
   simple past (*did*), 19–27, 30–32, 34–38,
     40–41, 50, 129–133
   simple present (*do*), 2–8, 11–12, 14–17, 27,
     32, 40–41
    future meaning, 53
The, 163–169
Themselves, 76*fn.*
Time clauses:
   future, 46–48
   past, 30
   with *since*, 135
Time prepositions, 38
To + simple form (infinitive), 83, 111*fn.*
To with modal auxiliaries, 83
Too many/much, 151
Two, 150

U

Units of measure (*a cup of, a piece of*), 158
Used to (past habit), 33–34

V

Verbs:
   parallel structure with, 48–49
   vs. subjects and objects, 63
   (SEE ALSO Auxiliaries; Modal auxiliaries;
     Tenses; and individual items)

 # Answer Key

Answers to the Selfstudy Practices

Chapter 1: PRESENT TIME

◇ PRACTICE 1, p. 1.

A: Hi. My name __is__ Kunio.

B: Hi. My __name__ is Maria. I __'m__ glad to meet you.

KUNIO: I'm glad to __meet__ you, too. Where __are you from__ ?

MARIA: I __'m__ from Mexico. Where __are you from__ ?

KUNIO: I __'m__ from Japan.

MARIA: Where __are you__ living now?

KUNIO: On Fifth Avenue in __an__ apartment. And you?

MARIA: I'm living in a dorm.

KUNIO: __What's__ (What is) your field of study?

MARIA: Business. After I study English, I'm going to attend the School of Business Administration. How __about__ you? __What's__ your major?

KUNIO: Chemistry.

MARIA: __What do__ you like to do in your free time? __Do__ you have any hobbies?

KUNIO: I __like__ to swim. How __about__ you?

MARIA: I read a lot and I __collect__ stamps from all over the world.

KUNIO: Really? __Would__ you like some stamps from Japan?

MARIA: Sure! That would be great. Thanks.

KUNIO: I have __to__ write your full name on the board when I introduce __you__ to the class. __How__ do you spell your name?

MARIA: My first __name__ is Maria. M-A-R-I-A. My last __name__ is Lopez. L-O-P-E-Z.

KUNIO: My __first__ name is Kunio. K-U-N-I-O. My __last__ name is Akiwa. A-K-I-W-A.

MARIA: Kunio Akiwa. __Is__ that right?

KUNIO: Yes, it __is__ . It's been nice talking with you.

MARIA: I enjoyed it, too.

◇ **PRACTICE 4, p. 3.**
1. am sitting
2. am reading
3. am looking
4. am writing
5. am doing
6. sit . . . am sitting
7. read . . . am reading
8. look . . . am looking
9. write . . . am writing
10. do . . . am doing

◇ **PRACTICE 5, p. 3.**

Part I:
1. speak
2. speak
3. speaks
4. speak
5. speaks

Part II:
1. do not (don't) speak
2. do not (don't) speak
3. does not (doesn't) speak
4. do not (don't) speak
5. does not (doesn't) speak

Part III:
1. Do you speak
2. Do they speak
3. Does he speak
4. Do we speak
5. Does she speak

◇ **PRACTICE 6, p. 4.**
1. like __s__
2. watch __es__
3. do __es__ n't like __l__
4. climb __l__
5. Do __l__ . . . like __l__
6. Do __es__ . . . like __l__
7. like __s__
8. wash __es__
9. go __es__
10. make __l__
11. visit __s__
12. get __s__
13. get __l__
14. Do __es__ . . . get __l__
15. do __es__ n't get __l__
16. carr __ies__
17. play __s__
18. catch __es__
19. live __l__
20. live __s__

◇ **PRACTICE 8, p. 5.**

Part I:
1. am speaking
2. are speaking
3. is speaking
4. are speaking

Part II:
1. am not speaking
2. are not (aren't) speaking
3. is not (isn't) speaking
4. are not (aren't) speaking

Part III:
1. Are you speaking
2. Are they speaking
3. Is she speaking
4. Are we speaking

◇ **PRACTICE 9, p. 6.**
1. does
2. Do
3. /
4. is
5. Are
6. are
7. Is
8. Do
9. /
10. is
11. is
12. are
13. /
14. /
15. Do
16. Does
17. Is
18. Are
19. are
20. /
21. are
22. is

◇ **PRACTICE 11, p. 7.**
1. often
2. rarely/seldom
3. always
4. usually/often
5. sometimes
6. usually
7. rarely/seldom
8. rarely/seldom
9. never
10. always
11. often
12. rarely/seldom
(also possible: sometimes)

◇ **PRACTICE 13, p. 9.**
Expected answers:
1. He is (He's) swimming.
   He's doing the crawl.
2. He's cutting her hair.
   He's using scissors.
   She's getting a haircut.
3. She's sleeping.
   She's dreaming.
   She's having a pleasant dream.
4. He's crying.
   He's wiping his tears with his hand.
5. She's kicking a ball.
   She's playing soccer.
6. He's hitting a golf ball.
   He's playing golf.
   He's golfing.
   He's swinging a golf club.
7. She's riding a motorcycle.
   She's wearing a helmet.
8. They're dancing.
   They're smiling.
   They're having a good time.

PRACTICE 15, p. 11.

1. is snowing
2. takes
3. drive
4. am watching
5. prefer
6. need
7. are playing
8. is looking . . . sees
9. sings
10. bite
11. writes
12. understand
13. belongs
14. is shining . . . is raining

PRACTICE 16, p. 12.

1. A: Are   B: I am   OR   I'm not
2. A: Do   B: they do   OR   they don't
3. A: Do   B: I do   OR   I don't
4. A: Does   B: she does   OR   she doesn't
5. A: Are   B: they are   OR   they aren't
6. A: Do   B: they do   OR   they don't
7. A: Is   B: he is   OR   he isn't
8. A: Are   B: I am   OR   I'm not
9. A: Is   B: it is   OR   it isn't
10. A: Does   B: it does   OR   it doesn't

PRACTICE 19, p. 14.

1. is . . . is blowing . . . are falling
2. eats . . . don't eat . . . do you eat
3. A: Do you shop   B: don't . . . usually shop
   A: are you shopping   B: am trying
4. am buying . . . buy
5. A: Do you read
   B: do . . . read . . . subscribe . . . look
6. B: am . . . am trying   A: is resting
7. A: am I studying . . . do I want . . . need
8. lose . . . rest . . . grow . . . keep . . . stay . . . don't
   grow . . . don't have . . . Do trees grow

PRACTICE 23, p. 18.

1. of
2. to
3. to
4. with
5. for
6. to
7. with/at
8. of
9. from
10. to
11. at
12. for

Chapter 2: PAST TIME

PRACTICE 1, p. 19.

1. walked . . . yesterday
2. talked . . . last
3. opened . . . yesterday
4. went . . . last
5. met . . . last
6. Yesterday . . . made . . . took
7. paid . . . last
8. Yesterday . . . fell
9. left . . . last

PRACTICE 2, p. 20.

1. started
2. went
3. saw
4. stood
5. arrived
6. won
7. had
8. made
9. finished
10. felt
11. fell
12. heard
13. sang
14. explored
15. asked
16. brought
17. broke
18. ate
19. watched
20. built
21. took
22. paid
23. left
24. wore

PRACTICE 3, p. 20.

1. A: Did you answer
   B: I did . . . I answered
   OR I didn't . . . I didn't answer
2. A: Did he see
   B: he did . . . He saw
   OR he didn't . . . He didn't see
3. A: Did they watch
   B: they did . . . They watched
   OR they didn't . . . They didn't watch
4. A: Did-you understand
   B: I did . . . I understood
   OR I didn't . . . I didn't understand
5. A: Were you
   B: I was . . . I was
   OR I wasn't . . . I wasn't

PRACTICE 4, p. 21.

1. shook
2. stayed
3. swam
4. jumped
5. held
6. fought
7. taught
8. froze
9. thought
10. called
11. rode
12. sold

PRACTICE 6, p. 22.

Expected answers:

1. swept
2. flew
3. caught/held/took
4. taught
5. froze
6. felt
7. drew/got/made
8. heard
9. fell . . . broke
10. won
11. drove/took
12. fought
13. sold
14. hid/put
15. sheet
16. ran
17. led
18. paid
19. drank/had
20. bought/chose
21. wore
22. gave/lent

◇ PRACTICE 10, p. 26.

END OF VERB	DOUBLE THE CONSONANT?	SIMPLE FORM	-ING	-ED
-e	***NO***	*excite*	***exciting***	***excited***
Two Consonants	***NO***	*exist*	***existing***	***existed***
Two Vowels + One Consonant	***NO***	*shout*	***shouting***	***shouted***
One Vowel + One Consonant	***YES***	ONE-SYLLABLE VERBS *pat*	***patting***	***patted***
	NO	TWO-SYLLABLE VERBS (STRESS ON **FIRST** SYLLABLE) *visit*	***visiting***	***visited***
	YES	TWO-SYLLABLE VERBS (STRESS ON **SECOND** SYLLABLE) *admit*	***admitting***	***admitted***
-y	***NO***	*pray* *pry*	***praying*** ***prying***	***prayed*** ***pried***
-ie	***NO***	*tie*	***tying***	***tie***

◇ PRACTICE 11, p. 26.
1. wai__**t**__ing ... wait
2. pa__**tt**__ing ... pat
3. bi__**t**__ing ... bite
4. si__**tt**__ing ... sit
5. wri__**t**__ing ... write
6. figh__**t**__ing ... fight

7. wai__**t**__ing ... wait
8. ge__**tt**__ing ... get
9. star__**t**__ing ... start
10. permi__**tt**__ing ... permit
11. lif__**t**__ing ... lift

12. ea__**t**__ing ...eat
13. tas__**t**__ing ... taste
14. cu__**tt**__ ... cut
15. mee__**t**__ing ... meet
16. visi__**t**__ing ... visit

◇ PRACTICE 12, p. 27.
1. A: Did you hear
   B: didn't ... didn't hear ... was
2. A: Do you hear   B: don't ... don't hear
3. A: Did you build   B: didn't ... built
4. A: Is a fish   B: it is   A: Are they
   B: they are   B: don't know
5. A: want ... look ... Do you want
   B: have ... bought ... don't need
6. offer ... is ... offered ... didn't accept
7. took ... found ... didn't know ... isn't ... didn't want ... went ... made ... heated ... seemed ... am not
8. likes ... worry ... is ... trust ... graduated (also possible: was graduated) ... went ... didn't travel ... rented
   ... rode ... was ... worried (also possible: were worried) ... were ... saw ... knew

◇ PRACTICE 13, p. 28.
1. was standing
2. was eating
3. was answering
4. was singing
5. was walking

6. were climbing
7. was beginning
8. was counting
9. was melting
10. was looking ... was driving

◇ PRACTICE 15, p. 30.

1. While I was climbing the stairs, the doorbell rang.   OR   The doorbell rang while I was climbing the stairs.
2. I gave Alan his pay after he finished his chores.   OR   After Alan finished his chores, I gave him his pay.
3. The firefighters checked the ashes one last time before they went home.   OR   Before the firefighters went home, they checked the ashes one last time.
4. When Mr. Novak stopped by our table at the restaurant, I introduced him to my wife.   OR   I introduced Mr. Novak to my wife when he stopped by our table at the restaurant.
5. While the kitten was sitting on the roof, an eagle flew over the house.   OR   An eagle flew over the house while the kitten was sitting on the roof.
6. My father was listening to a baseball game on the radio while he was watching a basketball game on television.   OR   While my father was watching a basketball game on television, he was listening to a baseball game on the radio.

◇ PRACTICE 16, p. 30.

1. began (also possible: was beginning) . . . were walking
2. was washing . . . dropped . . . broke
3. hit . . . was using
4. was walking . . . fell . . . hit
5. knew . . . were attending . . . mentioned . . . were . . . were staying (also possible: stayed)
6. was looking . . . started/was starting . . . took . . . was taking . . . (was) enjoying . . . came . . . asked . . . told . . . thanked . . . went . . . came . . . covered . . . went

◇ PRACTICE 19, p. 33.

1. used to hate school
2. used to think
3. used to be a secretary
4. used to have a rat
5. used to go bowling
6. used to raise chickens
7. used to have fresh eggs
8. used to crawl under his bed . . . (used to) put his hands over his ears

◇ PRACTICE 25, p. 38.

1. on
2. at . . . in
3. in . . . on . . . At . . . In
4. In . . . at . . . in
5. in . . . at
6. at
7. In . . . In . . . on . . . on
8. in (also possible: during)

◇ PRACTICE 26, p. 39.

1. at . . . in
2. for . . . in
3. on . . . at . . . in . . . from . . . at/with . . . at
4. with . . . in (also possible: during)
5. on . . . of . . . on . . . in
6. of . . . in

Chapter 3:   FUTURE TIME

◇ PRACTICE 1, p. 40.

1. a. arrives
   b. arrived
   c. is going to arrive OR will arrive
2. a. Does . . . arrive
   b. Did . . . arrive
   c. Is . . . going to arrive OR Will . . . arrive
3. a. does not (doesn't) arrive
   b. did not (didn't) arrive
   c. is not (isn't) going to arrive OR will not (won't) arrive
4. a. eats
   b. ate
   c. is going to OR will eat
5. a. Do . . . eat
   b. Did . . . eat
   c. Are . . . going to eat OR Will . . . eat
6. a. do not (don't) eat
   b. did not (didn't) eat
   c. am not going to eat OR will not (won't) eat

◇ PRACTICE 2, p. 41.

1. B: Do . . . get
   A: do . . . get
   B: Did . . . get
   A: did . . . got
   B: Are . . . going to get
   A: am . . . am going to get
2. B: Do . . . study
   A: do . . . study
   B: Did . . . study
   A: did . . . studied
   B: are . . . going to study
   A: am . . . am going to study

◇ **PRACTICE 4, p. 41.**
1. A: are you going to do   B: am going to finish
2. A: is Ryan going to be   B: is going to be
3. A: Are you going to have   B: am not going to eat
4. A: Are you going to finish   B: am going to finish
5. A: Are you going to call   B: am not going to call her . . . am going to write
6. A: is Laura going to talk   B: is going to discuss

◇ **PRACTICE 7, p. 43.**
1. A: Will you help   B: I will   OR I won't
2. A: Will Paul lend   B: he will   OR he won't
3. A: Will Jane graduate   B: she will   OR she won't
4. A: Will her parents be   B: they will   OR they won't
5. A: Will I benefit   B: you will   OR you won't

◇ **PRACTICE 8, p. 43.**
1. probably won't   5. will probably
2. will probably   6. probably won't
3. will probably   7. will probably
4. probably won't   8. will probably

◇ **PRACTICE 11, p. 45.**
1. I am going to   5. am going to
2. will   6. will
3. am going to   7. am going to . . . will
4. will

◇ **PRACTICE 12, p. 46.**
1. am going to   6. am going to
2. will   7. A: are . . . going to
3. will   B: am going to
4. am going to   8. will
5. will

◇ **PRACTICE 13, p. 46.**
1. When I call Mike tomorrow, I'll tell him the good news.   OR
   I'll tell Mike the good news when I call him tomorrow.
2. Ann will lock all the doors before she goes to bed.   OR
   Before Ann goes to bed, she'll lock all the doors.   OR
   (Before she goes to bed, Ann will lock all the doors.)
3. When I am in London, I'm going to visit the Tate Museum.   OR
   I'm going to visit the Tate Museum when I am in London.
4. The show will start as soon as the curtain goes up.   OR
   As soon as the curtain goes up, the show will start.
5. Nick is going to change the oil in his car after he takes a bath.   OR
   After Nick takes a bath, he's going to change the oil in his car.   OR
   (After he takes a bath, Nick is going to change the oil in his car.)
6. We'll call you before we drive over to pick you up.   OR
   Before we drive over to pick you up, we'll call you.
7. I'll call you when I get an answer from the bank about the loan.   OR
   When I get an answer from the bank about the loan, I'll call you.
8. I'll pay my rent as soon as I get my paycheck.   OR
   As soon as I get my paycheck, I'll pay my rent.

◇ **PRACTICE 14, p. 47.**
1. will read . . . take
2. will call . . . returns
3. won't be . . . come
4. go . . . will prepare
5. visits . . . will take
6. will move . . . graduates . . . finds

◇ **PRACTICE 15, p. 47.**
1. is . . . won't go
2. get . . . will pay
3. will be . . . don't go
4. will stop . . . tells
5. gets . . . will eat . . . is . . . will be

◇ **PRACTICE 17, p. 48.**
1. was listening . . . (and) (was) doing
2. are going to meet . . . (and) (are going to) study
3. will rise . . . (and) (will) set
4. was carrying . . . (and) (was) climbing
   flew . . . (and) sat
   dropped . . . (and) spilled
5. is going to meet . . . (and) (is going to) go
6. moves . . . (and) starts
7. slipped . . . (and) fell
8. am getting . . . (and) (am) walking
9. arrived . . . (and) started
   was . . . (and) felt
   was watching . . . (and) (was) feeling
   knocked . . . (and) asked
   see . . . (and) usually spend
   are borrowing . . . (and) (are) going
   are going to take . . . (and) (are going to) go

◇ **PRACTICE 18, p. 49.**
1. will retire . . . (will) travel   OR
   are going to retire . . . (are going to) travel
2. close . . . think
3. is watching . . . (is) studying
4. takes . . . buys
5. go . . . tell
6. will take . . . (will) forget   OR
   am going to take . . . (am going to) forget
7. will discover . . . (will) apologize   OR
   is going to discover . . . (is going to) apologize
8. saw . . . ran . . . caught . . . knocked . . . went . . .
   sat . . . was waiting . . . got . . . understood . . . put
   . . . took

◇ **PRACTICE 20, p. 51.**
1. is traveling (travelling)
2. are arriving
3. am meeting
4. am getting

5. is . . . taking
6. am studying
7. am leaving
8. is attending . . . am seeing
9. is speaking
10. am spending . . . am visiting

◇ **PRACTICE 21, p. 52.**
Possible answers:
1. Fred is eating/having dinner with Emily on Sunday.
2. He is seeing Dr. Wood at 1:00 p.m. on Monday.
3. He is going to Jean's birthday party at 7:00 p.m. on Tuesday.
4. He is probably eating lunch with Jack on Wednesday.
5. He is meeting Tom's plane on Thursday at 2:00 p.m.
6. He is attending a financial seminar on Friday.
7. He is taking his children to the zoo on Saturday.

◇ **PRACTICE 24, p. 53.**
1. A: does . . . begin/start   5. A: does . . . close
   B: begins/starts   B: closes
2. opens   6. begins/starts
3. arrives/gets in/lands
4. B: begins/starts
   A: does . . . end/finish
   B: ends/finishes

◇ **PRACTICE 25, p. 54.**
1. The chimpanzee is about to eat a banana.
2. Sam is about to leave.
3. The plane is about to land.
4. The woman is about to answer the phone.

◇ **PRACTICE 26, p. 54.**
1. don't need
2. is planning/plans . . . Are you coming/Are you going to come
3. A: do you usually get
   B: take
4. was watching . . . became . . . stopped . . . found
5. A: am going/am going to go
   B: are going/are going to go
6. will probably call/is probably going to call . . . go
7. A: is . . . are flashing
   B: know . . . know . . . see
   A: is going . . . Are you speeding
   B: am going   A: is passing
8. is going to land/will land . . . think
9. ride . . . was raining . . . drove . . . arrived . . . discovered
10. will give
11. are you wearing/are you going to wear . . . am planning/plan . . . bought . . . is . . . will show . . . will get . . . (will) bring
12. B: is wearing
    A: didn't lend
    B: will be/is going to be

◇ PRACTICE 27, p. 56.

(1) made . . . did not have . . . were not . . . wore
(2) make . . . comes . . . buy
(3) is . . . wear . . . wear
(4) exist . . . wear . . . are
(5) will probably be/are probably going to be . . . will wear/are going to wear . . . Will we all dress/Are we all going to dress . . . show . . . do you think

◇ PRACTICE 31, p. 60.

1. at
2. at
3. in
4. with
5. for
6. to . . . with
7. for
8. from
9. about
10. for

◇ PRACTICE 32, p. 60.

1. to
2. from . . . for
3. to . . . at
4. to
5. of
6. from . . . for
7. in . . . with
8. for . . . with . . . to

Chapter 4: NOUNS AND PRONOUNS

◇ PRACTICE 1, p. 61.

1. <u>Chicago</u> has busy <u>streets</u> and <u>highways</u>.
2. <u>Boxes</u> have six <u>sides</u>.
3. Big <u>cities</u> have many <u>problems</u>.
4. <u>Bananas</u> grow in hot, humid <u>areas</u>.
5. <u>Insects</u> don't have <u>noses</u>.
6. <u>Lambs</u> are the <u>offspring</u> of <u>sheep</u>.
7. <u>Libraries</u> keep <u>books</u> on <u>shelves</u>.
8. <u>Parents</u> support their <u>children</u>.
9. <u>Indonesia</u> has several active <u>volcanoes</u>.
10. <u>Baboons</u> are big <u>monkeys</u>. They have large <u>heads</u> and sharp ***teeth***. They eat <u>leaves</u>, <u>roots</u>, <u>insects</u>, and <u>eggs</u>.

◇ PRACTICE 2, p. 61.

1. mouse
2. pockets
3. tooth
4. tomato
5. fish
6. woman
7. branches
8. friends
9. duties
10. highways
11. thief
12. beliefs
13. potatoes
14. radios
15. offspring
16. child
17. seasons
18. customs
19. businesses
20. century
21. occurrences
22. phenomenon
23. sheep
24. loaf

◇ PRACTICE 5, p. 63.

1. [Bridges *S*]   [cross *V*]   [rivers *O*].
2. [A terrible earthquake *S*]   [occurred *V*]   [in Turkey *PP*].
3. [Airplanes *S*]   [fly *V*]   [above the clouds *PP*].
4. [Trucks *S*]   [carry *V*]   [large loads *O*].
5. [Rivers *S*]   [flow *V*]   [toward the sea *PP*].
6. [Salespeople *S*]   [treat *V*]   [customers *O*]   [with courtesy *PP*].
7. [Bacteria *S*]   [can cause *V*]   [diseases *O*].
8. [Clouds *S*]   [are floating *V*]   [across the sky *PP*].
9. [The audience *S*]   [in the theater *PP*]   [applauded *V*]
[the performers *O*]   [at the end *PP*]   [of the show *PP*].
10. [Helmets *S*]   [protect *V*]   [bicyclists *O*]   [from serious injuries *PP*].

◇ PRACTICE 6, p. 63.

1. v.	9. n.	16. n.
2. n.	10. v.	17. n.
3. n.	11. v.	18. v.
4. v.	12. n.	19. v.
5. v.	13. v.	20. n.
6. n.	14. n.	21. n.
7. n.	15. v.	22. v.
8. v.		

◇ PRACTICE 8, p. 65.

Expected answers:

1. old	9. hard/difficult	17. expensive
2. old	10. narrow	18. light
3. hot	11. dirty	19. light
4. slow	12. full	20. private
5. happy	13. safe	21. right
6. bad	14. quiet	22. right
7. dry	15. deep	23. strong
8. hard	16. sour	24. short

◇ PRACTICE 9, p. 65.

1. Paul has a (loud) voice.

2. Sugar is (sweet.)

3. The students took an (easy) test.

4. Air is (free.)

5. We ate some (delicious) food at a (Mexican) restaurant.

6. An encyclopedia contains (important) facts about a (wide) variety of subjects.

7. The child was (sick.)

8. The (sick) child crawled into his (warm) bed and sipped (hot) tea.

◇ PRACTICE 11, p. 66.

1. newspaper articles
2. page numbers
3. paper money
4. apartment buildings
5. key chains
6. city governments
7. duck ponds
8. shoulder pads
9. pocket knives
10. traffic lights

◇ PRACTICE 12, p. 66.

1. bottles ... caps
2. seats
3. students ... experiments ... classes
4. Houseflies ... pests ... germs
5. Computers ... operators
6. kinds ... flowers
7. reporters ... jobs
8. manners
9. tickets
10. lives ... ways ... years ... lamps ... candles ... houses ... chickens ... fires

◇ PRACTICE 14, p. 68.

1. me (*O of vb*)
2. I (*S*) ... me (*O of prep*)
3. He (*S*) ... it (*O of vb*) ... It (*S*) ... him (*O of vb*)
4. me (*O of prep*) ... We (*S*) ... her (*O of vb*) ... she (*S*) ... us (*O of vb*) ... We (*S*) ... her (*O of prep*)
5. He (*S*) ... them (*O of vb*) ... them (*O of vb*) ... They (*S*)
6. I (*S*) ... him and me (*O of prep*) ... He and I (*S*)

◇ PRACTICE 15, p. 68.

1. She = *Janet* ... it = *a green apple*
2. her = *Betsy*
3. They = *Nick and Rob*
4. they = *phone messages*
5. him = *Louie* ... He = *Louie* ... her = *Alice* ... She = *Alice*
6. She = *Jane* ... it = *letter* ... them = *Mr. and Mrs. Moore* ... They = *Mr. and Mrs. Moore* ... her = *Jane*

◇ PRACTICE 16, p. 68.

1. It
2. He ... them
3. They ... her
4. it
5. it ... it ... him ... he
6. they ... them ... they
7. them
8. it
9. it ... It
10. them ... They ... They ... them

◇ PRACTICE 17, p. 69.

1. me
2. He
3. him
4. he
5. her
6. She
7. me ... He ... us
8. her ... They
9. I ... They ... us ... it ... We ... them
10. them
11. me ... him
12. she
13. I ... him and me

◇ PRACTICE 18, p. 70.

1. friend's	9. person's
2. friends'	10. people's
3. son's	11. teacher's
4. sons'	12. teachers'
5. baby's	13. man's
6. babies'	14. men's
7. child's	15. earth's
8. children's	

◇ PRACTICE 19, p. 70.
1. A king's chair
2. Kings' chairs
3. Babies' toys
4. a baby's toys
5. the caller's words
6. A receptionist's job . . . callers' names
7. yesterday's news . . . today's events
8. The pilots' seats
9. the earth's surface
10. Mosquitoes' wings
11. A mosquito's wings
12. A cat's heart . . . an elephant's heart
13. the elephants' tricks
14. the animals' bodies
15. an animal's footprints

◇ PRACTICE 22, p. 73.
1. your . . . yours
2. her . . . hers
3. his . . . his
4. your . . . yours
5. their . . . our . . . theirs . . . ours

◇ PRACTICE 24, p. 74.
1. myself
2. himself
3. ourselves
4. yourself
5. yourselves
6. herself
7. themselves

◇ PRACTICE 25, p. 74.
1. blamed myself
2. are going to/will cut yourself
3. introduced myself
4. was talking to himself
5. work for ourselves
6. taught themselves
7. killed himself
8. wished myself
9. is taking care of herself
10. believe in ourselves
11. felt sorry for myself
12. help themselves

◇ PRACTICE 26, p. 75.
1. me . . . him
2. yourselves
3. itself
4. its . . . its
5. hers
6. him
7. yourself . . . your
8. our . . . our
9. ours
10. themselves
11. itself
12. himself

◇ PRACTICE 28, p. 77.
1. The other
2. a. Another
3. b. The other
3. a. Another
   b. Another
   c. Another
   d. another
4. The other
5. Another
6. The other
7. a. Another
   b. the other
8. a. another
   b. another
   c. another
   d. another
   e. another

◇ PRACTICE 29, p.78.
1. The other
2. The others
3. a. Other
   b. Others
   c. Others
   d. Other
4. a. the other
   b. The others
5. a. other
   b. others
6. others
7. other
8. Others
9. Other
10. a. The other
   b. The others

◇ PRACTICE 30, p.79.
1. A
2. C
3. D
4. B
5. E
6. C
7. A
8. D
9. B
10. E

◇ PRACTICE 32, p. 80.
1. **R**obert **J**ones
2. (*no change*)
3. **U**ncle **J**oe . . . **A**unt **S**ara
4. (*no change*)
5. **S**usan **W**. **M**iller
6. **P**rof. **M**iller's
7. **J**anuary
8. (*no change*)
9. **M**onday
10. **L**os **A**ngeles
11. **C**alifornia
12. (*no change*)
13. **U**nited **S**tates of **A**merica
14. (*no change*)
15. **A**tlantic **O**cean
16. (*no change*)
17. **M**arket **S**treet . . . **W**ashington **H**igh **S**chool
18. (*no change*)
19. **H**ilton **H**otel . . . **B**angkok
20. **J**apanese . . . **G**erman

◇ PRACTICE 33, p. 81.
1. for
2. A: to . . . about
   B: at . . . for
3. to
4. from
5. for
6. A: on
   B: about
7. in
8. of
9. with . . . about/on
10. to

◇ PRACTICE 34, p. 82.

1. about
2. from
3. of
4. to . . . with
5. to
6. for
7. from
8. with
9. with
10. to
11. in
12. at
13. for . . . at
14. at
15. A: with . . . about
    C: to
    A: to . . . about . . . with

Chapter 5: MODAL AUXILIARIES

◇ PRACTICE 1, p. 83.

1. must <u>Ø</u>
2. has <u>**to**</u>
3. should <u>Ø</u>
4. ought <u>**to**</u>
5. May I <u>Ø</u>
6. can <u>Ø</u>
7. must <u>Ø</u>
8. can't <u>Ø</u>
9. have got <u>**to**</u>
10. A: Should I <u>Ø</u>
    B: have <u>**to**</u> . . . could <u>Ø</u>
    A: ought <u>**to**</u> . . . might <u>Ø</u> . . .
       Would <u>Ø</u>
    B: should <u>Ø</u> . . . can <u>Ø</u> . . .
       will <u>Ø</u>
    A: must <u>Ø</u> . . . can't <u>Ø</u>

◇ PRACTICE 3, p. 84.

1. zebra
2. cat
3. Elephants
4. Monkeys
5. camels
6. cow
7. horse
8. donkey
9. squirrel
10. ants

◇ PRACTICE 6, p. 86.

1. can . . . can't
2. may
3. can
4. may . . . may not
5. may
6. may
7. can't
8. may
9. might . . . might not
10. can . . . can't
11. might
12. can . . . might . . . might not
13. can't . . . Can . . . might

◇ PRACTICE 7, p. 87.

1. A
2. B
3. B
4. B
5. B
6. A
7. B
8. A

◇ PRACTICE 10, p. 88.

1. Can
2. may
3. Would
4. could
5. Can
6. A: Could
   B: May
7. A: Can
   B: Will
8. Could

◇ PRACTICE 12, p. 89.

1. A
2. C
3. B
4. A
5. B
6. C
7. A
8. C .
9. B
10. C

◇ PRACTICE 14, p. 90.

1. C
2. A
3. D
4. C
5. B
6. A
7. D
8. C

◇ PRACTICE 16, p. 91.

1. must not
2. don't have to
3. must not
4. don't have to
5. don't have to
6. must not
7. don't have to
8. must not
9. must not
10. don't have to

◇ PRACTICE 17, p. 92.

1. have to/must
2. doesn't have to
3. don't have to
4. must not
5. has to/must
6. doesn't have to
7. has to/must
8. must not

◇ PRACTICE 20, p. 94.

1. must
2. must not
3. must
4. must
5. must not
6. must not
7. must

◇ PRACTICE 22, p. 95.

1. Wait
2. Don't wait
3. Read
4. Don't put
5. Come in . . . have
6. Don't cross
7. Don't just stand . . . Do
8. Call
9. Take . . . Go . . . Walk . . . give
10. Capitalize . . . Put . . . use

◇ **PRACTICE 24, p. 96.**

1. A: go . . . fly
   B: see
2. B: get
   A: take
3. A: go
   B: play
4. A: take
   B: take . . . save
5. A: stop . . . fill up
   B: pick up/get
6. A: go
   A: call . . . see

◇ **PRACTICE 26, p. 98.**

1. prefer
2. like
3. would rather
4. prefer
5. would rather
6. A: prefer
   B: likes
   B: would rather
7. would rather
8. would rather
9. B: prefer
   A: like
10. prefer

◇ **PRACTICE 28, p. 99.**

1. A
2. C
3. A
4. A
5. B
6. C
7. B
8. C
9. B
10. A
11. C
12. A
13. B
14. C
15. B

◇ **PRACTICE 32, p. 104.**

1. A: with/to
   B: about
2. for
3. to
4. of
5. A: in
   B: for
6. to
7. of
8. for
9. of (also possible: about)
10. for
11. of
12. for
13. from

Chapter 6: QUESTIONS

◇ **PRACTICE 1, p. 106.**

Possible completions:
1. (*Supply your own name.*)
2. What is (What's) your name?
3. Is that your first name? / Is Anna your first name?
4. What's your last name?
5. How do you spell that? / How do you spell your last name?
6. Where are you from? / What country are you from? / What country do you come from?
7. What city? (What city are you from?) / Where in Poland? (Where do you come from in Poland?) / What's your hometown?
8. When did you come to (*name of this city/country/school*)? / When did you arrive here?
9. Why did you come here?
10. What is your major? / What are you going to study? / What are you studying? / What field are you in? / What's your field?
11. How long are you going to stay here? / How long do you plan to stay?
12. Where are you living?
13. Do you live far from / a long way from school? / Is their house far from school?
14. How far is it? / How far is their house from school? / How far away are you?
15. How do you get to school every day?
16. How do you like going to school here? / Do you like it here too?

◇ PRACTICE 2, p. 107.

1. A: Do
   B: I don't
2. A: Is
   B: it is
3. A: Do
   B: they don't
4. A: Are
   B: I am
5. A: Does
   B: it does
6. A: Are
   B: they aren't
7. A: Do
   B: they do
8. A: Are
   B: I am
9. A: Is
   B: it isn't
10. A: Do
    B: they do
11. A: Does
    B: it does

◇ PRACTICE 3, p. 108.

helping verb	subject	main verb	rest of sentence
1. Do	you	like	coffee?
2. Does	Tom	like	coffee?
3. Is	Ann	watching	TV?
4. Are	you	having	lunch with Rob?
5. Did	Sara	walk	to school?
6. Was	Ann	taking	a nap?
7. Will	Ted	come	to the meeting?
8. Can	Rita	ride	a bicycle?

form of *be*	subject		rest of sentence
9. Is	Ann		a good artist?
10. Were	you		at the wedding?

◇ PRACTICE 5, p. 109.

(question word)	helping verb	subject	main verb	rest of sentence
1. Ø	Did	you	hear	the news yesterday?
2. When	did	you	hear	the news?
3. Ø	Is	Eric	reading	today's paper?
4. What	is	Eric	reading	Ø?
5. Ø	Did	you	find	your wallet?
6. Where	did	you	find	your wallet?
7. Why	does	Mr. Li	walk	to work?
8. Ø	Does	Mr. Li	walk	to work?
9. Ø	Will	Ms. Cook	return	to her office at one o'clock?
10. When	will	Ms. Cook	return	to her office?

(question word)	form of *be*	subject		rest of sentence
11. Ø	Is	. the orange juice		in the refrigerator?
12. Where	is	the orange juice		Ø?

◇ PRACTICE 6, p. 110.

1. What time/When do the fireworks start
2. Why are you waiting
3. When does Rachel start
4. What time/When do you usually leave
5. Why didn't you get
6. Where can I buy★
7. What time/When are you leaving
8. Where did you study . . . Why did you study . . . Why didn't you go
9. When do you expect
10. Where will the spaceship go

★ Also possible: *Where can* **you** *buy?* In this case, *you* is used as an impersonal pronoun meaning *someone, anyone,* or *all people.*

◇ **PRACTICE 10, p. 113.**
S
1. Who knows?
O
2. Who(m) did you ask?
S
3. Who knocked on the door?
O
4. Who(m) did Sara meet?
S
5. Who will help us?
O
6. Who(m) will you ask?
O
7. Who(m) is Eric talking to on the phone?   OR
O
To whom is Eric talking on the phone?
S
8. Who is knocking on the door?
S
9. What surprised them?
O
10. What did Mike learn?
S
11. What will change Ann's mind?
O
12. What can Tina talk about?   OR
O
About what can Tina talk?

◇ **PRACTICE 11, p. 113.**
1. Who taught you to play chess?
2. What did Robert see?
3. Who got a good look at the bank robber?
4. Who(m) are you making the toy for?   OR
   For whom are you making the toy?
5. Who(m) does the calculator belong to?   OR
   To whom does the calculator belong?
6. What do you have in your pocket?
   [also possible: What have you (got) in your pocket?]
7. What did the cat kill?
8. What killed the cat?
9. Who(m) did you get a letter from?   OR
   From whom did you get a letter?
10. Who wrote a note on the envelope?
11. What makes an apple fall to the ground from a tree?

◇ **PRACTICE 12, p. 114.**
1. What is Alex doing?
2. What should I do if someone calls while you're out?
3. What do astronauts do?
4. What should I do?
5. What are you going to do Saturday morning?
6. What do you do when you get sick?
7. What can I do to help you?
8. What did Sara do when she heard the good news?

◇ **PRACTICE 16, p. 116.**
1. Which
2. What
3. Which
4. What
5. What . . . Which
6. What
7. Which
8. which

◇ **PRACTICE 17, p. 117.**
1. Who
2. Whose
3. Whose
4. Who
5. Who
6. Whose
7. Whose
8. Who

◇ **PRACTICE 19, p. 118.**
1. hot . . . hot
2. soon
3. expensive
   (also common: how much)
4. busy . . . busy
5. serious . . . serious
6. well . . . well
7. fresh . . . fresh . . . fresh
8. safe

◇ **PRACTICE 20, p. 119.**
1. far
2. long
3. far
4. far
5. long
6. far
7. long
8. long
9. far
10. long

◇ **PRACTICE 21, p. 119.**
1. often
2. long
3. many
4. far
5. many
6. many
7. long
8. many
9. often
10. many
11. long
12. often
13. far
14. many
15. often
16. far
17. long

◇ PRACTICE 23, p. 121.

1. When are you going to buy a new bicycle?
2. How are you going to pay for it?
3. How long (How many years) did you have your old bike?
4. How often (How many times a week) do you ride your bike?
5. How do you (usually) get to work?
6. Are you going to ride your bike to work tomorrow?
7. Why didn't you ride your bike to work today?
8. When did Jason get his new bike?
9. Who broke Jason's new bike?
10. What (Whose bike) did Billy break?
11. What (Whose bike) is broken?
12. How did Billy break Jason's bike?
13. Does your bike have a comfortable seat?
    [also possible: Has your bike (got) a comfortable seat?]
14. What kind of bicycle do you have?
    [also possible: What kind of bike have you (got)?]
15. Which bicycle is yours, the red one or the blue one?
16. Where do you keep your bicycle at night?
17. Who(m) does that bike belong to?   OR
    To whom does that bike belong?
18. Whose bike did you borrow?
19. Where is Rita?
20. What is she doing?
21. How far did Rita ride her bike yesterday?
22. How do you spell "bicycle?"

◇ PRACTICE 28, p. 125.

1. a. don't
   b. doesn't
   c. don't
   d. doesn't
   e. isn't
   f. aren't
   g. does
   h. is
2. a. didn't
   b. did
   c. were
   d. wasn't
3. a. aren't
   b. is
   c. is
   d. weren't
   e. was
4. a. can't
   b. will
   c. shouldn't
   d. wouldn't
   e. do
   f. didn't

◇ PRACTICE 29, p. 126.

1. wasn't he
2. can't they
3. don't they
4. is he
5. wouldn't you
6. aren't they
7. isn't it
8. can it
9. shouldn't you
10. won't she
11. doesn't he
12. did you
13. is it
14. do I
15. is it
16. weren't they
17. will she
18. doesn't it

◇ PRACTICE 32, p. 127.

1. about
2. with
3. to
4. at
5. to
6. A: to
   B: for
7. about/of
8. for
9. about . . . about
10. from

Chapter 7: THE PRESENT PERFECT AND THE PAST PERFECT

◇ PRACTICE 1, p. 128.

1. A: Have you ever eaten
   B: have . . . have eaten   OR
      haven't . . . have never eaten
2. A: Have you ever talked
   B: have . . . have talked   OR
      haven't . . . have never talked
3. A: Has Erica ever rented
   B: has . . . has rented   OR
      hasn't . . . has never rented
4. A: Have you ever seen
   B: have . . . have seen   OR
      haven't . . . have never seen
5. A: Has Joe ever caught
   B: has . . . has caught   OR
      hasn't . . . has never caught
6. A: Have you ever had
   B: have . . . have had   OR
      haven't . . . have never had

◇ PRACTICE 2, p. 129.

1. have used
2. has risen
3. have never played
4. have won
5. hasn't spoken
6. hasn't eaten
7. has given
8. haven't saved
9. Have you ever slept
10. have never worn
11. has improved
12. have looked

◇ PRACTICE 3, p. 129.

1. have already called . . . called
2. have already begun . . . began
3. have already eaten . . . ate
4. have already bought . . . bought
5. has already left . . . left
6. have already locked . . . locked

◇ PRACTICE 4, p. 130.

1. began . . . have begun
2. bent . . . have bent
3. broadcast . . . has broadcast
4. caught . . . have caught
5. came . . . have come
6. cut . . . have cut
7. dug . . . have dug
8. drew . . . has drawn
9. fed . . . have fed
10. fought . . . have fought
11. forgot . . . have forgotten
12. hid . . . have hidden
13. hit . . . has hit
14. held . . . has held
15. kept . . . have kept
16. led . . . has led
17. lost . . . has lost
18. met . . . have met
19. rode . . . have ridden
20. rang . . . has rung
21. saw . . . have seen
22. stole . . . has stolen
23. stuck . . . have stuck
24. swept . . . have swept
25. took . . . have taken
26. upset . . . have upset
27. withdrew . . . have withdrawn
28. wrote . . . have written

◇ PRACTICE 6, p. 134.

1. since	8. for
2. for	9. since
3. since	10. for
4. for	11. since
5. for	12. for
6. since	13. since
7. since	14. for

◇ PRACTICE 7, p. 135.

1. have known . . . were
2. has changed . . . started
3. was . . . have been
4. haven't slept . . . left
5. met . . . hasn't been
6. has had . . . bought
7. A: have you eaten . . . got up
   B: have eaten
8. had . . . was . . . left . . . have taken . . . have had . . . have learned

◇ PRACTICE 10, p. 136.

1. A: has Eric been studying
   B: has been studying . . . two hours
2. A: has Kathy been working at the computer
   B: has been working . . . two o'clock
3. A: has it been raining
   B: has been raining . . . two days

4. A: has Liz been reading
   B: has been reading . . . half an hour/thirty minutes
5. A: has Boris been studying English
   B: has been studying English . . . 1990
6. A: has Nicole been working at the Silk Road Clothing Store
   B: has been working at the Silk Road Clothing Store . . . three months.
7. A: has Ms. Rice been teaching at this school
   B: has been teaching at this school . . . September 1992
8. A: has Mr. Fisher been driving a Chevy
   B: has been driving a Chevy . . . twelve years
9. A: has Mrs. Taylor been waiting to see her doctor
   B: has been waiting to see her doctor . . . an hour and a half
10. A: have Ted and Erica been playing tennis
    B: have been playing tennis . . . two o'clock

◇ PRACTICE 11, p. 137.

1. B
2. B
3. A
4. B
5. A
6. A
7. B
8. A

◇ PRACTICE 15, p. 140.

PART I:

1.	∅	*is*	always
2.	always	*finishes*	∅
3.	always	*finished*	∅
4.	∅	*will*	always
5.	∅	*has*	always
6.	always	*helped*	∅
7.	∅	*are*	always
8.	always	*help*	∅
9.	∅	*have*	always
10.	∅	*can*	always
11.	∅	*are*	usually
12.	usually	*help*	∅
13.	∅	*have*	usually
14.	∅	*can*	usually

PART II:

15.	*Do*	∅	you	usually
16.	*Is*	∅	Mike	usually
17.	*Did*	∅	your mom	usually
18.	*Were*	∅	you	usually
19.	*Can*	∅	students	usually
20.	*Do*	∅	you	ever
21.	*Is*	∅	Mike	ever
22.	*Did*	∅	your mom	ever
23.	*Were*	∅	you	ever
24.	*Can*	∅	students	ever

PART III:

25. probably *won't* Ø
26. probably *isn't* Ø
27. probably *doesn't* Ø
28. probably *hasn't* Ø
29. Ø *won't* ever
30. Ø *isn't* ever
31. Ø *doesn't* always
32. Ø *hasn't* always

◇ **PRACTICE 17, p. 142.**

1. B	6. A
2. D	7. C
3. A	8. D
4. D	9. B
5. C	10. C

◇ **PRACTICE 19, p. 143.**

1. a. 1st	5. a. 1st
b. 2nd	b. 2nd
2. a. 2nd	6. a. 2nd
b. 1st	b. 1st
3. a. 1st	7. a. 1st
b. 2nd	b. 2nd
4. a. 2nd	8. a. 2nd
b. 1st	b. 1st

◇ **PRACTICE 20, p. 145.**

1. has already left
2. had already left
3. have already slept
4. had already slept
5. have already met
6. had already met
7. have already seen
8. had already seen
9. have made
10. had made

◇ **PRACTICE 21, p. 145.**

1. B	5. B
2. A	6. A
3. A	7. B
4. B	8. B

◇ **PRACTICE 22, p. 146.**

1. was sleeping
2. have never been
3. had already heard
4. was still snowing
5. had passed
6. were making
7. Hasn't he come
8. had never been
9. was wearing . . . had never worn . . . hasn't worn

◇ **PRACTICE 23, p. 147.**

1. A	6. B
2. C	7. D
3. B	8. C
4. D	9. D
5. A	10. B

◇ **PRACTICE 25, p. 148.**

1. (up)on
2. from
3. of
4. (up)on
5. to
6. to . . . for . . . for . . . (up)on
7. for
8. to/with
9. of
10. for

Chapter 8: COUNT/NONCOUNT NOUNS AND ARTICLES

◇ **PRACTICE 1, p. 149.**

1. / furniture → noncount
2. **one** table → count
3. **one** ring → count
4. / jewelry → noncount
5. / homework → noncount
6. **one** assignment → count
7. **one** job → count
8. / work → noncount
9. **one** question → count
10. / information → noncount
11. **one** new word → count
12. / new vocabulary → noncount

◇ **PRACTICE 2, p. 149.**

1. **some** furniture
2. **a** table
3. **a** ring
4. **some** jewelry
5. **some** homework
6. **an** assignment
7. **a** job
8. **some** work
9. **a** question
10. **some** information
11. **a** new word
12. **some** new vocabulary

◇ PRACTICE 3, p. 150.

1. furniture /
2. table **s**
3. ring **s**
4. jewelry /
5. homework /
6. assignment **s**
7. job **s**
8. work /
9. question **s**
10. information /
11. word **s**
12. vocabulary /

◇ PRACTICE 4, p. 150.

1. (*no change*)
2. **two** tables
3. **two** rings
4. (*no change*)
5. (*no change*)
6. **two** assignments
7. **two** jobs
8. (*no change*)
9. **two** questions
10. (*no change*)
11. **two** new words
12. (*no change*)

◇ PRACTICE 5, p. 151.

1. **a lot of** furniture
2. **a lot of** tables
3. **a lot of** rings
4. **a lot of** jewelry
5. **a lot of** homework
6. **a lot of** assignments
7. **a lot of** jobs
8. **a lot of** work
9. **a lot of** questions
10. **a lot of** information
11. **a lot of** new words
12. **a lot of** new vocabulary

◇ PRACTICE 6, p. 151.

1. **much** furniture
2. **many** tables
3. **many** rings
4. **much** jewelry
5. **much** homework
6. **many** assignments
7. **many** jobs
8. **much** work
9. **many** questions
10. **much** information
11. **many** words
12. **much** new vocabulary

◇ PRACTICE 7, p. 152.

1. **a little** furniture
2. **a few** tables
3. **a few** rings
4. **a little** jewelry
5. **a little** homework
6. **a few** assignments
7. **a few** jobs
8. **a little** work
9. **a few** questions
10. **a little** information
11. **a few** new words
12. **a little** new vocabulary

◇ PRACTICE 8, p. 152.

1. **a** game
2. **a** rock
3. **a** store
4. **an** army
5. **an** egg
6. **an** island
7. **an** ocean
8. **an** umbrella
9. **a** university
10. **a** horse
11. **an** hour
12. **a** star
13. **an** eye
14. **a** new car
15. **an** old car
16. **a** used car
17. **an** uncle
18. **a** house
19. **an** honest mistake
20. **a** hospital
21. **a** hand
22. **an** aunt
23. **an** ant
24. **a** neighbor

◇ PRACTICE 9, p. 153.

1. **a** letter
2. **some** mail
3. **some** equipment
4. **a** tool
5. **some** food
6. **an** apple

7. __some__ clothing

8. __an__ old shirt

9. __some__ advice

10. __a__ suggestion

11. __an__ interesting story

12. __some__ interesting news

13. __a__ poem

14. __some__ poetry

15. __a__ song

16. __some__ Indian music

17. __a__ new idiom

18. __some__ new slang

◇ **PRACTICE 10, p. 153.**

1. grammar _/_
2. noun _s_
3. language _s_
4. English _/_
5. makeup _/_
6. scenery _/_
7. mountain _s_
8. traffic _/_
9. automobile _s_
10. sand _/_
11. dust _/_
12. beach _es_
13. slang _/_
14. mistake _s_
15. information _/_
16. fact _s_
17. game _s_
18. weather _/_
19. thunder _/_
20. water _/_
21. parent _s_ . . . health _/_
22. circle _/_ . . . degree _s_
23. Professor _s_ . . . knowledge _/_
24. family _/_ . . . luck _/_
25. neighbor _s_ . . . help _/_
26. factor _ies_ . . . pollution _/_
27. pride _/_ . . . children _/_
28. people _/_ . . . intelligence _/_

◇ **PRACTICE 13, p. 155.**

1. many letter **s** _are_
2. much mail _/_
3. many **men** _have_
4. many famil **ies** _are_
5. many word **s** _are_
6. many sentence **s** _are_
7. much chalk _/_ _is_
8. much English _/_
9. much English literature _/_
10. many English word **s**
11. much gasoline _/_ (much petrol _/_)
12. much homework _/_
13. many grandchild **ren**
14. many page **s** _are_
15. many librar **ies** * _are_
16. many bone **s** _are_
17. many **teeth** _/_
18. much water _/_
19. many cup **s**
20. much tea _/_
21. many glass **es**
22. much fun _/_
23. much education _/_
24. much soap _/_
25. many island **s** _are_
26. many people _/_ _were_
27. many human being **s** _are_
28. many people _/_
29. many zero **es** OR zero **s** _are_
30. many butterfl **ies** *

◇ **PRACTICE 14, p. 156.**

1. a little music _/_
2. a few song **s**
3. a little help _/_
4. a little English _/_
5. a few more apple **s**
6. a little honey _/_
7. a little advice _/_
8. a few suggestion **s**
9. a few question **s**
10. a few people _/_
11. a few more minute **s**
12. a little light _/_
13. a little homework _/_

_____

*The -y is changed to -i and then -es is added. Example: *baby* → *babies*. (See Chart 4-1.)

◇ PRACTICE 15, p. 157.

1. How many children do the Millers have?
2. How much money does Jake make?
3. How many players are there on a soccer team?
4. How much homework do you have tonight?
5. How many feet are there in a mile?
6. How many meters/metres are there in a kilometer/kilometre?
7. How many suitcases did you take on the plane to Florida?
8. How much suntan oil did you take with you?
9. How many pairs of sandals did you take?
10. How much toothpaste/How many tubes of toothpaste did you take?
11. How long did the flight take?
12. How many times have you been in Florida?
13. How many apples are there in the two baskets?
14. How much fruit is there in the two baskets?

◇ PRACTICE 16, p. 158.

Expected answers. Others may be possible.
PART I:
1. can/jar
2. box
3. bottle
4. jar
5. can
6. box
7. can
8. bag/box
9. bottle
10. can/bag
11. can/bag
12. bag
13. bottle/can
14. can

PART II:
15. cup/glass
16. bowl
17. slice/piece
18. slice/piece
19. slice/piece
20. glass
21. bowl/cup
22. piece
23. glass
24. bowl/cup
25. glass/cup
26. bowl
27. slice/piece
28. bowl/cup
29. bowl

◇ PRACTICE 20, p. 160.

1. D
2. G
3. F
4. B
5. E
6. C
7. A

◇ PRACTICE 22, p. 161.

1. **A** bird . . . Birds have feathers.
2. Ø Corn . . . (*none possible*)
3. Ø Milk . . . (*none possible*)
4. **A** flower . . . Flowers are beautiful.
5. Ø Water . . . (*none possible*)
6. **A** horse . . . Horses are strong.
7. Ø Jewelry . . . (*none possible*)
8. Ø Honey . . . (*none possible*)
9. **A** shirt . . . Shirts have sleeves.
10. Ø Soap . . . (*none possible*)

◇ PRACTICE 23, p. 161.

1. **a** bird . . . I saw some birds.
2. **some** corn . . . (*none possible*)
3. **some** milk . . . (*none possible*)
4. **a** flower . . . I picked some flowers.
5. **some** water . . . (*none possible*)
6. **a** horse . . . I fed grass to some horses.
7. **some** jewelry . . . (*none possible*)
8. **some** honey . . . (*none possible*)
9. **a** new shirt . . . Tom bought some new shirts.
10. **some** soap . . . (*none possible*)

◇ PRACTICE 24, p. 161.

1. **a** dog
2. **the** dog
3. **the** radio
4. **a** radio . . . **a** tape player
5. **a** desk, **a** bed, **a** chest of drawers
6. **the** desk . . . **the** top drawer
7. **the** basement
8. **a** basement
9. **a** subject and **a** verb
10. **the** subject . . . **the** verb
11. **a** meeting
12. **the** meeting
13. **a** long distance . . . **a** telephone
14. **The** distance . . . **the** sun . . . **the** earth
15. **the** telephone
16. **a** question
17. **the** problem
18. **a** poem
19. **the** lecture . . . **The** speaker . . . **an** interesting talk
20. **a** cup . . . **the** cafe . . . **the** corner

◇ PRACTICE 25, p. 163.

1. Ø Dogs
2. **the** dogs
3. Ø Fruit
4. **The** fruit
5. Ø Children
6. **the** children
7. Ø Paper . . . Ø trees
8. **The** paper
9. **the** potatoes
10. Ø Potatoes . . . Ø vegetables
11. Ø Nurses
12. **the** nurses
13. Ø Frogs . . . Ø small animals . . . Ø tails . . .
    Ø turtles . . . Ø tails . . . Ø hard shells
14. **The** frogs . . . **The** turtles
15. Ø books . . . Ø textbooks . . . Ø workbooks . . .
    Ø dictionaries . . . Ø encyclopedias . . .
    Ø entertainment . . . Ø novels . . . Ø poetry
16. **The** books
17. Ø plants . . . Ø fruit . . . Ø vegetables . . . Ø plants
    . . . Ø meat . . . Ø plants
18. **The** plants
19. **An** engineer . . . Ø engineers . . . Ø bridges . . .
    Ø rivers . . . Ø valleys . . . Ø highways . . . Ø
    railroad tracks . . . Ø other places
20. **the** bridges

◇ PRACTICE 26, p. 164.

1. **a** banana . . . **an** apple . . . **the** banana . . . **the** apple
2. **some** bananas . . . **some** apples . . . **the** bananas . . .
   the apples
3. **some** coffee . . . **some** milk . . . **The** coffee . . . **The**
   milk
4. **a** desk . . . **a** bed . . . **The** desk . . . **The** bed
5. **a** pen . . . **some** paper . . . **the** pen . . . **the** paper
6. **a** bag . . . **some** sugar . . . **some** cookies . . . **The**
   sugar . . . **the** flour . . . **the** flour . . . **some** little
   bugs . . . **the** little bugs . . . **a** new bag . . . **The** new
   bag
7. **some** birds . . . **a** tree . . . **a** cat . . . **the** tree . . . **The**
   birds . . . **the** cat . . . **the** cat . . . **the** birds
8. Once upon a time, ___**a**___ princess fell in love
   with ___**a**___ prince. ___**The**___ princess wanted to
   marry ___**the**___ prince, who lived in a distant
   land. She summoned ___**a**___ messenger to take
   ___**some**___ things to ___**the**___ prince to show him her
   love. ___**The**___ messenger took ___**the**___ jewels
   and ___**a**___ robe made of yellow and red silk to
   ___**the**___ prince. ___**The**___ princess anxiously
   awaited ___**the**___ messenger's return. She hoped
   that ___**the**___ prince would send her ___**some**___
   tokens of his love. But when ___**the**___ messenger
   returned, he brought back ___**the**___ jewels and

___**the**___ beautiful silk robe that ___**the**___ princess
had sent. Why? Why? she wondered. Then
___**the**___ messenger told her: ___**The**___ prince
already had ___**a**___ wife.

◇ PRACTICE 28, p. 166.

1. **An** egg . . . **the** egg
2. Ø Eggs
3. **a** scientific fact . . . Ø steam . . . Ø water
4. **the** tape player . . . **the** shelves . . . **the** batteries
5. Ø Chalk . . . **a** necessity
6. **the** plumber . . . **The** sink . . . **the** water supply . . .
   the house . . . **the** leak
7. Ø Water . . . **the** water . . . **The** pollution
8. **a** taxi
9. **the** car . . . **a** minute . . . **the** kids . . . **the** car . . . **a**
   minute
10. Ø Newspapers . . . **an** important source . . .
    Ø information
11. **The** sun . . . **a** star . . . **the** sun . . . Ø heat . . .
    Ø light . . . Ø energy
12. Ø Ducks
13. **the** letter . . . **A** strong wind . . . **the** floor . . . **the**
    dog . . . **the** scraps . . . **the** wastebasket
14. **An** efficient transportation system . . . **an** essential
    part
15. **the** alarm . . . **the** door . . . **the** stove . . . **the**
    windows . . . **the** lights
16. **an** exceptionally talented person
17. Ø Money . . . Ø trees
18. Ø sick people . . . **A** farmer . . . Ø crops . . . **An**
    architect . . . Ø buildings . . . **An** artist . . . Ø new
    ways . . . **the** world . . . Ø life
19. Ø Earthquakes . . . Ø relatively rare events
20. **an** earthquake . . . **the** earthquake . . . **The** ground

◇ PRACTICE 30, p. 170.

1. one
2. it
3. one
4. it . . . it
5. it
6. one
7. one
8. it
9. one
10. it

◇ PRACTICE 32, p. 171.

1. it
2. some
3. some
4. it
5. them
6. some
7. any
8. it

◇ PRACTICE 34, p. 173.

1. from
2. about ... for
3. to ... about
4. to ... from ... into ... by
5. for
6. on
7. about/of ... with
8. from ... to
9. about ... from

◇ PRACTICE 35, p. 174.

1. for
2. in
3. In ... to
4. for
5. with
6. at
7. of
8. to
9. at
10. in ... on
11. of
12. to
13. to
14. from ... of
15. for
16. about/of ... at
17. of ... for ... (up)on ... for ... In
18. for ... to
19. A: about ... about ... with/at
    B: from ... in ... to ... for
20. of ... on